How to Talk Language Science with Everybody

Do you want to talk about the linguistic research that you think is important, but you don't know where to start? Language is a topic that is relevant to everyone, and linguists are often asked to speak publicly about their research, to a range of lay audiences in the media, politics, festivals and fairs, schools, museums, and public libraries. However, relaying this vital information in an engaging way can often feel like an insurmountable task. This accessible guide offers practical advice on how to talk about language to a range of nonacademic audiences. It draws on the linguistics behind effective communication to help you have cooperative conversations, and to organize your information for a diverse range of people. It is illustrated with a wealth of examples from real-life scenarios and includes chapter-by-chapter worksheets, enabling you to make your own fun and interesting language science activities to share with others.

Laura Wagner is a professor in the Department of Psychology at The Ohio State University. She directs the Language Sciences Research Lab at the Center of Science and Industry in Columbus, OH.

Cecile McKee is a professor in the Department of Linguistics at The University of Arizona, where she directs the Developmental Psycholinguistics Lab. The American Association for the Advancement of Science recently recognized her service in promoting public awareness of the significance of linguistic study.

How to Talk Language Science with Everybody

Laura Wagner The Ohio State University
Cecile McKee The University of Arizona

CAMBRIDGE
UNIVERSITY PRESS

Shaftesbury Road, Cambridge CB2 8EA, United Kingdom

One Liberty Plaza, 20th Floor, New York, NY 10006, USA

477 Williamstown Road, Port Melbourne, VIC 3207, Australia

314–321, 3rd Floor, Plot 3, Splendor Forum, Jasola District Centre, New Delhi – 110025, India

103 Penang Road, #05-06/07, Visioncrest Commercial, Singapore 238467

Cambridge University Press is part of Cambridge University Press & Assessment, a department of the University of Cambridge.

We share the University's mission to contribute to society through the pursuit of education, learning and research at the highest international levels of excellence.

www.cambridge.org
Information on this title: www.cambridge.org/9781108841511

DOI: 10.1017/9781108894227

First published 2023

A catalogue record for this publication is available from the British Library.

Library of Congress Cataloging-in-Publication Data
Names: Wagner, Laura (Professor of linguistics), author. | McKee, Cecile, author.
Title: How to talk language science with everybody / Laura Wagner, Ohio State University; Cecile McKee, University of Arizona.
Description: Cambridge ; New York, NY : Cambridge University Press, 2023. | Includes bibliographical references and index.
Identifiers: LCCN 2023001157 (print) | LCCN 2023001158 (ebook) | ISBN 9781108841511 (hardback) | ISBN 9781108794923 (paperback) | ISBN 9781108894227 (epub)
Subjects: LCSH: Outreach programs in linguistics. | Linguistics–Public relations.
Classification: LCC P53.6122 .W34 2023 (print) | LCC P53.6122 (ebook) | DDC 410.1/4–dc23/eng/20230228
LC record available at https://lccn.loc.gov/2023001157
LC ebook record available at https://lccn.loc.gov/2023001158

ISBN 978-1-108-84151-1 Hardback
ISBN 978-1-108-79492-3 Paperback

Contents

Figures

Preface

Becoming an expert is a narrowing process. We start by wanting to answer the broad questions: What makes people tick? How does the universe work? But the only way to answer such questions is to break them down into smaller pieces. By the time that you become an actual expert in something, the question you're trying to answer can look downright tiny. What's important is that you never lose sight of what the bigger picture is. For example, there are people who spend their whole lives studying how children learn the meanings of verb endings (or, as one of our mothers once said: "You're only studying parts of words? You can't even study how children learn whole words?"). Verb endings are a very tiny piece of language, but understanding how children learn them tells us a little bit about how children learn their native language, which in turn tells us something about what the human mind is capable of learning, which in turn tells us something about what it means to be human at all. Verb endings are a tiny piece of a very broad question.

This book is about how to do effective science communication, and our goals are both broad and narrow. Our broad concern is to help someone with scientific expertise (or really, any kind of expertise) communicate what they know and why it is important to people who don't have the same knowledge. Effective science communication is important because it genuinely matters for societal problems. We wrote this book during the COVID-19 pandemic, which illustrated to us daily what happens when people don't trust scientific experts. Scientists who know how to connect with people, how to explain their science, and how to engender trust as they do so are a rare commodity. We hope our book can help make more of them.

However, science communication is too broad a topic area to focus our advice: We needed to narrow ourselves down to one particular science so that our points could be concrete and understandable (which are important properties for effective communication). And we feel very lucky that the science we know best is language science because it's a really good domain to use to illustrate our broader ideas. Language is a piece of the world that people have a lot of personal experience with, making it easy to find relevant examples and also to connect with people's lived experiences. It doesn't hurt that our science also helps explain why many core practices in science communication are effective.

These two different levels are on display right in our title. Broadly, our book is about how to talk science with everybody. More narrowly, we are aware that our specific scientific topic is language and that this book will have special resonance for people who are interested in language specifically. We've made the language part of the book's title look a bit different typographically, though, to help us remember that other topic areas fit there too.

Acknowledgments

We have many people to thank, both individually and collectively, for helping us with our engagement work as well as with this book specifically.

We thank the major institutions that have supported us: our home universities, The Ohio State University (OSU) and The University of Arizona (UA); the National Science Foundation for its generous funding of our regular research as well as our public engagement work; the Linguistic Society of America; and the venues that have hosted us in ways large and small: the Center of Science and Industry (COSI), Children's Museum Tucson (CMT), the Tucson Festival of Books, Tucson Meet Yourself, Mission Garden, the USA Science and Engineering Festival, and the American Association for the Advancement of Science (AAAS) Family Science Days festival.

We thank the colleagues and students who have been integral to our engagement efforts. Joan Maling was an extraordinary champion for us and for the importance of connecting language science with larger communities. The Language Science for Everyone group, led by Colin Phillips, has also been an important source of support and inspiration. We also benefited from an outstanding workshop led by Liz McCullough at Seattle's Pacific Science Center.

LW wants to especially thank the executive committee of the Language Pod at COSI: Kathryn Campbell-Kibler, Cynthia Clopper, Rachael Holt, Leslie Moore, Nikole Patson, and Shari Speer. In addition, Jan Weisenberger at OSU and Andy Aichele at COSI have done more than they probably realize to make this book possible. Kathryn Campbell-Kibler and Leslie Moore deserve extra thanks: Creating OSU's public engagement training course with them was a critical starting point for this book, and their ideas are embedded throughout all of my work. Hundreds of students have used (and improved) the demos used in the Language Pod and beyond. The following students made substantive contributions to specific demos described in this book: Nick Bednar, Shasteny Cabrera, Sherman Charles, Luana Lamberti, Madeleine Manly, Nathaneal Miller, Emily Perko, Mike Phelan, Abigail Sarver-Verhey, Victoria Sevich, Alexis Wilson, and the Spring 2018 5700 training class. And thanks to Jory Ross, who created the vowel plot shown in Chapter 15.

CM wants to especially thank CMT colleague Autumn Rentmeester, who welcomed her into the museum world and so taught her a great deal more about it than one finds in books and articles. UA colleague Sally Stevens introduced CM to the funds of knowledge approach, which radically affected everything after that. The following students made substantive contributions to specific demos described in this book: Nikolis Atkinson, Marg (Max) Beltran, Yamile Diaz, Genesis Grijalva, Sean Harley, Jaycie Martin, Joe McDonough, Matt Mutterperl, Donovan Pete, Mia Vento, and especially Elly Zimmer. The students in the Spring 2016 LING 392/492 course contributed critically to the CMT-based project described here: Marissa Amezcua, Yahaira Garcia, Julia Ribeiro, Noemi Rodriguez, Lexie Sorrentino, Lisa Winslow, and Hannah Zedek.

Many of the photos of people used in this book were taken in public venues (such as the AAAS Family Science Days festival), which grant the use of images taken there. We would like to thank the students (and former students) who are pictured here: Maram Alrjub, Nikolis Atkinson, Lian Arzbecker, Marg (Max) Beltran, Christina Brindley, Michelle Bullock, Donna Green, Sean Harley, Chris Heffner, Rachel Hughes, Izabela Jamsek, Dosia Kumbe, Marissa LaVigna, Shea Mangan, Joe McDonough, Donovan Pete, Daniel Puthwala, Mikayla Perry, Jory Ross, Kelly Schroeder, Victoria Sevich, Anna Sies, Hannah Zedek, and Elly Zimmer.

The development of this book owes thanks to a few particular people and places. We are grateful to the Linguistic Society of America's Linguistic Institute at UC Davis (2019) for including our workshop on public engagement. We honed several ideas (and our collaborative working process) at that workshop. Special thanks go to Sue Allen. Not only has her work inspired us, but she deserves credit for suggesting that we explain core informal science education practices in terms of linguistic theory in this book. In addition, we want to thank a few other people who inspired us, although we never met. Emily Dawson's work was important for shaping our thinking on many things, especially the importance of inclusion in informal spaces. Our index benefited from us attending a virtual Planet Word talk by Dennis Duncan (see his book *Index, A History of the*).

We are extremely grateful to the people who read through this manuscript in full or in part at various stages of its development: Nick Bednar, Chris Heffner, Rachael Holt, Dan Reynolds. They helped us improve many things in the book (and, of course, all remaining errors are our own). Thanks also go to our reviewers (both of the proposal and of the manuscript) and to our contacts Helen Barton and Izzie Collins at Cambridge University Press, who also provided invaluable feedback. Our editor, Helen Barton, deserves special thanks for being willing to take on a book that was a little different from the typical linguistics title at Cambridge University Press. In fact, the whole field of linguistics owes her thanks, as she's shepherded a number of wonderful books through Cambridge University Press's processes.

On a more personal note, LW gives love and thanks to Dan Reynolds. Beyond all the things he deserves thanks for every day, he has always been a stalwart supporter of my engagement work, which has meant, among other things, carrying boxes, bringing snacks, posing for pictures, traveling to events, testing out demos, proofreading materials, and generally holding me together. He has more than earned every language science T-shirt he's gotten (including the one he is pictured in within this book)!

CM is also grateful for her personal paladin. Though not a scientist, Jesse Zoernig memorizes the periodic table and reads about astronomy and ornithology for fun. She believes in the enterprise that we describe here like we do. Jesse responds enthusiastically to my every request (including demonstrating some vowels for this book). Indefatigable and dauntless, Jesse has run emergency errands during the maddest of events, entertained students, and helped improve several of the demos we describe here.

Most of this book was written during the COVID-19 pandemic, and we both worried at times that we might be writing about something that was forever past: a time when people met face-to-face and actually had a chance to talk with each other. We are profoundly grateful that we all do again have the opportunity to engage with people in real life.

1 Why Bother?

OPENING WORKSHEET

What does PUBLIC ENGAGEMENT mean to you?

When you think about talking with the general public about language, what are you picturing? The focus of this book is going to be on how to talk with the public in free-choice learning locations – museums, festivals, libraries. What do you imagine engaging with people in these settings might be like?

Why are you reading this book?

We assume you're reading this because you have some interest in communicating about language with nonexperts in public spaces. But let's go deeper and get personal. You know your own interests, strengths and weaknesses, and long-term goals. Why do **you** want to engage with a public audience? Write down three reasons that are meaningful to you.

This book is about how to talk with members of the general public about science, particularly in informal, free-choice settings. If you have a strong interest in language and how it works, and if you have a genuine interest in sharing that interest with nonexperts, then this book is for you.

Throughout this book, we're going to argue that the best way to engage the general public about language science (or really, any complex topic) is to have honest-to-goodness conversations with people, one-on-one and in small groups. We'll be giving practical advice for how to have good conversations, and we'll guide your development of what we'll call your DOABLE DEMO. By the end of the book, you should be able to use your doable demo to get such conversations going. But we also have a long-term agenda: We believe that engaging with the public in an accessible way should be a regular part of the job of working scientists.

If you're currently a working language scientist – whether you call yourself a linguist, a psychologist, an audiologist, a computer scientist, a speech pathologist, an anthropologist, an English teacher, or something else – this book is for you. We appreciate that people are interested in language for lots of different reasons and study it from many different perspectives. We've included examples throughout this book that span a wide range of language topics to illustrate how any part of language science can be used to engage with people. We also suspect that your training up to now didn't include much on how to talk with the public, and we hope you will see this book as a form of continuing education.

If you're still getting your training – whether that means you're a graduate student working toward becoming a full-fledged language scientist, or you're an undergraduate who has only recently discovered how amazing the study of language can be – this book is also for you. Engaging with the public is a skill, and the more you do it, the better you're going to get at it. We (both authors!) have taught many college students the core lessons in this book and we have a healthy respect for their ability to use them well. You don't need to be the world's leading expert on a topic in order to convey a sense of excitement about language. What you need is a willingness to try.

Why Bother?

Most language science classes ask you to learn about how language is structured, how people use it, how children learn it, how it changes, what happens when it breaks down, and so on. Language science has been a very successful field for the last hundred (or more!) years, so there is a lot to know about. If you're passionate about language science, you can easily devote your entire life to learning the field. And traditionally, that's what most experts in the field have in fact done.

So if the science has moved forward so nicely without much engagement with the general public, why should we bother to do it now? One reason is that language is something that impacts our everyday lives in many ways. We believe that understanding how language works is critical for making certain choices, at both the personal and societal levels.

Should parents worry if their child uses a funny past tense form like *runned*? Is it OK to raise your child bilingual? What's the best way for a school system to educate multilingual children? Why is English hard to learn to read? Should we invest government money to encourage people to learn multiple dialects of Arabic? Why do computer assistants like Alexa and Siri regularly misunderstand people who use certain dialects of English? Can people tell what race you are from a telephone call? How can we help children born with hearing loss learn to read? To what extent do face masks make it difficult to understand what someone is saying?

Language scientists know the answers to such questions, and this information can be relevant to social issues such as parenting, immigration, education, law, national security, and technology development. We would be delighted if the general public came to be more knowledgeable about all of these areas, and your public engagement just might move us toward that goal in a small way.

But the very act of public engagement does something else: It demonstrates that language is studied by scientific experts. There is a wonderful world of language out there, and there are guides who can help you navigate it. When an issue arises that touches on language, the public does have someone they can turn to for expert advice: language scientists.

Of course, if you need a more personal reason to engage with the public, the skills you need to do it well are relevant in many other situations. Knowing how to communicate effectively with a range of people is just plain useful. If your goal is to be an academic, the skills we promote here will come in handy. The average introductory classroom is just a room full of nonexperts. The dean of your college is also likely to be a nonexpert in your field, and trust us, it's good to be able to explain to your dean why your work is interesting and worthwhile. Doing interdisciplinary work requires you to be able to talk with people whose backgrounds and goals differ from yours. Even talking with your fellow professors within your own department, you will find that background knowledge differs and it's useful to be able to explain your work in a way that builds bridges to others.

If your goal is not to become an academic, effective communication skills are just as necessary. Outside of the ivory tower, you are likely to interact with a very large range of people coming from very diverse backgrounds. Being able to explain complicated, technical information is highly prized. It is common practice for businesses to foster collaboration among teams of people with different skill sets, so being able to communicate with people who have different perspectives will help you succeed. The principles for being clear and interesting will help you give an excellent professional presentation in any field. Mastering the core lessons in this book will make you a more marketable commodity.

Whether you're motivated by a desire to improve society, your field, or yourself, this book is for you.

Talking with the Public in Informal Free-Choice Learning Environments

One distinctive thing about this book is that it will focus on talking with the public in INFORMAL FREE-CHOICE LEARNING ENVIRONMENTS. Before we tell you why we chose to focus there, let's be clear about what these environments are.

What we have in mind are places such as festivals, libraries, and museums. These are places where people visit in order to have fun and learn a little something. They are *informal learning* environments because they are not in classrooms with a podium or a screen at the front of the room. That means you don't get the usual tools of a classroom to work with – no quizzes, no reading assignments, no homework, no grades. Also, these environments aren't structured like classrooms, where students are often sitting in specific places and the main talker is typically the teacher. These locations are *free-choice* because visitors come and go freely. You might be in a crowd or in front of a booth or behind a cart, and you will need to capture the interest of people passing by and sustain that interest long enough to inspire new thinking about language. If people don't like what you're doing, they will freely choose to go somewhere else!

What kinds of people go to these locations? All kinds. And lots of them. People spend a lot more of their lives outside of school than inside school, and they do a lot of their lifetime learning in informal free-choice locations. The graph in Figure 1.1 comes from research by scholars of free-choice science learning, John Falk and Lynn Dierking. It shows how much exposure people get to any kind of science education over their lifetime. As you can

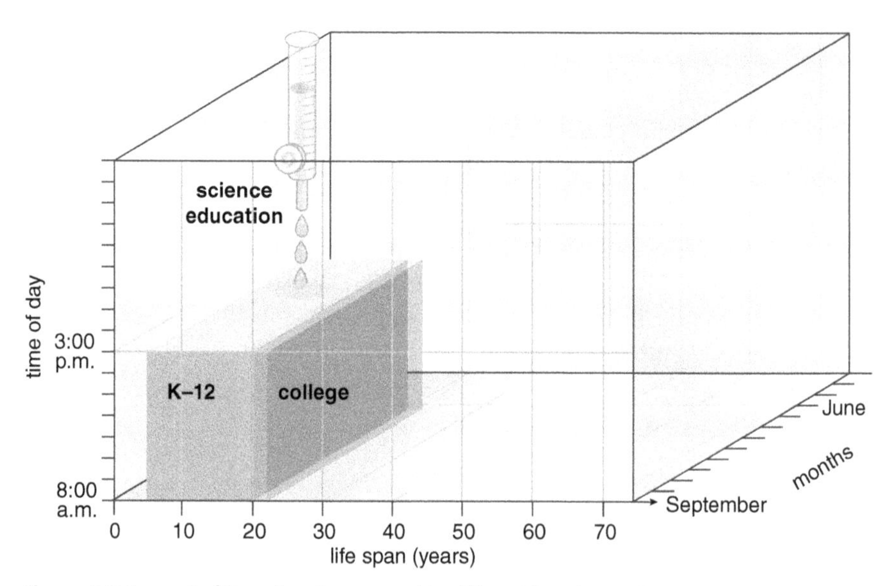

Figure 1.1 Amount of time Americans spend in different learning environments
Note. This elegant figure from Falk and Dierking (2010) shows that Americans may spend on average only about 5 percent of their whole lives in formal classrooms. The amount of time they spend getting formal science education is so small, it can only be shown in droplets. Used with permission.

see, at least for Americans, most of that isn't coming from standard schooltime.

This research also found that the percentage of people from all around the world who had visited an informal learning location was high. From these same researchers, the graph in Figure 1.2 shows that a high percentage of people visit public libraries, zoos/aquariums, natural history museums, and science/technology museums. Language science fits well in at least three of these places (and you might even bring language science into a zoo/aquarium through a connection with animal communication!).

Beyond major institutions that are devoted to informal learning and free-choice settings, there are many event-based opportunities as well. Many organizations host science festivals, and language science makes for a terrific booth. Language science can fit into other kinds of festivals – arts festivals,

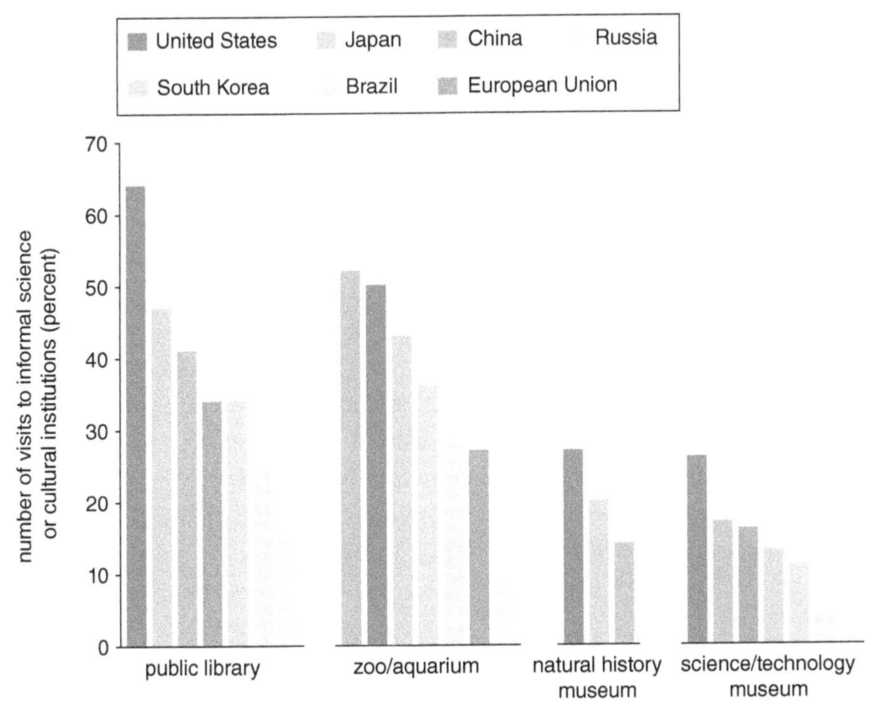

Figure 1.2 Attendance at several types of informal learning venues
Note. This graph from Falk and Dierking (2010) shows that all kinds of informal learning venues are popular around the globe. Moreover, Falk and Dierking suggested that the fact that the US public visits science-oriented institutions at particularly high rates may account for why American adults have similar proficiency in science to other adults worldwide even though American children tend to lag behind: Americans learn science in informal venues all through their lives. Used with permission.

food festivals, children's festivals, and cultural festivals all have room for language connections. Often for these kinds of events it's worth tailoring your focus to fit the event, but with the breadth of topics that language science covers, that's rarely a problem.

What's more, if you are connected to a university or college, it's likely that your home institution has events that would welcome you. The events might target local students (freshman orientation and meet-your-major fairs are great!), or they might be events intended to reach the wider community. Either way, they offer some infrastructure to support engagement with the public. Toward the end of this book (Chapters 18 and 19), we'll offer some more specific suggestions for places you might practice your new public engagement skills, and provide some advice for how to be a good partner with institutions or groups you might want to work with.

Our own public engagement efforts have centered on free-choice learning environments (see the Worked Example Box in this chapter). We like them for many reasons. First, they allow us to reach a lot of people, both in terms of raw numbers (as you saw above, lots of people go to these kinds of locations) and in terms of types of people (not just college students, but families; and in many of the venues, families from diverse backgrounds). Second, they are great places for our students to get training in how to talk with the public. Most of the interactions we have at these locations are relatively short (often fifteen minutes or less), which means our students get many opportunities to practice. They also get feedback from the people they talk with – there is nothing more satisfying than hearing someone walk away saying, "That was so cool!" Finally, we believe the challenge is worth it! To paraphrase a famous song by Kander and Ebb, "If you can make it in a free-choice learning setting, you can make it anywhere!" For most people, talking with the public doesn't come naturally, and mastering the relevant skills takes effort and practice. But your communication abilities and public speaking confidence will improve dramatically.

What You Won't Find in This Book, at Least Not Directly

There are lots of different ways to engage with the public around language science. As we laid out above, this book focuses on something we have a lot of experience with: encouraging informal learning in free-choice environments. But often when we tell people that we train people to talk with the public, they assume we're doing something different – like helping people talk to politicians, or helping people create a podcast or a social media page. We think reaching various kinds of nonexperts and using different media are worthwhile, and if that's what you're interested in, we encourage you to do it. But it's not what **this** book is about. The core lessons of this book will be useful if you talk to politicians or create online materials, but they aren't targeted toward those goals. And we certainly appreciate – and we hope that you do as well – that there are going to be differences between working with the general public at a festival and talking to your local elected representative.

LINGUISTIC ACTIVISM is another sort of public engagement that has a strong presence in the language sciences. Many researchers, especially those whose work depends on linguistic data from distinctive speech communities, have a tradition of giving back to those communities. Sometimes these efforts involve creating educational materials to help preserve a local language or dialect; sometimes they involve combating prejudice against the community; sometimes they involve celebrating the history and culture of the community. We have the greatest respect for these activist efforts, but that's not what this book is about either.

Our emphasis is much more general than most linguistic activism. We believe that just about every dimension of language science is worth sharing broadly, from highly theoretical topics in syntax and phonology to experimental results in language processing and acquisition to the sociolinguistics of identity. We will recommend that you tailor your messages to the needs and interests of your audience, and that can mean being sensitive to the cultural background of the people you're talking with. But we're not expecting that your activities will be embedded within a specific community or that your language science topics will necessarily be connected to classic issues of social justice or combating prejudice.

We do, however, think that the kind of engagement we're promoting in this book can be seen within the activist tradition. Ultimately, the goals of this engagement are to encourage a field that is committed to communicating with broad audiences, and to creating a public that is more informed about language science. But we see these as very long-term goals. What you will be doing with each conversation with a nonexpert is contributing in a small, incremental way to these long-term goals.

It's Language Science All the Way Down

The science content that we know best is language science, and the examples in this book emphasize language and how it works. But language science is not only important as our core content; it has also created some of the most important insights for how to effectively communicate with others. As you'll see in the upcoming chapters, our advice draws heavily on two foundational results from language science: Grice's principles of COOPERATIVE CONVERSATION and the information processing principle of GIVEN BEFORE NEW.

We're not trying to suggest that you need a degree in linguistics to prepare to talk with the public. If you've taken an introductory course on linguistics, you've likely run across both of our core ideas. If you've taken a course on informal science learning, you will likely have met these ideas there too. But communication is a part of language science, and it shouldn't be a big surprise that our field has helped uncover how communication works, and what can make it work better (or worse). We take our science seriously and encourage you to put some trust in the results of the very field you are interested in. We consider it a privilege that it is **our** science that we draw on to guide our efforts.

How to Use This Book

We think of this book as a guidebook for communication, and it can be used in a few different ways. We've organized ideas into bite-sized chunks, so if you're looking for ideas about how to avoid using jargon, or about how to make your work relevant to others, or want advice on where to go to do public engagement, you can jump to the chapters that emphasize those topics. If you read the book straight through, you'll get the full story, from theory all the way to very practical advice. If you want a slightly deeper dive into details – including pointers for more to read – you can check out the further reading section at the end of each chapter. Each chapter ends with a worksheet designed to help you make a demo that should be doable by the end of the book. Collectively, these worksheets will help you develop an activity on language science that you can use with the public in a free-choice learning environment.

CRITICAL TAKE-HOME MESSAGE

Informal learning venues are good places to reach a lot of people. This book will help you engage people with language science at these locations.

WORKED EXAMPLE BOX

Who are we? Why do we bother?

Laura Wagner

I'm a professor in the Department of Psychology at the Ohio State University. My PhD is in linguistics, and I have spent my career doing interdisciplinary research, mostly involving children's language development. My bread-and-butter research is on children's understanding of aspect, and I have also worked on children's developing understanding of indexical information such as social register and regional dialect.

A number of years ago I helped start the Language Sciences Research Lab (https://u.osu.edu/thebln/language-pod/). The lab is embedded inside of my local science museum, the Center of Science and Industry (COSI) in Columbus, OH. I collect my regular research data at the lab (alongside several other language scientists), and the visitors to the museum are my participant pool. Museum visitors can just watch, or ask questions about what we're doing, or participate in live research. At the lab, we think of our research as a form of public engagement: One of our missions is to demystify science for the public by showing them what the actual practice looks like, from the inside (Wagner et al., 2015).

Because of the special location, the lab is also a permanent museum exhibit that attracts hundreds of thousands of people every year. And that's more people than even our team of scientists can work with! So we also use the lab as a platform to engage with the public using just the kind of activities featured in this book. Another one of the lab's missions is to show people the range of things that language science has discovered and help people to experience the wonder and joy of language.

I think there are lots of societally important reasons to do this kind of work (and we laid those out in the chapter), but I think that what really keeps me doing it is how much fun it is. I love to think about language and science, and people regularly say things that are surprising and make me think about both of them in new ways. For example:

One of our demo activities uses an iPad app that lets you record someone speaking and then play it back for them (the app is called Singing Fingers and is produced by the MIT Media Lab). It's great fun to use with little kids because they get permission to shout on the museum floor and hear their own voices. One of this app's features lets you play the recorded sounds backward as well as forward, and that leads to some fun discussions about coarticulation effects and how we can only produce sound in the forward direction. I once watched a student doing this activity, and she started with a thought-provoking question to a young child. The child had just recorded her name, and the student asked,

(cont.)

"Do you think your name will sound the same backward as it did forward?" The child said her name, then turned around so her back faced the student and said it again. She triumphantly returned to the student and confidently announced that her name did in fact sound the same when she said it backward.

I cracked up laughing, as did the student. But truly, the child was a natural experimentalist and taught me something about space-time metaphors in the process. You don't need to be an expert in order to have insight or to come up with the perfect example. Every time I go out on our museum floor is another chance for me to learn something cool (and often to get to laugh while I do it!).

Figure 1.3 The authors on the job
Note. Cecile (left) and Laura (right) at the Family Science Days festival of the American Association for the Advancement of Science (AAAS), 2016.

(cont.)

Cecile McKee

I'm a professor in the Department of Linguistics at the University of Arizona, but I'm also affiliated with units such as the Department of Psychology. Before my university-based career, I was a K-12 teacher. I was also Director of the Linguistics Program at the National Science Foundation (NSF) 2001–2003. This latter experience is what crystallized for me the importance of public engagement. This particular agency is a sophisticated pipeline for distributing public monies to research on and education about what's called STEM (science, technology, engineering, and mathematics) here in the United States, including both formal and informal settings. I came to realize while working on that pipeline that many of us who generate new STEM knowledge share it through relatively narrow channels. The points we just discussed regarding the popularity of informal learning venues suggest that scientists who are so inclined should get out more. I myself was so inclined, and fortunately, so are many of our colleagues (McKee et al., 2015).

While I've emphasized working at events like festivals more than anything else, I've dipped my toes into some other streams as well. For example, I took a workshop on public discourse a few years ago, which led to publications and presentations for audiences outside of academia. I volunteer at an agricultural heritage museum featuring edible plants of Arizona, California, and Mexico (called Mission Garden); and I've worked bits of linguistics into interactions with the public that I have through that work. I've also collaborated with Children's Museum Tucson for both teaching and research activities. I do this for all the reasons we touched on above. Because my research concerns language and literacy development, my favorite interactions with members of the public include ones like the following:

I was in a museum playing one of the games that my students and I designed to engage children in science practices and to study their practices. The game started with a demo of how mouth shapes relate to vowels. Players produce the vowels [i], [u], and [ɔ] and then come up with words having those vowels (like *see*, *sue*, and *saw*). Our conversations with caretakers after children played this game emphasized that changing something and noticing effects of the change was a science practice that very young children could enjoy and that adults could encourage. A Latina mother whose child had just finished a bilingual version of our game stayed to talk about her family. Sharing that she and her husband

(cont.)

were native speakers of Spanish, she expressed concern that they disagreed on whether to use Spanish at home. She called him over for a spontaneous conversation on multilingual development, a topic that experts across language sciences have studied extensively and that is critically relevant where I live in Arizona and also more broadly.

This anecdote highlights one benefit of the free-choice setting, namely that we can take more time with people who want to keep a conversation going or who want to take it in their own direction. For me, then, it's not so much the chance to teach someone about vowels or young children's science practices. It is instead that such one-on-one conversations give me the chance to show that science is flexible and relevant and even fun, that scientists care about the applications of their expertise, and that science engagement can happen anywhere.

CLOSING WORKSHEET

Making a doable demo

The goal of this book is to inspire you to engage with the public, and to provide some practical advice about creating an activity that you can use for such engagement. We'll be calling these kinds of activities *demos*, which is our shorthand for *demonstration activities*. The Closing Worksheets at the end of each chapter offer specific suggestions to help you apply the lessons from that chapter to the demo you yourself make for public engagement.

So let's begin!

First, brainstorm topics that you might turn into a doable demo. Try to think broadly at this stage and consider a wide range of possibilities. Don't worry about coming up with a specific activity at this point – that's what the rest of the book is about. For now, try to think big. Write down three topics.

Now, for each of your three ideas, think about the following three things:

- How knowledgeable are you about the topic area?
- How societally relevant is your topic area?
- How much fun would your topic area be to work with?

We recommend that you keep a file (or a notebook, or a set of index cards, or a website – whatever works for you) where you save your responses to these Closing Worksheets. These sheets will build on each other as you go through the book, and the later worksheets will be a lot easier to do if you have a record of what you did for earlier ones. If you do all the worksheets, at the end of this book you will have what you need to do your very own (language) science demo!

Further Reading

1 *What does public engagement mean to you?*

Public engagement is our first technical term. We think that most readers will start with a sense of what the term means, in part because they're reading this book. We'll be using this term in the context of science education that occurs outside the formal classroom. But it can also refer to decision-making processes that various governing entities might use, as you can see in this guide published by the city of Fort Collins, CO (USA): www.fcgov.com/excellence/files/publicengagementguide.pdf.

Researchers whose work has implications for public health often use public engagement to share their results, not only to inform the public of the research conclusions but also to inform the researchers of the concerns and questions of the public. To get a sense of the breadth in each element of this term, see Duncan et al. (2017): www.publicengagement.ac.uk/sites/default/files/publication/reviewing_pe_in_ref_2014_final.pdf.

2 *If you're currently a language scientist*

People study language in all kinds of fields and from all kinds of perspectives! This blog post from computational sociolinguist Rachael Tatman gives a nice rundown: https://makingnoiseandhearingthings.com/2021/05/11/who-all-studies-language-%f0%9f%a4%94-a-brief-disciplinary-tour/.

3 *There is a lot to know about*

If you're interested in getting some general background in language science, we have some recommendations! *An Introduction to Language*, by Vicki Fromkin, Robert Rodman, and Nina Hyams (Fromkin et al., 2018), is a terrific introductory textbook of a traditional sort, and The Ohio State Linguistics Department's *Language Files* (Dawson & Phelan, 2016) is full of bite-sized introductions to language topics. If you'd rather read something aimed at a more popular audience, David Crystal's *How Language Works* (Crystal, 2007) is a good choice. And if you'd rather learn via video, the *Crash Course – Linguistics* YouTube channel or Moti Lieberman's *The Lingspace* YouTube channel are both entertaining and informative. And if you just want more, we recommend checking out Gretchen McCulloch's *All Things Linguistic* website (https://allthingslinguistic.com), which curates a list of podcasts, blogs, and other resources to scratch your language itch.

4 *Engagement with the general public*

Many people refer to what we're talking about here as *outreach* rather than *engagement*. In fact, we ourselves have on occasion used the term *outreach* (e.g., reaching out from the university to another institution). However, throughout this book, we're going to use the term *engagement*.

We think it's a better choice for several reasons. First, *engagement* is an everyday kind of word, while *outreach* may sound more technical. As people who value plain speaking, we are in favor of using an everyday word for what we do. Second, we like the way that the word *engagement* suggests participation from multiple people. Engagement is something that you do **with** other people, while outreach is more likely to be something you do **to** them. As you'll see (for example, in Chapter 4), we believe that it is important to respect the funds of knowledge that your conversational partner brings to the table. *Engagement* captures that cooperation and reciprocity better. A final reason to go with *engagement* is that it is the genuinely modern term for what we're doing. As we know from historical linguistics, the popularity of words changes over time, and right now, the popular word for our kind of work is *engagement*. Google's Ngram Viewer can show this! We used it to chart the frequency of use of the words *engagement* and *outreach* for a couple of hundred years, as represented in texts Google has access to (see Figure 1.4).

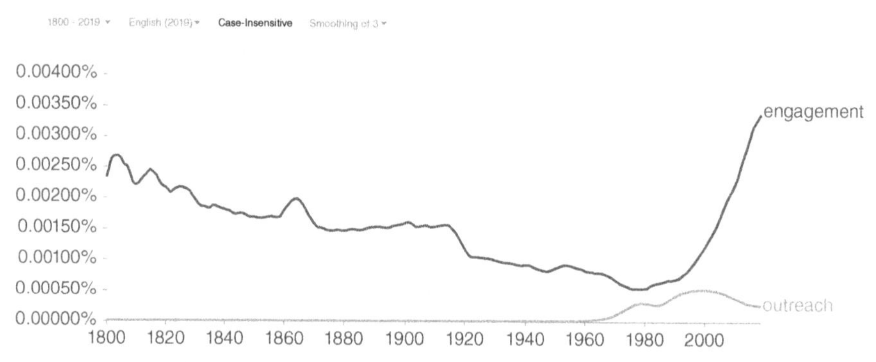

Figure 1.4 A Google Ngram graph comparing usage of *engagement* and *outreach*
Note. This graph was created with Google Books Ngram Viewer. See https://books.google.com/ngrams/info.
Source: Michel et al. (2010).

As you can see, around the year 2000, the word *outreach* peaked in popularity; since then, *engagement* has really taken off. We like to think that this rise is because of the two reasons we started with above, but regardless of the reasons, it does appear to be the word that everybody is using. Including us.

5 *Informal learning environments*

Informal learning can be thought of as being the learning that people do outside of a formal classroom situation. However, it's a bit more useful to think of it as consisting of a set of positive features. Callanan et al. (2011) identifies five distinctive dimensions to informal learning: It is less didactic, it is socially collaborative, it is embedded in a meaningful context, it is initiated by the learner's choice, and it has no consequential assessment (like a grade). These are all features that are common in the venues we are focusing on here, but they are found in other kinds of places as well. For example, Rogoff et al. (2016) takes an ethnographic perspective and discuss how many cultures depend on informal learning practices in the home and community, and how they are even present "on the side" in many formal learning contexts as well. Critically, informal learning is something that happens a lot. Thinking about learning as something that only happens in what Rogoff et al. calls the "factory model of instruction" is missing an enormous part of how we all develop knowledge and skills.

6 *Science education over their lifetime*

Falk and Dierking (2010) emphasizes the disconnect between where or how most Americans get most of their science knowledge and the policies or funding sources that typically support primary and secondary schooling in the United States – what the authors call a "school-first" paradigm. Interestingly, science education in American high schools and colleges is generally good, but these experiences aren't available to everyone. If public engagement like what we advocate here contributes to the public's science literacy, there is considerable democratizing potential in such activities.

7 *Linguistic activism*

There are many linguists who engage in linguistic activism. We can't mention them all, but a few to consider include Ofelia Zepeda (University of Arizona), Rebecca Wheeler (Christopher Newport University), and Walt Wolfram (North Carolina State University). We also think it's worth mentioning some of the linguists who collaborate with the K-12 school system, like Maya Honda (Wheelock College), Kristin Denham (Western Washington University), and Wayne O'Neil (MIT). Denham and Lobeck (2010) describes a number of these collaborations.

8 *Cecile McKee [Worked Example Box]*

See Cecile McKee and her team in action: www.youtube.com/watch?v=6kXK6W8sOII

9 *STEM*

While NSF originally emphasized education in mathematics and the physical sciences, it has long taken a much broader approach. The 1945 report to the US president that motivated NSF's establishment showed visionary attention to science education (Bush, 1945). (This pdf has the original report, as well as NSF's current context: www.nsf.gov/about/history/EndlessFrontier_w.pdf.) NSF added social sciences to its portfolio in 1957. It now uses the term STEM (standing for Science, Technology, Engineering, and Mathematics) to include the many fields where it funds basic research. Interestingly, though, Charles E. Vela coined this term in the early 1990s as a way of referring to an integrative approach to education in these broad areas (Raupp, 2020). Vela developed this emphasis on integrative education at the

Center for the Advancement of Hispanics in Science and Engineering Education. In 2001, when Judith Ramaley became head of NSF's education arm, NSF was referring to its portfolio as SMET. Fortunately, Ramaley took up Vela's term (Chute, 2009). And now, the term is used everywhere English is spoken and beyond. Though sometimes conveying a relatively narrow view (e.g., excluding the social sciences), we ourselves follow Vela and Ramaley in using the term STEM more inclusively. If you want to read more of this history, see www.nsf.gov/about/history/nsf50/science_policy.jsp.

10 *Making a doable demo*

The Closing Worksheets in each chapter will guide you through making your own demo. Throughout the book, we'll be talking about a variety of demos that we've used in the past that cover a wide range of topics. In the index, we refer to these demos using names that we hope are clear for readers. You'll find each demo in the index at least twice – once under the general header "Demos" and again under the linguistics topic area that they exemplify. We also note that our own actual day-to-day references to these are often different and somewhat more fun. For example, we actually call the lexical stress demo the "taco demo"; we actually call the word learning demo "mystery words."

2 You Can Be the Expert

OPENING WORKSHEET

What does an expert look like?

Write down the names of three different people that you think of as real experts in their field – they can be people who taught you (your eighth grade history teacher, a college calculus professor), people who are famously smart (Nobel prize winners, legendary scientists), people who are public experts (in government, or on TV and online), or anybody else that you think is the kind of person you'd want to learn from.

What are some key strengths and weaknesses of your favorite experts?

Are your favorite experts

Knowledgeable? Informed? Questioning?
Passionate? Calm? Funny? Quiet?
Single-minded? Interested in lots of different things? Well-rounded?
Preachy? Didactic? Long-winded? Inclusive? Responsive?
Friendly? Stern? Warm? Scary?

Write down one or two strengths and at least one weakness for each of the people you identified.

What are some of your key strengths and weaknesses? Write down at least one key strength and one key weakness of your own.

Do any of your strengths or weaknesses overlap with those of your favorite experts? Are there any features of your favorite experts that you wish you had? Are there things that you are good at that your favorite experts are not?

Both of us writing this book have similar styles when we engage with the public: We're both high-energy, extroverted people. We also both have a research background in children's language development. But you don't need to share our personality traits any more than you need to share our academic specialty in order to be good at public engagement. This book will lay out some principles to help you have good conversations about your science. The personal style that you bring to those conversations will always be your own. And **your** style is one of your strengths as you engage with others. As you'll see in Chapter 16, **you** are one of the core ingredients for creating a good engagement activity.

If you look at some of the best public science figures out there, you can see how different styles can work well. For example, if you watch some classic Bill Nye (the Science Guy) videos from the 1990s, you'll see that he is super goofy – he cracks jokes, does wacky things with his camera and his body, has a nifty theme song, and wears outrageous bow ties. But if you check out Bill Nye later (he's got a nice Twitter profile), you'll see that he is now more restrained. (In Figure 2.1, you'll see both versions.) The bow ties are still there, but there's less slapstick and his tone is less silly. You might prefer early Bill Nye to later Bill Nye (or vice versa), but both versions of him are really effective at what they do.

Or consider the best language science talks you've been to. Some speakers are larger than life and give you a sense of the whole sweep of the field. Others impress with clever examples and tightly constructed arguments that address every objection. Again, which kind of talk you prefer is totally up to you. Both are great models to analyze and even aspire to.

In the course of training students to engage with the public, we've learned that plenty of styles different from our own can be effective. Bringing a calm, even-keeled presence can help young children focus on your content. Being really careful as you walk someone through an International

Figure 2.1 Photos of early (1993) and later (2017) Bill Nye
Note. Early Bill Nye is reprinted with permission from the Everett Collection (Photo credit: PBS). Later Bill Nye is used under Creative Commons Attribution 2.0 (Photo credit: Neil Grabowsky).

Phonetic Alphabet (IPA) chart can be a very effective way of explaining how it works. Being a little bit shy or even awkward can help put some people at ease.

In addition to your personal style, you also bring other properties of yourself to the situation. We are conscious of the fact that we are both female, and we enjoy representing the fact that women can be scientists. Our students often tell us that some of their favorite interactions involve connecting with families that don't typically get to see someone who looks like them being the expert – whether that means someone who is Black, or wears a hijab, or is transitioning genders, or speaks Korean, or any of the many ways we could describe our students.

In the ageless words of Muhammad Ali, sometimes you need "different strokes for different folks." Just as each person reading this book has a different personality, so do the people who you'll interact with: Different styles will appeal to different people. Whatever your own style is will likely be the perfect way to connect with somebody. And as Mr. Ali would also appreciate, sometimes just being who you are in these informal learning spaces will help you connect with people in a special way.

You've undoubtedly had a lot of practice being yourself, so you're probably very good at that. Lean into it! Living up to the principles in this book – making your topic exciting and relevant, organizing information for your audience, expressing yourself in an accessible way, really listening to what your conversational partner is saying – isn't easy. We can't imagine trying to do those things while also trying to act like people we're not. Luckily, all kinds of people can be good communicators and all kinds of styles can be effective. There's not just one way to be good at this!

Attitude Counts for a Lot

One of the most important attributes that you can bring to this process is a genuine interest in your topic area. Making a doable demo will take time and effort, and you're more likely to put that in if you enjoy what you're working on. But interest will matter even more when it comes time to use your demo with public audiences. To get good at working with the public takes practice. If you aren't interested enough in your topic to talk about it over and over (and over and over) again, then you're not going to get the practice on the demo that you need. If you are genuinely interested in what you're trying to communicate, then it's fun to spend the time putting in the work.

Being genuinely interested in your topic will also make you more engaging. People will respond to you and your enthusiasm. If you don't think that your activity is worthwhile, then they probably won't either. People are very good at reading social cues, and they can tell if you think you're doing something stupid or boring. Would you want to take a class from someone who hated the material? Make sure you're working on a topic that you really do think is interesting. That will help people think that you're someone worth talking with.

A slightly different concern that you might have is that only real language nerds will think that your topic is interesting. We appreciate the fact that many of the people reading this book are probably some kind of language nerd – after all, you think language is so cool that you want to talk with other people about it. You might worry that your passion for templatic morphology or tone sandhi or syllabaries will just come across as, well, weird.

Don't worry! Showing off your passion is a good thing and most people will react positively to it. That said, the lessons in this book will help you channel your passion in a productive way. You'll want to think carefully about how to make your topic interesting (Chapter 6) and relevant to the people you're talking with (Chapter 7). We emphasize that one route to relevance involves finding out what your conversational partners already know – their funds of knowledge. And you'll want to make sure that you don't overload people with technical terms (Chapter 14). We are confident that any topic within language science can be turned into a fun and fascinating activity. But it may take more effort to get some topics there than others – so it's a good thing you have the passion to motivate you!

But How Much Do I Really Need to Know?

A critical part of being an expert is, of course, knowing something. If you're a tenured professor, then you're probably used to being an expert on a topic or two, and are pretty confident about what you know. But tenured professors are also very aware of all the things that they don't know! Syntacticians may not feel comfortable talking about phonology. And even among syntacticians, an expert on reference may not feel comfortable talking about argument structure. One of the things that happens as you go on in school is that you are trained to be narrow: It takes a lot to become an academic expert on a topic and you need a suitably small topic in order to earn an advanced degree in it.

But public engagement has a goal that differs from that of a senior thesis or a graduate program. We'll talk more about this in the next chapter, but your aim shouldn't be to prove that you deserve a graduate degree or to promote academic standards of erudition. Your goal is to talk with a member of the public about some piece of language so that they know why it's interesting and a little bit about how it works. Your approach may start in different places, depending on what your conversational partners already know. You don't need to be the world's expert on a topic in order to do those things.

So just how much knowledge do you need? The bare minimum you need is an understanding of the basic science behind your doable demo and how the examples within your demo work. Anything beyond that is terrific, but not strictly speaking necessary. Take for example an activity we've used about sign languages.

The main point of the sign languages demo is to show that sign languages are like any other language. They aren't just an advanced game of charades. Instead, each has rules about how to produce the signs; many signs are arbitrary in nature; and in fact, there are multiple sign languages around the world that are different from each other. How do we show this? We teach people how to count to ten in American Sign Language (ASL) and in British Sign Language (BSL). If you are working in the United States, the idea that there are rules about how to produce individual signs usually comes up when we ask people to guess how to sign *three* in ASL – Americans count to three with different fingers than the ones ASL uses to sign the number three, and it is very rare for anybody in the United States to guess the right three fingers to put up. The more general point that many signs are arbitrary (that is, they can't be guessed at all) comes up when we ask people to guess how to sign *six* in ASL – people don't even come close to suggesting what the actual sign is. The idea that different sign languages are truly different from each other is highlighted by contrasting BSL and ASL. Even though the spoken languages of the United Kingdom and the United States are quite similar, BSL and ASL don't even use the same signs to count to ten!

You might think that in order to effectively do this demo you need to be fluent, or at least proficient, in ASL. But that's simply not the case. The number of signs that you need to know to do the activity is exactly twenty: You need to know how to count to ten in ASL and BSL. It's pretty easy to learn those twenty signs – the structure of the demo actually expects the general public to be able to learn those signs in just a few minutes. And there are many helpful videos online that will show you what the signs look like. One of us (LW) has used this demo many times, and the signs in this activity represent a large proportion of the ASL signs she knows (and 100 percent of the BSL signs she knows).

What you do need to know in order to do this activity is something more general about the status of sign languages and what it means for a sign to be arbitrary (as opposed to iconic). It takes a little bit of reading to learn the core facts, but not more than you would find in an introductory textbook or an encyclopedia.

If you happen to have rich knowledge about ASL (or any other sign language), then you can likely have a richer conversation with people about how sign languages work. On the other hand, if your expertise is shallow, you are likely to be asked a question you don't know the answer to. For the ASL counting demo, people frequently ask how to sign different numbers – 11, 100, 69, etc. If you don't how to sign those numbers, what do you do? You say, "I don't know!" There's no shame in not knowing the answer to something. Nobody knows all the answers. Admitting what you don't know doesn't make you sound dumb – it makes you sound humble. Real experts can admit the limits of their expertise, and people respect experts who are honest about their limits. If you like, you can always suggest how to find the answer. In the case of ASL, it's easy enough to look the answer up online. For other cases, people might ask about something that actually isn't yet known by anybody and would require a whole scientific program to figure out. "I don't know" is the first step to moving science forward.

You might be worried that someone with a lot more expertise on your topic area will come and talk with you. What should you do if you're talking about sign languages and someone who is fluent in ASL comes to talk with you and your knowledge is very shallow? In our experience, have fun. The people who are most likely to appreciate your efforts to engage the public on a particular topic are the people who are deep experts on that topic. They aren't going to give you a hard time about the details of what you're saying; they are more likely to be grateful that someone is trying to promote their topic area. Fluent signers won't be mad because you're not fluent yourself; they will be happy that you're explaining how sign languages are complex and have all the same properties as spoken languages to people who might not realize that. You might even learn your twenty-first sign from such an expert.

On occasion, you might in fact get corrected by someone who knows more than you. (It turns out it matters which direction the palm of your hand is facing when you sign the numbers in ASL!) What should you do if that happens? Thank the person. Because your topic interests you, you should appreciate learning something new about it!

Figure 2.2 An Ohio State University student teaching a child how to make a few signs in ASL at the AAAS Family Science Days festival
Note. The student pictured here is quite knowledgeable about ASL, and she knows far more than the twenty signs used in the activity described in the text.

Build on Your Strengths and Work on Your Weaknesses

Like any skill you are honing, you'll get better with practice. Learning how to present yourself as an expert and getting comfortable in that role is no different.

When you first start working with members of the public, we recommend playing to your strengths. For the first activity that you put together, pick something where you feel like you have a comparatively strong background. Students working with us regularly draw on coursework they have done with other instructors. The audiology majors love talking about how people hear – they take a lot of classes on how the ear works and mechanisms of speech processing and have a lot of details to draw on. By contrast, the psychology majors are more likely to want to center their demos around a topic such as how language can serve as a chunking guide for memory retrieval. And students coming from more humanities-oriented fields often draw on phenomena they have encountered there, such as the difficulty of translating poetry across languages.

It's also good to think about what your own personality is. Are you an extrovert? An introvert? Do you like kids or adults? Do big gangs of teenagers freak you out? Does working with technology relax you or make you nervous? Design your demo to play to your personality strengths. For example, if you're a total extrovert, then the ASL activity is a lot of fun – there's nothing between you and the public except your hands! However, if you're more of an introvert, it can be reassuring to have a physical object that focuses the attention of the visitor – perhaps a game involving a set of cards or blocks, or an app on an iPad. As you create your materials, it's fine to realize that you are the person who is going to have to use them. Make the demo be something that you are comfortable doing.

Once you start engaging with public audiences, remember to be kind to yourself. Nobody is born being good at this kind of activity. One thing we often hear from (mostly senior) colleagues is that they just don't have the "natural ability" that you need in order to talk with the public. But many skills don't rest on natural ability. Instead, we gain them from a lot of practice. Research by psychologist Carol Dweck has shown that when you emphasize the importance of natural ability instead of effort, you are less successful at persevering through a challenging situation (Dweck, 2008). She encourages people to adopt a "growth mindset," which really just means that you think of your mistakes as things to learn from. When the going gets tough, the smart thing to do is to think about what went wrong and keep on trying.

No matter who you are, your first efforts won't be ideal. Don't beat yourself up if you have problems at the beginning. Instead, keep track of the things that aren't working and try to learn from them. Developing your skill at talking with the public is a process that you will never stop working on! For example, both of us (LW and CM) struggle with the fact that we are fast-talkers and we don't like long pauses in the conversation. Sometimes we go so fast that people can't keep up, and sometimes we don't leave space for others to get their chance to speak. We're both better than we used to be, but it's hard, and it requires conscious effort for us to slow down the whole interaction.

One thing that is helpful about working in free-choice settings is that you will get feedback about how you're doing. How do people interact with you – do they stay and chat for a long time (that's good!)? Do they sneak away as soon as you pause for breath (that's not so good)? The public gets to vote with their feet in these settings. Pay attention to how people respond to you, and you'll figure out what is working better or worse. One of the many virtues of working in a free-choice setting is that you will have many, brief, interactions with people. Or as we like to think of it, many chances to learn from them.

CRITICAL TAKE-HOME MESSAGE

There's not just one right way to be good at engaging with the public. Be enthusiastic and let your personal style work for you. The most important thing to do is practice, practice, practice!

WORKED EXAMPLE BOX

A common experience for our students is that members of the public – usually children – will ask them if they are "real scientists." For some students, this question can create a bit of anxiety: They see themselves as students, as trainees, as assistants, as learners. They don't necessarily have *scientist* as part of their self-image. In fact, many professional science communicators resist identifying as scientists because they feel like you have to do hands-on work in a lab setting in order to earn that label.

We, however, want to encourage you to think about what it means to be a scientist more broadly, and to accept *scientist* as part of your self-image in general. We definitely want to encourage you to incorporate it into your self-image while you are talking about language science!

Some of you, we expect, are actual practicing language scientists. Your lab may not have any test tubes or beakers. But if you're using evidence to test hypotheses about some phenomena – whether that phenomenon is the trajectory of sound change in Albanian or the neural organization of Broca's area – then you're a scientist. If you're a research assistant in one of these labs, then you're also a scientist: You're using the scientific method to learn more about how the world works. You don't need to have an advanced degree to be a scientist; you just need to be someone who believes in the scientific method and who wants to learn more about how the world works by using it.

What's more, when you are engaging with your doable demo, you are presenting knowledge that language scientists have generated through the traditional processes of hypothesis testing, evidence gathering, and theory revision. Disseminating scientific information – whether you generated it yourself or someone else did – is part of the job of a scientist.

When we train students, we now warn them that this question may be coming their way. And the right answer to "Are you a real scientist?" is "Yes, I am!"

CLOSING WORKSHEET

In the previous chapter, we asked you to identify three possible topics for a doable demo and think about what you know about each topic, how relevant each would be for other people, and how much fun each would be to do. We hope you wrote all that down!

Now we want you to rank order your three ideas along each of the dimensions you considered. Which one do you know most about? Which one is most socially relevant for people? Which one sounds like the most fun to do?

Now for the hard part: Pick one.

There is no single right answer for what makes the best topic area for a doable demo. You don't have to be the world's expert on your topic (though if you are, that's fine too). You don't have to work on a topic that is ripped from today's headlines (though it's fine if you want to do that too). We do, however, think that it's a good idea to pick a topic that you believe would be fun to work with. It will take you some time to create your demo in the first place, and once you have it, you will be spending a lot of time using it! That's all going to be easier to do if you pick something that you'll enjoy working on.

For the rest of the Closing Worksheets in this book, we'll be referring to your doable demo choice: We mean the one you picked right here. Each chapter will provide advice for how to develop your idea into an activity that members of the public might enjoy and learn from.

Further Reading

1 *Early Bill Nye and later Bill Nye*

In case you're not up on older vs. newer Bill Nye, you might want to read this overview of his background from the *New York Times*: www.nytimes.com/2013/06/18/science/bill-nye-firebrand-for-science-is-a-big-man-on-campus.html.

(Fair warning: The *New York Times* has a paywall and only allows you to read a limited number of articles for free. Contact your library for help.)

But there's no substitute for hearing from the man himself! Bill Nye's Official website is https://billnye.com/, and many clips are available on the YouTube channel *Nye Labs*. If you watch any of Bill Nye's videos, pay special attention to the words he uses. He illustrates Chapter 14's points about having a clear critical take-home message rather amazingly!

2 *Attitude counts for a lot*

If you need some inspiration to bring your attitude with you, we recommend this short piece by Naomi Dalchand about channeling your inner Lady Gaga when presenting (Dalchand, 2021): www.sciencemag.org/careers/2021/02/how-i-transformed-myself-confident-presenter-thanks-lady-gaga.

3 *Many signs are arbitrary*

Most of the words in spoken languages arbitrarily relate to their meanings. That is, the word "shoes" doesn't actually sound anything like shoes, and it isn't directly connected to other shoe properties. A language could pick any old sequence of sounds, and it would work just as well to represent the meaning SHOE. In fact, other languages do pick other sound sequences, and they work just fine. The word for shoes in Japanese is *kutsu*, and in French it is *chaussures*. In sign languages, most of the signs don't look like what their meanings are. In ASL, the sign for shoes involves tapping your fist-shaped hands together twice. (You can see it here: www.lifeprint.com/asl101/pages-signs/s/shoes.htm.) However, there are a significant number of signs in ASL (as well as in other sign languages) where the signs do look a lot like what they refer to. For example, the ASL sign for book involves opening your hands as if you were opening a book (https://lifeprint.com/asl101/pages-signs/b/book.htm). These signs are called "iconic" because the sign is like a pictorial representation (an icon) of what it means. When and how these iconic signs are leveraged for language learning is an interesting domain of research. To learn more, we recommend reading Caselli and Pyers (2020).

4 *Sign languages around the world are different*

Many people are surprised to learn that there are at least 125 sign languages used by deaf communities in the world (www.ethnologue.com/subgroups/sign-language). As with spoken languages, the histories of these languages explain some of their similarities and differences. In this light, it is interesting that the sign languages of the United Kingdom and the United States are not very similar even though spoken English dominates in these places. It turns out that ASL is more similar to French Sign Language than it is to BSL. This reflects an early and critical collaboration between the American Thomas Hopkins Gallaudet (Gallaudet University is named after him) and the French Laurent Clerc. In 1817, they founded the American School for the Deaf, where Clerc became the school's first deaf teacher. If you're interested in learning more about this, the book *When the Mind Hears* tells this specific story and much more about the many interconnections across the deaf communities in France and the United States, including linguistic similarities across these languages (Lane, 1989).

5 *Growth mindset*

You can watch a Ted Talk of Carol Dweck talking about her theory of growth mindset: www.ted.com/talks/carol_dweck_the_power_of_believing_that_you_can_improve?language=en.

6 *Many public science communicators resist identifying as scientists*

The idea that "real science" is limited to work on just a few disciplines (usually things like biology, physics, and chemistry) is widespread, as is the notion that to be a "real scientist" you have to be actively engaged in creating new knowledge in one of these disciplines. James (2020) interviewed science communicators who were working at pop culture conventions to explore how they perceived their scientific identities even as they were engaging in scientific communication. It appears that for many individuals, being a scientist is conceived quite narrowly.

3 Cooperative Conversations

OPENING WORKSHEET

Think about a time when you had an argument, or even just a minor misunderstanding, with someone who you were talking with.

Briefly write down at least one factor that caused the misunderstanding. You might want to consider the following list:

- Were you and the other person both being truthful? Did you tell each other **all** of the truth or only part of it?
- Did you and the other person agree about what the **real** topic of the conversation was? Were you arguing about the same thing, or were you talking past each other?
- Were you and the other person using the same words to mean different things? (For example, "out late" could mean different things to different people.)
- Were you able to say as much as you wanted, or were you unable to get a word in edgewise?
- Did the other person say enough for you to get their point? Or did they say so little that you had to figure everything out for yourself? Did you figure things out the way the other person wanted you to?

In this book, we're talking a lot about conversations. The key to effectively sharing your ideas with other people is to approach your interaction like you're having a conversation. Conversations are a core language experience, and the field of language science has found out a lot about how they work: what we expect when we are going into one, what kinds of things make conversations run smoothly, what kinds of things make them go horribly wrong. In this chapter, we're going to briefly cover what language science teaches us about successful conversations.

Conversations Succeed When They Are Cooperative

At the heart of a good conversation is two people working together to communicate with each other. The insight that conversations are fundamentally cooperative goes back to at least the 1970s, thanks to a philosopher named Paul Grice (Grice, 1975). Grice's ideas were very influential, and we're going to use a lot of his terminology as we describe conversations.

Once you put cooperation front and center, it's easy to see that understanding people is essential for understanding conversations. Words don't cooperate with each other; **people** cooperate with each other. Luckily, cooperation is something that comes pretty naturally. Infants and toddlers value it and know how to do it. For example, the psychologist Felix Warneken has shown that children who weren't even two years old would spontaneously try to help unfamiliar adults having problems opening doors and finding objects (see Warneken & Tomasello, 2006, for one compelling study in Warneken's program). Without being directly asked or getting any kind of reward (besides the warm fuzzy feeling that comes with being a nice person), these toddlers volunteered to work with someone to get something done. This drive to cooperate with others seems to be a deep human instinct.

When we talk with others, we are drawing on this instinct to cooperate. But for cooperation to be effective, you have to pay attention to the people you're cooperating (conversing) with. What do they know? What do they expect? What do they want? The fields of communication and psychology have a lot to say about how we track the mental states of other people, and we'll talk more about that angle in Chapters 11 and 12. For now, we'll just mention that keeping track of what's going on in other people's minds can be tricky, and it's very easy to mix up what you know (and expect, and want) with what other people know (and expect, and want).

Our Opening Worksheet asked you to think about arguments. If anything feels like it doesn't involve cooperation, surely it's an argument – right? Not necessarily! First, think about something that's more like a disagreement, or a debate. You want to go out for Italian food, say, and I'd rather stay home and cook Indian food instead. To talk through this, we need to agree on what the problem is (type of cuisine, location of dinner) and each of us needs to make our positions clear to the other person. That is, we need to create a common understanding about what each of us wants and how important it is to us. Once we have this mutual understanding, we still might not agree with each other; our desires and interests might be so incompatible that we each end up eating on our own. But if we had a cooperative argument, then at least we will have made our decision based on an accurate understanding of each other.

Now think of something a bit more heated – a real honest-to-goodness fight with someone. Sometimes these fights are just like cooperative arguments, but with more intense feeling (maybe I **hate** Italian food). But sometimes arguments break all the rules that make a cooperative conversation work: We may not believe each other, or understand each other, or feel like we're even talking about the same topic, and we might just go round in circles. Our fight about where to go to dinner might really be about money, or politics, or the fact that you never clean the dishes – and we might not even agree about what we're fighting about!

But in these cases, it's not clear that we're having a conversation at all. What Grice's approach tells us is that our default assumption when talking with others is that they are trying to communicate with us so that we will understand them. Grice proposed four core rules for a cooperative conversation – he called them MAXIMS. When we follow all the rules, we are more likely to have a **successful** conversation. When we don't follow them, there are unfortunate consequences: We don't connect effectively, we misunderstand each other, we fail to communicate; we may even offend each other. Of course, you can break the rules if you want to (there isn't a conversation cop out there!). In general, though, people don't expect you to. Your goal in public engagement should be to have a conversation where you connect, communicate, and foster understanding. To do that takes cooperation. Let's see how this all works.

MAXIM OF QUALITY: Tell the Truth

The first rule for successful conversation is to be truthful. Most people, most of the time, are telling you the truth. And most people, most of the time, believe that you are telling the truth. We expect our friends to talk with us honestly about their interests, their feelings, their plans, and even their whereabouts. We even expect total strangers to give us honest answers to all kinds of questions: What time is it? Has the bus stopped here recently? How do I make this thing work?

Of course, not everybody tells the truth all the time. If you lie just a little bit, you can often get away with it because you can free-ride off the fact that everyone expects you to tell the truth. But there are consequences to being caught out in a lie, and even bigger consequences to being viewed as a habitual liar. We'll be talking about how to have a conversation of a particular kind – one where you're the expert and you're talking with a member of the public. Following the Maxim of Quality has a special resonance in this case. We are all familiar with conspiracy theories, "fake news," and "alternative truth," as well as the distrust that these bring. One way to think about such issues is to see them as breakdowns in the Maxim of Quality: We are all so used to having this rule broken by (some) public figures calling themselves experts that for many people, quality is no longer their default expectation for experts. In Chapter 8, we'll talk a bit about how to occupy the role of expert so people take you at your word, as a person of true quality!

MAXIM OF QUANTITY: Say as Much as You Need to, but Not More

The second rule for having a successful conversation is about quantity. Grice's analysis is that Goldilocks had it right: You don't want too much, and you don't want too little. You want to make sure you say just the right amount!

How do you know what the right amount is? It helps to have some idea about what your conversational partner knows and needs. Suppose you hear someone exclaim, "I got in!" If you don't know that person at all, you might wonder what they got in to. Did they just get admitted to college? Did they just crack a government security system? Did they just dive into a pool? For a stranger, there's not enough information in that exclamation for you to know. But if you're a close friend, you would know if the person had recently applied to college, or was an inveterate hacker, or hated cold water. And having that background knowledge would allow you to understand what they meant. As a general guideline, the better you know somebody, the more background information you share and the less you need to actually say directly in your conversation.

How about the other direction? Have you ever had a conversation with someone where they kept telling you things you already knew? It's annoying! "The Eiffel Tower is located in the 7th Arrondissement in the left bank in Paris. In France. In Europe." If you can already understand something with less information, getting more feels wrong. Often it feels very condescending, as if the person has a very low opinion of what you already know. (Come on! I know that Paris is in France!) In fact, this particular way of violating the Maxim of Quantity can be more than off-putting; it can be downright offensive.

Just like we have a default expectation that people will be truthful, we also expect that people will give us the right quantity of information. If they tell us something we already know, they must think it is something we don't know: That's what makes it seem condescending. And if they give us too little information, we might feel uncomfortable asking about what's assumed or we might feel that the speaker doesn't care about our understanding. In that case, the speaker seems to think we know enough to fill in the gaps, so if we can't, we might worry that's because we're missing something important. Either way, as the listener, getting the wrong amount of information feels like the speaker isn't being respectful of what you know.

Getting the quantity right helps make for a better, and more respectful, interaction. We will come back to this point in Chapter 9, where we talk about how to balance the desire to tell the (whole) truth and the need to tailor your message to what can usefully be related in a brief conversation.

MAXIM OF RELEVANCE: Stick to the Point

The third rule for a successful conversation rests on relevance. Conversations are about topics, and our default expectation is that everything we say is going to make a positive contribution to the conversational topic. Part of how we interpret phrases like "I got in" is because we expect it to be relevant to the topic of conversation. If we're talking about hacking computers, then what you got into should be relevant to security systems; if we're talking about swimming, then what you got into should be something relevantly wet.

Relevance is very tightly connected to the foundational idea of cooperation. As we mentioned earlier, one route to relevance involves exploring your conversational partner's funds of knowledge. This takes cooperation between you and them. A conversation is something we are building together, but that only works if everybody is trying to contribute to this goal. If we're building a house out of Legos, I won't be helping if I bring a hammer and nails. I need to bring something that will fit with the rest – the things that fit are relevant. Relevance is an extremely strong default assumption, so much so that extreme violations of it are often taken as conversational signals. For example, if we are talking about something that I find distasteful, uncomfortable, or boring, I might offer an out-of-the-blue statement that is clearly unrelated to the topic ("Very fine weather we've been having these days"). The statement is typically taken as being very relevant – not about the topic under discussion directly, but about my interest in continuing with the topic (clearly, I'm not).

Many researchers have argued that this is the maxim from which the other ones flow. Truth is usually far more relevant than untruth. And we interpret the quantity of information that people provide in light of its relevance. If it looks like someone hasn't given enough information to be understood, we might try to connect what they said to the conversational topic. If the topic is swimming, for example, we can assume that "I got in" relates to the topic and so is more likely to refer to getting into a pool than cracking a security system. Similarly, if it looks like someone has provided too much information, we might try to figure out why that extra information is especially relevant to the topic, perhaps in an unexpected way. (Is France considering leaving the European Union?) Even the way that we say something (the Maxim of Manner, coming up next) can provide a clue to what the speaker wants us to think about the topic.

So can there be genuine violations of relevance in a conversation? Actually, yes. It is possible for two people to be talking and to not notice that one of them is using Legos while the other is using a hammer and nails. Earlier, we mentioned arguments as a place where cooperation sometimes fails; in our experience, many arguments have just this kind of problem. But another place where this kind of problem can arise is in exactly the kind of conversations that this book is about: when experts are trying to communicate with the public. In upcoming chapters (especially Chapter 5), we will talk about where your audience is likely to be coming from and suggest some ways to help make sure that you and your audience are building a conversation together.

MAXIM OF MANNER: Be Clear!

The last rule for successful conversations concerns clarity. Ideally, speakers should try to communicate clearly and concisely, ordering their contributions to help their conversational partner. This rule is actually the same advice that every writing teacher has given to every student they've ever taught. This rule sometimes seems like it's more about style than substance. But the fact is that if people can't follow what you're saying, it doesn't matter how accurate, appropriate, on-topic, or otherwise awesome it is. They won't be able to stick with it, and that means you won't be building anything together.

People sometimes underestimate the importance of manner in communication and feel like it just takes care of itself. We're not sure that's ever true, but it is definitely not true for the kinds of conversations we're focusing on in this book: conversations where you are sharing complex language science information with someone who likely has little expertise on that specific topic. For these conversations, it is absolutely critical that you be clear and organized. Creating a clear explanation is hard, and it does require thought and planning. We think it's hard enough that we devote Chapters 11–16 to talking about ways to describe phenomena clearly and ways to organize your information to facilitate real understanding.

CRITICAL TAKE-HOME MESSAGE

Our default assumption when talking with someone is that they are trying to communicate with us so that we will understand them. The cooperative rules (or maxims) are what we do to participate in a successful conversation. When we don't follow these rules, there are unfortunate consequences: We don't connect effectively, we misunderstand each other, we fail to communicate. Our goal when talking with the public is to have a conversation where we connect, communicate, and foster understanding. To do that takes cooperation.

WORKED EXAMPLE BOX

Cooperation isn't always easy to achieve in conversations! Sometimes, even when everybody is trying to communicate helpfully, things still go wrong. For example, in the 1970s there was a staff morale problem at Heathrow Airport. The baggage handlers (mostly white men) felt like the new food service workers (mostly Pakistani women) were being rude, leading to bad interactions that made the food service workers feel discriminated against. To help figure out what was going on, the airport administrators brought in linguist John Gumperz to see if he could help. He discovered that the heart of the problem was a communication misunderstanding.

In the lunch line, the food service workers would ask their customers if they wanted gravy with their food. In English (including the dialect spoken by most of the baggage handlers), a fast way to ask that question is to use one word (*gravy*) with rising intonation. However, drawing on the intonation patterns of their native language, the food service workers were asking that one word question with falling intonation. So instead of sounding like they were asking a question ("Gravy?") it sounded like they were insisting on adding it ("Gravy!").

The way in which a single word was uttered led to different interpretations. The food service workers thought they were politely asking about preferences, but the baggage handlers thought their preferences were rudely ignored.

Where did the cooperative breakdown come from?

When it comes to Quality and Relevance, there doesn't seem to be much of a problem. The food service workers and the baggage handlers were surely talking about the same general topic: What did the baggage handlers want to eat? And gravy definitely seems to have been an option for them.

The troubles here came from Quantity and Manner. You have to give the food service workers credit for being concise – a one-word question is about the least wordy way to ask something! But as it happens, the one word wasn't clear enough. The food service workers were assuming that the baggage handlers shared all the same assumptions they did about how to ask that question, and so they didn't spell everything out. But since the baggage handlers didn't share the same assumptions, they filled in the gaps in a different way.

(cont.)

This example also shows the special problems that can arise when conversations are between people from very different backgrounds – whether that means different languages, cultures, or levels of expertise in a subject. Getting Quantity and Manner right depends on correctly assessing what the other person knows; the more different someone is from you, the more likely it is that you will know different things.

You can read more about this example and more about John Gumperz's remarkable life in his *New York Times* obituary (Fox, 2013).

CLOSING WORKSHEET

Remind yourself of the topic you selected for your doable demo (see the Closing Worksheet in Chapter 2). Now think about how you can apply the different conversational maxims to it!

- Establish your base of Quality: Write down five true things about your topic.
- Find an ideal level of Quantity: From that set of five true things, identify the two that are the most important ones to talk about.
- Anticipate what is Relevant: Write down two reasons why your topic area matters in people's everyday lives.
- Practice your Manner: Write down your two most important true things in language that is clear, concise, and easy to understand. Now do that for your two reasons that the topic area is relevant.

Further Reading

1 *The philosopher Paul Grice*

Paul Grice is a foundational figure in the fields of philosophy and linguistics. He's important enough that you can read about him in most textbooks, or here: https://plato.stanford.edu/entries/grice/. But it is worth noting that Grice laid out his theory in the 1970s, and there has been a substantial amount of technical work on this topic written since then. If you're interested in finding out more about what this subfield of language science has discovered, we recommend starting with the book *Relevance*

(Sperber & Wilson, 1986), or articles by the linguists Craige Roberts (Roberts, 2012) and Judith Degen (Degen & Tanenhaus, 2019).

2 *The psychologist Felix Warneken*

To learn more about Warneken's work, a good place to start is Warneken and Tomasello (2006). Or, you can watch some delightful videos on Warneken's website of children engaging in cooperative behavior: https://sites.lsa.umich.edu/warneken/study-videos/.

3 *You and your audience*

This book refers to audiences a lot, so we want to note that we do not use this term to refer to any conventional group of hearers or spectators. Instead, we use *audience* to refer to our immediate conversational partners and to the people who attend events like festivals and places like museums. We emphasize in several chapters how important it is to learn what your immediate audience knows and then to calibrate your contributions to the conversation accordingly. Further, as the glorious *Oxford English Dictionary* (2013) tells us, the etymology of *audience* starts with the Latin *audire*, meaning to hear. But this book concerns an interactive audience made of people who both talk and listen.

4 *Facilitate real understanding*

We (like Grice) recognize that it isn't always possible to satisfy all the maxims equally well all the time. Sometimes, in order to deeply satisfy one maxim, you have to violate one of the other maxims. But nobody ever said having a successful conversation was going to be easy! In Chapter 9, we will talk about one of the places where you may have to work to find the right compromise between the maxims of Quality and Quantity.

4 Conversational Goals

OPENING WORKSHEET

Think about how things work in a regular classroom. Write down the answers to a few of the following questions:

- Who is present and why are they there?
- Who does most of the talking?
- Who are the experts in the room?
- When do you talk and when do you stay quiet?
- How does a teacher make you feel that it's OK to ask a question?
- What do you do when you're confused? How do you ask questions?
- Have you ever felt like you asked a 'dumb' question in a class? What happened to make you feel that way? What did you do?
- What do you do when you're bored or tired?
- What classroom activities are truly fun for you?

Now think about a free-choice learning environment – a museum, a fair, a festival, a café, a library. Which of your answers to the questions above are the same and which are different?

The purpose of most everyday conversations is pretty general – to catch up with a friend, to discuss a movie, to get some advice. For these kinds of conversations, you don't need much of an agenda or a plan to make them go smoothly. But for conversations supporting your public engagement, some planning will help. Before you begin, it's helpful to reflect on your goals and to have some ideas about how you'll accomplish them. If you know what you're trying to do with your conversation, you will be better able to choose what to say (and what not to say) and you'll be better prepared to handle the conversation when it takes an unexpected turn.

School's Out!

You may be most familiar with the learning situation in the school setting. You're probably someone who liked school, and maybe you even did (do!) pretty well in your classes. You're probably very comfortable with the idea of an expert explaining complicated material to a room full of quiet students there to master that material. Get ready to leave that zone! Engaging with the public in an informal learning setting is not like being in a classroom, and if you approach it as if it is, you will turn people off and likely fail to spark their interest in your topic.

The public who you will be talking with are not your students. They didn't sign up to be in your class, and they don't need your course for their major. There are also no external incentives for them to learn from you – they won't get an A for learning about your topic and there are no penalties for not paying attention. People will converse with you because they want to. That means that one of your core goals is to make your conversation interesting enough that people want to talk with you.

But no matter how interesting you are, the people you talk with in these environments are not as invested as students are in a typical class. Partly that's a product of time considerations – most of your interactions in these locations will be relatively short (often fifteen minutes or less) and you'll interact with each person (or group) just once. That's just a tiny fraction of the time that students spend with a teacher in a regular semester. And that means that the amount of content that you'll be able to get across will be just a tiny fraction of what would be covered in a regular class. Your goals need to be tailored to what can be accomplished in that short time.

Another factor that affects these interactions is the fact that people are likely to engage with you in an opportunistic rather than a planned way. That is, many people come to festivals and museums because they want to learn some new things. But they are very unlikely to be expecting to learn about your specific topic. You can't expect that anyone is coming in having read a lot in your area, or even that they are coming with any passion for your particular science.

Imagine that you are just one offering on a large buffet table (or tapas bar). If you are appealing, then lots of people will want to put you on their plates. But there are usually lots of things for people to choose from in these locations, and most people don't want to load up their plate with just one offering. People are looking for a bite-sized chunk of your science to think about.

In Chapter 9, we will cover the idea that it is not just OK to emphasize only some elements of your topic; it is in fact ideal. Being incomplete doesn't mean that what you're saying is incorrect. You're setting people up to learn more about the wider world. Giving people their first taste of a topic is an important part of that process.

Public Knowledge: Deficits vs. Funds

Getting out of the school mindset can be hard. And there is a long, unfortunate, tradition of scientists bringing the worst kind of school teaching into their interactions with the public. There's even a name for assumptions behind this unfortunate approach: the DEFICIT MODEL. On this model, the general public lacks knowledge (they have a deficit), and what they need is for the expert to provide what they're missing. A common thing to say from this perspective is, "The reason people believe X is because they just don't understand the facts." Depending on the week, that X might be "climate change isn't real" or "humans didn't evolve" or "vaccines give kids autism" or "bilingualism is bad for babies." Whatever the X, it is usually stated in an exasperated tone of voice. But this perspective convinces absolutely nobody.

People aren't empty vessels who are waiting to be filled up with scientific (or any other kind of) knowledge. People live in connected communities, and during the normal course of their lives they learn about all kinds of things. When they talk with an expert, they bring their own experiences and background knowledge with them. For hot-button issues, these background experiences can often be very emotional. The scientific facts you offer people may be in competition with ideas that they already have. And really, what would you expect someone to believe? Something they just heard from a person they just met, or something that a trusted member of their own community has told them and that they may have had personal experiences with?

In the case of language, people will likely be bringing with them a lifetime of experience with prescriptivism. Linguistic prescriptivism is the approach that aims to fix people's language by telling them (prescribing) correct language usage. People have had favorite teachers grade them for their use of 'right' and 'wrong' words; their parents have told them to avoid (or use) certain words; they probably have their own pet peeves about 'bad' things people say or ways to write. Language science, of course, embraces descriptivism: Everything that people say is important for understanding how the human mind creates and uses language. The fact that people judge others for their language choices is interesting primarily as a social (or perhaps sociolinguistic) phenomenon.

You could simply tell people that their prescriptivist attitudes are wrong, uninformed by modern linguistics, and that their attitudes reflect centuries of classism, sexism, and racism. Speaking as language scientists, we may be confident in what the facts are and the implications of those facts. But simply telling people they are wrong, or even explaining to them the history of grammar policing, is unlikely to convince them of much. And you probably already know that: Most of us have tried the direct approach at least once with people in our lives. One reason it doesn't work is that it flies in the face of what people already know: Their lived experiences tell them that standard forms of language do matter in some circumstances. In other words, prescriptivism is real and it matters. Who are you to deny their personal histories?

So what's the alternative? Instead of treating people's prior experiences as baggage to be dismissed or wrestled with, treat their experiences as an asset that you can work with. There's a name for this perspective as well: the FUNDS OF KNOWLEDGE approach. In this approach, you assume that the knowledge that people already have is a valuable resource. People can draw on their own experiences to contribute to their conversation with you. You can make your contributions more interesting and more relevant for someone if you can connect your work to what they already know or believe. What's more, sometimes people will have knowledge that you can learn from yourself – their lifetime of language use means that they might have noticed something that you haven't. You and they are partners in a joint exploration of knowledge.

In the case of language, the funds of knowledge approach is a natural fit. People use language every day – everyone you talk with has thousands (and thousands and thousands) of hours of language use under their belt. Not only that, but most people have spent time thinking **about** language – they've likely noticed regional accents; they may appreciate a clever rhyme in a rap; they may have misheard some song lyrics; they may have taken a foreign language class or speak another language natively; they might have a dyslexia; they may have a grandparent with an aphasia; they may have struggled to find the perfect phrase to use in a wedding toast. Part of the reason that language is fun to talk about in informal learning settings is precisely because people have such a rich personal history with it!

How do you leverage these funds of knowledge? Here's an example. One of the activities we've done a lot involves showing people the International Phonetic Alphabet (IPA). At the end of the activity, we usually make name tags with people's names spelled in the IPA for them to take home. A not uncommon reaction, especially from children when you write out their names in the IPA, is that you did it wrong. They know the right way to spell their names, and depending on their age, they may be very proud that they know how to do it right! In effect, they are throwing up a strong prescriptivist objection: Their fundamental concern is with the language being 'correct.'

We don't tell these children that they're wrong and we're right. After all, there is real value to the prescriptive point of view in this case: We all care that people spell our names correctly. Instead, we have children show us how they spell their own names, and validate their knowledge. Then we talk with them about how hard it is to learn how to spell some words, an experience that is easy for (English-speaking) children to relate to. (If the child is young enough, there's a parent nearby who is appreciating this conversation.) That turn in the conversation connects to the core educational message of the IPA activity, namely that letters and sounds are different things: One reason spelling is so hard in English is because the mapping between sounds and letters isn't straightforward. Having highlighted spelling challenges for children, the motivation for using the IPA is clearer: Each IPA symbol maps simply to one sound.

Now we can ask children to compare the IPA way and the standard way of spelling their own name and get them to think about what sounds in their name are hard to spell. Children can often connect this discussion to their own experiences – teachers who have mispronounced their written names before, or friends who have similar names but spell them differently. If the child happens to come from a non-English-speaking background, they may also have experience with a different writing system or how their name looks different in different alphabets.

In fact, this activity is a wonderful way to draw explicitly on the funds of knowledge for these families because they know very well how English spelling doesn't always capture the sounds that they are saying. For example, if you're working with a Spanish-English bilingual family, you might focus on differences in vowels in the two languages. The letter "I" is used to represent a variety of sounds in English: It sounds very different in *pin*, *vine*, and *magazine*. But Spanish has five vowel sounds and five vowel letters, and the same letter is consistently linked to the [i] sound. In fact, this consistency is helpful! A child learning to read English will typically have a harder time than a child learning to read Spanish. The IPA is a good tool for helping people think about how sounds and letters are different things. People's background experiences provide a rich set of examples that you can draw on.

SIX STRANDS of Science Learning

The field of science communication has been working for a while on methods to promote good interactions between scientists and the general public – methods that avoid the deficit model, respect people's funds of knowledge, and in general, make learning about science fun. A national panel of experts in informal science learning put together a report that distilled the work in this field into six strands of science learning (Fenichel & Schweingruber, 2010). These are called strands in part because of how they work together, like elements in a rope. To clarify how the strands can be woven together to make coherent and strong links for people who we engage with, we've framed each one here as a goal to strive for when you are working with the public.

Strand 1: Generate interest and excitement.
Strand 2: Celebrate scientific knowledge.
Strand 3: Foster observations, explorations, and questions.
Strand 4: Invite people to reflect on science as a process.
Strand 5: Collaborate in using the tools of science.
Strand 6: Encourage people to think of themselves as science learners and as potential scientists.

It is hard to make a single activity embody all of these strands, and different strands are better suited for different audiences and topics and locations. The one strand that we encourage you to aim for with absolutely every person – no matter their age – is Strand 1. Capturing people's interest and getting them excited about your topic prolongs your conversation and so gives you more time to address your other goals. Your success here also means that your audience is enjoying the experience you've engineered for them. In addition, Strands 2 and 3 are usually pretty easy to incorporate into your activity. Strand 2 focuses on getting people to appreciate the content of your science – the phenomena that it describes. We hope that the previous part of this chapter has convinced you that this strand is one to be very careful with: Don't fall into the school trap or the deficit model! Try to focus more on celebrating what we know than on testing people on what they don't know. Strand 3 focuses on some principles of a good interaction style, principles that are helpful for achieving all the other strands.

The last three strands concern elements that may or may not fit well with a particular activity. For example, the IPA activity mentioned above is a great way to address Strand 5 (the IPA is definitely a tool of language science). And depending on who you are talking with, you might have a conversation about the IPA that naturally leads to Strand 4 – thinking about how a linguist might describe the sounds of a new language invites a discussion about the process of linguistic discovery. By contrast, our activity about teaching people to count in ASL (from Chapter 2) doesn't embody Strands 4 or 5 particularly well. But that's OK. Again, each individual activity and each individual encounter with a person doesn't have to accomplish all possible learning goals. You can't be all things to all people all the time.

And what about Strand 6? How do you get people to think about themselves as able to **do** science? The content of your demo is unlikely to be where this strand is going to come out. Instead, you can weave this strand in through the kind of interactions you have. Encouraging people to reflect on their experience with your demo and to come up with some new ideas about how your phenomenon works (that is, hypotheses!) is really encouraging people to think like scientists. We'll suggest some concrete ways (such as using juicy questions) to promote these kinds of interactions in Chapter 10.

In addition, your very presence makes you a model for one way to be a scientist. We hope you are modeling the idea that a scientist is someone who is interested and interesting, engaged, and friendly. That might be the kind of person that would inspire some children to want to be scientists themselves!

Two Mantras

It can be a little bit overwhelming to think about all the things you could, or should, do when you're talking with the public. We offer here two short mantras that can take some of the pressure off.

It's Not about You

Don't worry about being the smartest person there, or the biggest expert on your topic. Just as you don't have external rewards to give the people you're talking with, they also don't have any to give you. You're not on a job interview or defending your dissertation – you don't have to prove yourself here. In fact, if you're taking the funds of knowledge approach seriously, you will be hoping to learn new things from the people who you interact with. Just relax and have a conversation with people. It's OK if one of your goals is to have fun while you do your demo!

Take the Long View

Ultimately, you're trying to raise public awareness about language science: The big goal with this kind of work is to change the world. But you're not going to achieve that with any individual conversation. Or two. Or even three. People change gradually, and you're not likely to see an Aha! moment where people walk away changed for life. Each conversation contributes to incremental progress toward this big goal. So just try to make sure that your conversations encourage people to keep talking with you, or with some other scientist, again and again.

CRITICAL TAKE-HOME MESSAGE

Talking with the public in an informal learning setting is very different from a school-based setting, and your goals need to match where you are. The six strands of science learning provide a great framework. But focus on Strand 1 (generate interest and excitement), no matter what else is possible. We also advocate for the funds of knowledge approach: Find out what people already know. Respect and appreciate the prior experiences of the people you're talking with!

WORKED EXAMPLE BOX

Strands of science learning and the language lateralization demo

One activity we've done many times uses a finger tapper to show that our left hemispheres care about speech. We ask people to use their **right** index finger to tap a counter on a wooden board for thirty seconds. Each person decides whether to talk or stay silent while tapping. Anyone can do the tapping task, although it's ideal for people older than eight years (because of dexterity). Another reason we especially like this demo is that anyone speaking any language, including ones that we don't know, can participate.

When people are done tapping, we ask if the person is right- or left-handed and record their total number of taps on a poster. The poster has a grid on it that allows us to illustrate the results of a few comparisons. The rows are labeled for whether the person talked or stayed silent; the columns are labeled for whether the person is right- or left-handed. We don't do anything fancy with the data: We just write the tap totals of each person in the correct cell, and every so often we compute averages to make it easy to compare across the cells.

Even though we ignore factors like age and sex, the averages after a dozen or so right-handers show that people who talked while tapping tap slower (fewer taps in thirty seconds) and people who stayed silent while tapping tap faster (more taps). (It takes a long time to find enough left-handed or ambidextrous tappers to fill the rest of the cells. So we bring numbers from previous uses of the demo with us.)

(cont.)

Figure 4.1 A University of Arizona student doing the language lateralization demo with a child at the Tucson Festival of Books

Then we tell people one important fact about the brain while teaching them one technical term: The brain has contralateral connections. That means that the left hemisphere is primarily responsible for making the right hand do the tapping. With just that one fact and the pattern of data on our poster, people can compare the numbers in the talking and silent cells and say why they think the numbers in the silent cell are on average bigger. At the end of this demo, we offer each person a paper left-hemisphere headband (see photographs in Figure 4.2).

Here are a few possible ways to hit the six strands with this demo.

Strand 1: Generate interest and excitement

The tapper is relatively loud, which draws a small crowd, which draws a bigger crowd. Friendly competition makes this demo popular with groups, friends egging the tappers on as they tap madly away. The big poster with numbers that are constantly changing also gets some attention. And the headbands bring us more visitors as time passes. People often come to our booth asking, "Is this where I can get a brain?" All joking aside, this demo is super fun!

(cont.)

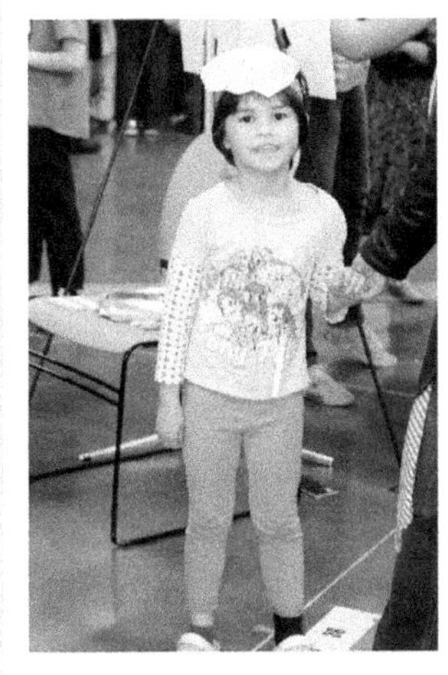

Figure 4.2 Children wearing left-hemisphere headbands after participating in the language lateralization demo

Strand 2: Celebrate scientific knowledge

Our core message is that spoken language is a processing load for left hemispheres. But the demo invites exploration of other topics too. Sometimes people want to talk about differences between right- and left-handers, or about how to classify people who are ambidextrous. Sometimes they want to talk about sex differences, or differences between children and adults. Sometimes they want to talk about different parts of language or about whether music and language work the same. We bring a collection of talking points with us so we're prepared to address different dimensions of brain organization and development.

Strand 3: Foster observations, explorations, and questions

The tap totals we put on the poster encourage observations and questions. We invite people to compare the averages in each of the cells on the poster and talk with them as they interpret the differences that they notice. For example, our data will typically show that the difference between the silent and talking cells is bigger for right-handers than for left-handers. And that can bring us to a larger conversation about variation in degrees of lateralization. It can also bring us to discuss the limits of using this kind of task (and see Strand 4).

(cont.)

People also have lots of ideas about variations on our task that might change the results. Would tappers get better if they could repeat the task in a quiet place? What about if they did the task with their other hand? If they are multilingual, they might ask how their data would look if they talked in different languages. Some of these ideas can even be explored right there on the spot! In addition, many people share stories of stroke patients in their own families, easily making connections between the demo and their own funds of knowledge.

Strand 4: Invite people to reflect on science as a process

When we write an individual's tap total on the poster, we explain that this activity is not a research study – that is, we're not collecting data as part of some ongoing investigation. This comment sometimes leads to interesting discussions about science in general. Why isn't this demo real research? In this context, people often note the noisy environment, the broad range of people who do the task (and we combine all their data), and some of the questions and comments noted above. In other words, they come up with the idea that scientists need to control their variables. How you get your data is a critical part of the scientific process!

Strand 5: Collaborate in using the tools of science

Our finger tapper doesn't look like a classic piece of scientific equipment. It's just a small mechanical gizmo that flips to a higher number every time you tap a tiny paddle. Modern researchers use much more impressive tools for questions about the brain (MRIs, ERPs, fNIRS, etc.). But gizmos like this simple tapper are still used in some research and clinical situations. Another tool we use is statistics. We calculate the means, and people are doing (informal) inferential statistical tests when they compare the numbers across the cells.

Strand 6: Encourage people to think of themselves as science learners and potential scientists

This activity actually asks people to do something that scientists really do: Look at patterns of data and draw inferences about them. It gives people a taste of that magic moment when you figure out what a pattern means. It's the feeling of scientific discovery!

Also, this activity is interdisciplinary: It is about both how the brain works and how language works. Because it is so broad, we often get

(cont.)

questions that we don't know the answers to. We are always happy to admit when we don't know something (see Chapters 2 and 8) and talk about how we – or the people we're talking with! – might go about learning more about it.

CLOSING WORKSHEET

Remind yourself of the topic you selected for your doable demo (see the Closing Worksheet in Chapter 2).

What funds of knowledge do people bring to your topic area?

Write down some general funds of knowledge that just about every person who you talk with would have about your topic.

Now consider some special groups of people who would bring specific funds of knowledge that might influence how you do your demo. For example, what would a parent bring? Or a multilingual person? Or a poet? Identify two special groups and write down the specific funds of knowledge they have, and also write down at least one idea about how you'd adjust your demo to make use of those funds.

Review the six strands of science learning. Pick two of them and write down an idea for how your doable demo topic might address them.

Further Reading

1 *Deficit model*

References to the "information deficit model" originated in studies of public communication of science. The term referred to a perspective that motivated and colored much of the work in that area – namely, that a lack of knowledge about science and technology made the public skeptical toward things like climate change and vaccinations. On this view, communicators who could fill these deficits would help change public perceptions so that people would see the benefits of science and technology. The deficit model matters in formal education as well, where students' failures have sometimes been attributed to their individual deficiencies or to disadvantages in their family or community rather than to problems in the education system.

The deficit model approach represents a top-down perspective. It assumes that "to know science is to love it" (Allum et al., 2008, p. 35). While this may be true to some extent, there are many factors that contribute to people's acceptance of and affection toward science. More important in the context of this book, a deficit approach ignores the role of trust in communication between experts and others. We urge replacing a presentation-based approach that reflects the deficit model with a conversation-based approach that sparks people's interest in a phenomenon, draws out the knowledge that they already have (i.e., their "funds of knowledge," González et al., 2005), and enhances their understanding (at whatever level it is) through asking juicy questions and listening to answers.

In the context of studying US-based scientists' communication objectives, Besley et al. (2018) overviewed possibilities that may help you think about what you are trying to do. A typical objective relates to conveying knowledge, but this often rests on a view of the audience as having a knowledge deficit. Another objective is sparking interest in science, which we emphasized above. Six other objectives that Besley et al. studied are: showing scientists' expertise; hearing what other people think about scientific issues; showing that scientists care about society's well-being; showing scientists' openness and transparency; showing that scientists share community values; and framing science so that it resonates with a community's values. You will see these ideas recurring through several chapters in this book as they relate to things like relevance and credibility.

2 *Funds of knowledge approach*

As several chapters note, we recommend consciously basing your public engagement on the funds of knowledge framework. This framework originated in research by anthropologists James Greenberg and Carlos Vélez-Ibáñez. After documenting the rich cultural backgrounds of children in the United States–Mexico borderlands, they argued for reforming educational systems that underestimate what these children know (Greenberg, 1989; Vélez-Ibáñez & Greenberg, 1992). Educator Luis Moll and colleagues developed the framework into a broader educational philosophy that emphasizes cooperative learning and explicitly addresses the assumptions of deficit or dysfunctionality that can hamper students from poor and minority families (González et al., 2005; Moll & Greenberg, 1990). The funds of knowledge framework asks educators and mentors to find and use the knowledge assets that may be hidden in people's everyday, real-world lives.

This framework is influential in a broad range of areas. For example, Cowie et al. (2011) describes research on multi-year science programming that supports Māori and Pasifika students in New Zealand. Another example is found in the office of the Superintendent of Public Instruction in the US state of Washington, which contains state-level guidance for classrooms with bilingual students. Also, Stevens et al. (2016) describes a mentoring program for young Native American girls and women in third to eighth grade.

3 *People have a rich personal history with language*

One situation where the people you're talking with have rich funds of knowledge to draw on is when you're interacting with people from a different cultural or linguistic group from your own. Their knowledge of a different language, a different communication style, and different cultural practices is information that can help you understand your science better. But of course, cross-cultural communication poses its own challenges. For example, in some cultures (e.g., some Hispanic and Native American cultures), there are wide differences in terms of history, cultural beliefs, social interaction style, and definitions of science from what dominates in Western cultures (Baez & Boyles, 2009). Both of us come from a Western perspective, and we find that it is important for us to adopt a conscious funds of knowledge mindset when engaging with individuals from other cultures. Learning is a mutual activity for us.

4 *A child learning to read English*

Seymour et al. (2003) makes this point with a fascinating study of literacy development in thirteen European countries. This research compared decoding skills in young children learning to read English and twelve other orthographies. The languages varied in syllabic complexity, and the orthographies varied in so-called depth (i.e., the transparency of relations between the phonology and the writing system). Examples at the extremes include Finnish and Spanish, which use relatively simpler syllable structures and are written with shallower orthographies; and Danish and English, which use relatively more complex syllable structures and are written with deeper orthographies. The children learning most of these orthographies did well by the end of their first year in school. But English was an outlier, with a much slower rate of literacy development. Seymour et al. suggests that readers of deep orthographies start out using both a logographic approach (i.e., learning to read frequently occurring words as wholes) and an alphabetic approach (i.e., learning letter-sound correspondences). This is harder than learning to read a shallow orthography, where an alphabetic approach works well from the start and for all words.

When parents watch their children do the IPA activity mentioned in the main text, we sometimes have conversations about reading, and some parents will want to discuss their children's challenges. One of us (CM) often follows up such conversations by offering to discuss the Seymour et al. study. Another resource that we recommend if you are interested in talking with people about writing systems is Omniglot: www.omniglot.com/.

5 *Strands of science*

If you'd like to find out more about the field that studies how people learn in informal settings, Fenichel and Schweingruber (2010) is an excellent place to start. This is a summary of the six strands, as well as the research behind them. The original Strands 2–5 were developed for elementary and middle school education and framed as learning outcomes for students, rather than as advice for how to teach students. Strands 1 and 6 were added especially for the kinds of environments that this book concerns. All six emphasize the importance of a learner's active engagement in science, and they are intertwined so that each strand supports a learner's progress on the other strands. As noted in Chapter 1, informal learning settings give learners considerable choice. This contrasts with formal settings. For example, classrooms usually have places where students are expected to sit while working, and students' tasks are usually designed for them, including how much time they spend at each task. By contrast, visitors to museums or festivals usually wander around on their own, stopping only at exhibits or doing activities that interest them and staying as long as they want. Thus, educators in informal settings need to be especially committed to learners' interests and motivations. People will be motivated to learn if exhibits and activities generate wonder, surprise, and curiosity. Learning and motivation to learn more are enhanced by emotional engagement and sometimes also by social connections.

6 *Listing of the strands of science*

We have recast the strands into our own words. We haven't changed their core meanings in any way, but we peeled them away from the physical science vibe that their original wording suggests. We also recast them to be more about what the educator does as opposed to what the learner receives, which fits better with what this book is all about.

7 *Finger tapper in the language lateralization demo*

The device that we use in this demo is part of the Halstead–Reitan Neuropsychological Test Battery. Factors like handedness, age, sex, education, and duration and repetition of tapping trials are of course controlled in research and clinical applications. The test battery is still used today, in part because it is easy to customize. It is often combined with measures of intelligence or of personality and supplements other assessments. See Schatz (2011) for more information.

5 Know Your Audience

OPENING WORKSHEET

What kinds of people do you think you will encounter while engaging with the public? Imagine people of different ages (e.g., a young child, a teenager, a middle-aged parent, a grandparent), people with different jobs (e.g., a teacher, an architect, a car mechanic, a nurse), people with different interests (e.g., a girl who loves dinosaurs, a boy who enjoys reading, a college student from a related discipline, a young couple who are interested in each other), and different group configurations (e.g., a family, a school outing, a single parent with several children, older adults on their own).

Pick two individuals to focus on and think about what each one of them wants from their interaction with you. Write down two aspects of your chosen topic area that would most appeal to these people.

A conversation is something you do **with** someone else. A good conversation requires at least two participants to contribute to the effort. When you first start out, you might feel like people don't get what you're trying to say. And your reaction to that feeling might be that those people should pay more attention, listen to you more carefully, or be better informed. That is, you might feel like it is their responsibility to do more work so that they can benefit from your wisdom and knowledge. That isn't how talking to people in a free-choice learning setting works.

As one of our mentors liked to say, "If people don't understand you, that's **your** problem, not theirs." It's not on them to pay more attention – it's on you to get and keep their attention. It's not on them to be well informed – it's on you to make your explanations understandable to someone who has a different background than you do. Whether you like it or not, you are the person responsible for making sure that your conversation is a good one. After all, you are the person who is there to share your love of language science and promote broader understanding of your favorite angle on language. If you want to accomplish such things, then you need to take the steps necessary to make it happen. Activities in free-choice environments are like TV shows, and the visitors who stop by to see you are the ones with the remote control. If your program isn't worth watching, they have plenty of other options and they will surely change the channel.

Everybody in the conversation brings something of themselves to the situation, and good audience design considers all the people involved. We'll start with you: Why are you there? What do you bring to your conversation? What are you trying to take away from your conversation?

Where Are You Coming From?

First, you're probably bringing to your own public engagement a certain amount of knowledge about how language works. Even if you've only taken one course or read one book on this, you probably have more technical knowledge than you realize. For example, you might know that languages can have different basic word orders; you might know that all languages change over time; you might know that people study language using experimental techniques; you might know that the position of the tongue affects which speech sound you're making. Keep in mind that your knowing these things doesn't mean that everybody knows them.

Even if you don't feel like you're an expert about all parts of language, one important thing you have learned how to do is to think analytically about language. You know that language can be an object of scientific study, and you know a little bit about how people do that. In Chapter 12, we'll talk more about how hard it is to remember what it felt like to not know such things. For now, though, it's important to just acknowledge that you do know something.

Of course, depending on who you are, you might be very aware that you know a lot about your topic area. If you're majoring in a language-related field, or you're a graduate student going after an advanced degree in linguistics, or you're someone who already has that degree, then you have a lot of technical knowledge about how language works. You're probably already fairly comfortable thinking of yourself as a language expert, and it's just good to keep in mind that part of what that means is that you have mastered specialized information.

But beyond your knowledge about language, the biggest assumption you are probably bringing to the conversation is the idea that language is worth talking about. You wouldn't be planning on talking with the general public about language if you didn't think language was fundamentally both interesting and important. Even more than the technical knowledge that you have, this assumption is what will make your conversations effective, because it is the key to interacting with others in a positive way.

Where Is Your Audience Coming From?

Now we consider the other half of the equation: the people who you're talking with. Why are they there? What do they bring to these conversations? What are they trying to take away from these conversations?

Your audience isn't a bunch of linguistics majors eager to take the hot new seminar on your favorite topic. But just because the public isn't coming to you with a technical mindset about language doesn't mean that they have no experience with language. For example, everybody you engage with is going to speak (or sign) at least one language, so they all have their personal language skills to draw on.

In addition, there are several common ways that people are likely to have encountered more formal study of language. Although it's often embedded in so-called language arts, schools are full of language science. Lots of people take foreign language classes and have received explicit instruction about the grammars of those languages. Just about everybody has received explicit instruction on writing in their native language. Of course, what people take away from their seventh-grade English class about grammar and spelling isn't always in line with the scientific perspective on language, but it does form an important part of what people know about how language works.

People are more likely to have encountered a scientific point of view on language if they have encountered it through a health profession. Many people have had experiences with speech language pathologists (SLPs) helping them with problems large and small. SLPs help children with articulation problems to improve the clarity of their speech, with reading challenges including dyslexia, and with more general language impairments. In fact, getting screened by an SLP in a school setting is a fairly common event for children. In addition, many people have had problems with their hearing, which often connects to language issues. Hearing aids and cochlear implants are increasingly common – not only among older adults but also among children and young adults with hearing loss. Adjusting to using these assistive devices requires people to adjust how they process language, a fact that is well known to the audiologists who help people get them. Or, people who you meet might know athletes who experienced language impairments after concussions. Language also interacts more generally with the aging process. Almost everybody will experience word-finding problems, and some adults may have experienced more dramatic issues, such as aphasias resulting from strokes.

A somewhat less formal place where people have a lot of language experience involves their own personal histories. Multilingualism is common across the world, including in the United States. Many people have therefore had lots of experience communicating in multiple languages themselves and with others who speak multiple languages in different contexts and with different degrees of fluency. It's worth thinking about the language landscape where you're going to be engaging with the public. Does it have a large population of people originally from somewhere else? One of us (CM) lives in the southwest United States where lots of people speak Spanish, as well as several Native American languages such as Navajo, Tohono O'odham, and Pascua Yaqui. The other one (LW) lives in the middle of the country, but in a city that happens to have a large Somali-speaking population. The language landscape of every place is different, but it's worth finding out what the landscape looks like where you are. Adding a few examples from the local language landscape will help make your demo relevant and interesting to your specific audience. It will also serve a broader goal of making people who speak these languages feel included. Not everybody feels equally comfortable in informal science learning settings, but reaching out to someone using their own language is a great way to make them feel more welcome.

And that's not all. Language is around us all the time and language science issues are everywhere. Parents are always interested in how their children learn to talk, and to read. Ever wondered how your phone talks with you? Or how Google finds what you're looking for even when you misspell your search terms? Those are language science questions. Word puzzles like Wordle and language games like Pig Latin are full of language science data. Language science also crops up in news stories and in popular culture on a regular basis. It's worth paying attention to the local news and movie reviews to find out what people are thinking about right now, whether it's vocal fry or Ebonics, or the movies *Arrival* or *The King's Speech*.

Who Is Your Audience?

As we mentioned in Chapter 1, institutions devoted to free-choice learning are well attended by the general public. Add in events that bring people together for just a few days (festivals and conventions of all kinds, library events), and there are even more people to consider. Each specific location is different, of course, and will attract a slightly different crowd. But there are some general types of people you will run across frequently.

Figure 5.1 Events like the AAAS Family Science Days festival attract a diverse audience

The first general type of person you'll encounter is people who are there to learn something. Some locations are basically designed for these kinds of people – science museums and science festivals advertise themselves as places where you can learn new things. But there are different motivations within this category. In a study from 2010, science education researchers John Falk and Martin Storksdieck interviewed hundreds of people who went to a science center about how they approached their visit. One of the most common approaches was taken by what the researchers called "Explorers." These were people who were generally interested in science and were looking for experiences that would feed their curiosity and spur more learning. A related approach was taken by the "Hobbyists." These were people who were hoping to learn more about a specific part of science that they already cared about. Both kinds of people came into the science center with some background knowledge (though the Hobbyists usually had more than the Explorers) and a desire to learn. But they differed a bit in how open they were to learning a wide range of things – the Hobbyists came in with more focus than the Explorers.

When it comes to language science, you're not very likely to be where people are expecting to learn about language. Outside of some library events, some special exhibitions, and a few very special museums, language science isn't a common focus for informal learning institutions or events. That won't cause any problems if you encounter an Explorer – Explorers are up for learning lots of things, and all you'll need to do is create some connection between language and whatever the main focus of your location is. For example, in the science museum where one of us (LW) works, there is a big exhibit about dinosaurs that visitors love. We don't know much about the language of dinosaurs, but we did create an activity that used dinosaur names to talk about compositional morphology: It turns out that all those complicated dino names break down into meaningful parts and language science helps you analyze them!

The Hobbyists that the researchers identified sometimes don't want to engage with an activity that's too far outside their area of interest. If you've come to a science center because you like astronomy, learning about the human vocal tract may not inspire you. But it turns out that language science has hobbyists of its own who are happy to discover that they are finally in a place that speaks directly to them! Parents who are interested in their children's language development, amateur dialectologists, and sci-fi conlangers are just a few of the types of people who get passionate about language. People who know more than one language count here as well – they have lots of experience navigating complex language situations; they aren't hobbyists so much as language professionals. If you're doing an enjoyable language activity of almost any type, these people will find you.

Another type of person you will encounter is people who are at your location to help others learn something. Falk and Storksdieck called these people "Facilitators" and found that they are among the most common types of visitors to a museum. These are people who are primarily motivated by a desire to help someone else get a good learning experience. They might be teachers bringing groups of students to an event, or they might be parents trying to make sure their children learn something important. Sometimes Facilitators accompany people who are delighted to be there – natural Explorers or Hobbyists. But sometimes Facilitators are with people who would rather be somewhere else, whether that's a kid in a bad mood, a teenager who is too cool to be there, or someone who just likes other things a lot more.

Working with a group that has a Facilitator adult in the mix can make things easier for you. Facilitators will encourage their charges to listen to you and ask and answer questions. They may also be willing to play along if you need someone to demonstrate how a game works or someone to break the ice with a first guess. As for the people getting facilitated, the best way to reach someone – whether they want to hear from you or not – is to be interesting. As we'll say in Chapters 6 and 7, it's important to make your activity relevant for people. You want to capture their interest right from the beginning and make connections to what they care about. Just do your activity as well as you can and trust that your language science is awesome enough to reach even the most distracted teenager.

The last general type of people you may encounter is those who aren't really there to learn; they are there to have fun. This type of person was less frequent than the other types, but there were enough for the researchers to identify two subtypes, who they called "Experience Seekers" and "Spiritual Pilgrims." Experience Seekers are just looking to see what you've got to offer. They'll actually try just about any activity you've got, if only to say that they tried it. Spiritual Pilgrims are looking for an experience that takes them outside their normal life and gives them a chance to contemplate something new. For most people, even the core phenomena of language science are new, so it is easy to hook these people in.

Regardless of the general type of person you're talking with, one thing that many visitors are looking for in these settings is access to real scientists. For example, the educator Eric Jensen and the director of the Centre of Science and Policy Nicola Buckley asked almost a thousand visitors to a science festival in Great Britain what they liked (and didn't like) about their experience (Jensen & Buckley, 2014). The festival-goers said they appreciated learning how science works and about new sciences; they also said they liked chatting with practitioners. In fact, one of the rare complaints that the festival-goers had was about scientists who didn't leave enough time for visitors to ask questions. If you're used to the academic environment, you may feel like you always have experts in the field around, and many of them are paid to answer questions. But outside the ivory tower, people are looking for access: They want to talk with people who know their stuff!

Embrace the Advantages of Difference

You might be wondering how you're going to make a single doable demo that will work with people of different ages who have different motivations and who come from different backgrounds. The trick is not to change the core activity but instead to have a variety of messages that you can illustrate with the same activity. It's useful to have three or four different angles that you could take so that you can flexibly respond to the specific person you're talking with.

For example, we mentioned above a dinosaur names activity one of us (LW) has used as a way to engage people about morphological analysis. Our critical take-home message for this activity is that language is compositional: If you know what the meanings of the small parts are and you know the rules for putting them together, you can figure out (or even create!) larger pieces of language. So we always talk about how to break down the long words into parts.

But for Explorers who have just visited the dinosaur exhibit, we focus more on the semantic content of the actual morphemes and the way they provide you with information about the dinosaur's properties. For example, the dinosaur name *Triceratops* actually describes that animal's head pretty well: *tri* = three; *cerat* = horned; *ops* = face. Our language science helps these Explorers see connections among the dinosaurs.

On the other hand, if we are talking with a Hobbyist who happens to be familiar with other languages, we are more likely to focus on the fact that most of the pieces in dinosaur names come from other languages (usually Latin or Greek). We might talk about how language borrowing occurs and how different languages become historically linked to special tasks, like scientific naming.

For Experience Seekers and Spiritual Pilgrims who seem like they just want to know something fascinating, we might talk about the metaphoric ways that dinosaur names describe properties. Elements such as *rex* (king) and *raptor* (robber) embody stories about the behavior and interactions of the animals. This point can lead to a nice discussion about how scientists often have a poetic side to them – even paleontologists like to play around with language!

The best way to do a demo is the way that keeps your audience engaged. Each time you do an activity, you are having a new conversation. It's great if each conversation is different and reflects the person who you are talking with. One of the wonderful things about supporting informal learning is that you're not giving a single speech to a unified audience; you're talking about your activity over and over again to specific individuals and small groups. Each conversation can be different.

Audience Inclusivity

The joy of language science is for everyone: It shouldn't be privileged information that is just for a select few. Depending on who you are, this point may seem so obvious that it is hard to imagine that it could be otherwise. After all, nobody is trying to keep language science a secret, and anybody who wants to learn about it is welcome to go and find out about it. You are developing an activity for the very purpose of promoting a general understanding of language science, right?

Unfortunately, science has a long history of exclusion, and so do informal science learning venues. Sociologist Emily Dawson has investigated how a wide range of people interact with informal learning institutions such as science museums (Dawson, 2014, 2019). She interviews people individually and in groups, and sometimes she even accompanies them as they visit these places. What she has found is that not everybody feels welcome in these environments or even that they have an equal right to partake in activities like what you are developing. In particular, people who are from low-income backgrounds or from minority communities often feel like these spaces are "not for them." As someone starting out with your activity, you're probably not in a position to influence who does and does not attend your venue. But what you can do is respect every single person who is there and make them feel welcome to do your activity.

Ideally, you'll be open to having a conversation about your science with everybody – old people, young people, people who look like you, people who don't look like you, people wearing religious clothing, people with purple hair, people in wheelchairs, people who wear novelty sweatshirts, people in three-piece suits. If someone is at your venue, then they are open to interacting with **you**. So you need to be open to interacting with them. As we mentioned in Chapter 2, you also bring distinctive attributes to the interaction. So also be open to the idea that everyone you talk with will be willing to interact with someone who looks like you. And once you are talking with someone, be sure to listen to them! In Chapter 10, we'll talk about how hard it can be to **really** listen to other people, but the more different someone is from you, the more important it is to pay attention to what they are saying.

And if you're working on language science, you should be aware that you have something special that can be very effective at fostering respect: Your science explicitly values people who speak different languages. In Emily Dawson's investigations, one of the reasons that non-native speakers often feel excluded at places like science museums and science festivals is because their language is not represented in the space. Moreover, their skill with the dominant language may make it more difficult for them to read signs or understand detailed explanations. But the presence of other languages in these spaces can make non-native speakers feel more welcome and encourage greater participation. The applied linguistic anthropologist Leslie Moore and her students followed families around in a science museum, focusing on ones who were not native English speakers (English being the dominant language of the region). They reported an anecdote about one Spanish-speaking family who dramatically changed their interaction style when they encountered an exhibit that had signs and instructions not only in English but also in Vietnamese and Spanish. The father in the group, who had been pretty hands-off until that point, became much more engaged with his children – reading the instructions and helping them do the activities. The mother in the group explicitly mentioned the Spanish signs as the reason for his change (Moore et al., 2019).

You can't control the signage where you are doing your demo, but many language science activities make a person's access to another language a particular asset. The funds of knowledge for a non-native speaker are different than those of a monolingual speaker of the dominant language; for a language science activity, those funds are valuable. Your science grants you an opportunity to make your setting more inclusive. Take advantage of that!

CRITICAL TAKE-HOME MESSAGE

People have many different motivations for coming to informal learning locations, and they also bring along a variety of different kinds of experiences with language. Everyone will respond well to an activity that is interesting and engaging, and you can and should tailor your messages to reflect the special properties of each conversation. Knowing your audience helps you do this.

WORKED EXAMPLE BOX

One dimension of audience design that we try to be sensitive to is the fact that some people we interact with speak languages different from the ones we speak. For example, one of us (CM) lives in the US Southwest. English is only one of several languages that people in this area speak. Our team typically meets many Spanish speakers in the festivals where we work. So we have a few demos that we can do in either English or Spanish, and we schedule volunteers to make sure there is always at least one native speaker of Spanish in our booth.

A demo that we designed specifically for young Spanish-speaking children combines lexical stress with the visualization of the speech signal that we can see in wave forms. This demo is in the form of a very simple game. We show a child something like this:

A Spanish-speaking volunteer explains two pictures on a page: One picture in Figure 5.2 shows *tacos de papa* (potato) and the other shows

Figure 5.2 Lexical stress demo

Note. A page from the booklet used in the lexical stress demo showing a wave form for *tacos de papá* (tacos of father).

(cont.)

tacos de papá (father). We then point to the wave form at the top of the page and ask children to figure out which of the two pictures goes with that image. (The wave form shows stressed syllables as bigger and darker than unstressed syllables.) Spanish-speaking children easily get that the difference between *papa* and *papá* has to do with where the stress goes. Once children make this connection between the wave form and the stressed syllable, they often want to flip through the booklet and 'read' it on their own! The task is so easy that children as young as three sometimes take the booklet and run the demo with other people in their group.

The core messages for this activity are that small differences can distinguish similar sounding words, and that we can see those differences in special images of speech. These messages are well understood by people who speak any language. But for Spanish speakers, this activity has special value. The small differences that the activity highlights are small differences in their own language!

You may have noticed that most of the activities we describe in this book use English-language examples. That reflects the fact that both of us are native speakers of English, and we often work in places where English is the most common language. But this activity explicitly draws on the funds of knowledge possessed by Spanish speakers. It creates a welcoming environment for Spanish speakers. And even better, it gives the youngest Spanish speakers who we engage with a chance to demonstrate their knowledge.

CLOSING WORKSHEET

Remind yourself of the topic you selected for your doable demo (see the Closing Worksheet in Chapter 2).

Think about how your topic could be used to engage someone who is an Explorer. Ideally, that is going to mean that your doable demo will be highly interactive, it will encourage exploration, and it will be fun to do.

Write down two ideas for ways that someone could do something interactive based on your topic. For each idea, what dimension of your topic would they be exploring? How much fun would it be to do your interactive activity?

Now think about how the interaction could be shifted to make it work better with a Hobbyist and an Experience Seeker. Write down one change you would make to adjust your interaction for each of these other kinds of visitors.

Further Reading

1 *Audience design considers all the people involved*

Audience design refers to various ways that speakers modify their speech to accommodate to those they are addressing. Some research that helped launch the field that studies this includes Bell (1984), Clark (1992, 1996), and Clark and Wilkes-Gibbs (1986). For more recent research, see Ferreira (2019) and Gann and Barr (2014). Many studies of audience design are concerned with automatic adjustments that speakers do or do not make for their conversational partners, such as changing how they repeat references to the same object or idea (e.g., "the governor" for a first reference and "she" for a second one). Speakers are rarely conscious that they make these adjustments: Some amount of audience design appears to be an intrinsic part of our language use. However, in addition to these automatic processes, it is also possible to consciously change how you express yourself in response to the communicative needs of your audience. It is this kind of purposeful and thoughtful process that we are concerned with here. And see Chapter 15, especially, for concrete advice about how to tailor your message for different kinds of people.

2 *The language landscape of every place is different*

Sometimes you may be surprised at how complicated the local language landscape is where you are! In central Ohio, where LW works, the local environment is sometimes classified as "superdiverse" linguistically (Moore et al., 2019). That is, the area is undergoing rapid demographic shifts, which has led to many different languages being spoken in the area, although from year to year, which languages have the most speakers locally can change fairly dramatically.

If you're interested in learning more about these landscapes, the terms *language landscape* and *linguistic landscape* are sometimes used interchangeably. But some scholars distinguish these terms. As the main text suggests, a language landscape usually emphasizes the languages that are used in a particular area (as you can get a sense of from maps like at this website: http://langscape.umd.edu/map.php). A linguistic landscape usually emphasizes language displayed in a particular place (Carr, 2019; Shohamy & Gorter, 2009). For example, a study of a linguistic landscape in a multilingual environment might analyze identity through billboards, road signs, and place names.

3 *Language crops up in popular culture*

There are lots of websites where you can find out the latest linguistics buzz. If you want to read academic linguists talking about current language-related issues, try the *Language Log* (https://languagelog.ldc.upenn.edu/nll/). But there are also many language experts outside the academy who are writing for a popular audience. If you want to read a real popular pro talking about language, try Gretchen McCulloch's site, *All Things Linguistic* (https://allthingslinguistic.com/). And many of the non-academic popular language writers have content in many places, so it's often easiest to just search for your favorite people. Some of our favorites are Arika Okrent, Michael Erard, Ben Zimmer, Lane Greene, and Julie Sedivy.

4 *Very special museums*

Full disclosure: Both authors of this book are on the advisory board of one museum devoted to language, Planet Word (https://planetwordmuseum.org/). So naturally we like that one! But there are other museums that center on language, like Mundolingua (www.mundolingua.org/en/).

5 *Sci-fi conlangers*

Artificial, or constructed languages (conlangs) have a long history that includes philosophically minded individuals trying to perfect a theory of concepts all the way to science-fiction enthusiasts trying to create a culture for Klingons. Arika Okrent's 2009 book, *In the Land of Invented Languages*, is an outstanding tour of these creations.

6 *Paleontologists like to play around with language*

Apparently, paleontologists also like classic rock, as they named a species of dinosaur they discovered in 2001 after the guitarist of Dire Straits: https://www.science.org/content/article/dire-straits-dinosaurs.

7 *Lexical stress demo*

Because the lexical stress demo is designed for Spanish speakers, it contrasts *papa* (potato) with *papá* (father), and *sabana* (savanna) with *sábana* (sheet). If you don't know Spanish, where the stress falls in each word affects the meaning. Roughly comparable examples from English include *contract* (legal agreement) – *contract* (to reduce) and *produce* (fruit and vegetables) – *produce* (to manufacture). Naturally, signed languages also use small differences to distinguish words even though their phonology rests on elements like handshape, hand movement, and location of the sign rather than manipulations of the vocal tract. Some noun–verb pairs in ASL differ only in movement. For example, the noun CHAIR is made with repeated short movements while the verb SIT is made with one big movement; the handshape and the location of these two signs are the same though. To truly appreciate this and several other ASL examples, watch this video: www.youtube.com/watch?v=4gc6fwXwFV0.

6 Creating Relevance by Generating Interest

OPENING WORKSHEET

Write down a brief description of a time when you were blown away by something you learned about the workings of your topic area.

Write down your answers to a few of the questions below.

What was the phenomenon? Was it dramatic? Did it make you smile? What was it that especially caught your attention?

Where did you encounter the phenomenon? Was it something you learned in class? Something that happened in real life? Something you read about in a book or heard about on a podcast? Something you noticed in a movie?

Why did this grab **you** in particular? Was it a puzzle that you solved? Was it completely unexpected? Was it unlike other things you had learned before? Was it funny? Was it relevant for your daily life?

If you have some experience with college classrooms, then you surely have encountered (or maybe been) the students who are taking the class because it satisfies a requirement, or just because it fits into their schedule. These students aren't there because they are passionate about the topic; instead, they are there because they have to be. In a school setting, these students will stay – and will often even pay attention and do the work – because the teacher is grading their performance. The teacher doesn't have to do anything special to convince these students that it's worth staying in the class. The grade and the credit are motivation enough.

Talking with the public in a free-choice environment is nothing like that! If you're talking with people at a museum, or at a festival, or in any kind of open public space, you're talking with people who don't have to be there. They can choose something else at any time. Either people choose to engage with you, or they choose not to. If your goal is to inspire and educate people about language science, then it is up to you to motivate people to want to talk with you.

Giving a lecture is one way that teachers educate adolescent and adult students in classrooms – and you may even have had great experiences with really inspiring lectures. But this approach just will not fly in a free-choice setting. Even if you give the **best** lecture in the world, a festival booth or a roving museum cart is not in a place that is friendly to any kind of lecture. It will likely be noisy, and crowded, and full of all kinds of distracting things (other booths to visit, cotton candy, school groups, fireworks, science cheerleaders). Your interactions will be shorter than a lecture, and they need to adapt to the people you are talking with and their immediate circumstances. What you need is a conversation, not a lecture.

To get started, you need to give people a reason to want to have a conversation with you. We know from Chapter 2 that a good conversation is cooperative and that one of the fundamental rules for maintaining cooperation is being relevant. We're going to talk about two big ways that you can make your conversations relevant to broader audiences. In Chapter 7, we'll talk about how to connect your language topic to the real world: How can you take what **others** care about and connect it to your topic? But in this chapter, we'll start with you. How can you take what **you** care about and make it seem relevant for someone else?

Generating Interest and Excitement

The best way to get people to want to talk with you is to show them that your science is interesting – it's something worth being excited about. In principle, this shouldn't be hard! After all, **you** must think your science is pretty interesting or you wouldn't want to share it with other people. You need to use your own excitement to encourage others to have a conversation with you.

The idea that the first step in this kind of engagement is getting people excited might sound familiar. As we mentioned in Chapter 4, when the National Research Council put together their guidelines for teaching people about science in informal learning settings, their number one strand was to "generate interest and excitement." Excitement is critical because it's what keeps people choosing you in the free-choice environment. The basic principle is familiar from the advertising world. Before you can sell your wares, you need to get your buyers in the door! Without the structures of a formal classroom, you need to offer a reason for people to come talk with you. You're proposing a topic of conversation; you have to make it a topic worthy of their cooperation.

For example, one demo that one of us (CM) has used to get a conversation started involves an ultrasound machine. Ultrasound imaging is a noninvasive tool that can record cross-sectional images of the moving vocal tract. Many people are familiar with these images because they are used to monitor the progress of pregnancies. Imagine visitors to a festival walking by your booth and seeing such a machine in use. The moving images are cool! The gel is yucky! You've just accomplished Strand 1 of the six strands of science learning: generate interest and excitement. One of the other reasons we like this demo is because it is also a great way to address Strand 5: Collaborate in using the tools of science. Tools can be a great way to capture attention and start the ball rolling. People will ask what this machine could possibly have to do with language. Many people think yucky = fun! and are not just willing but eager to have ultrasound gel under their chins and see the tool in action. If you have people produce words like *bar*, *door*, and *fur*, they can compare the ways their tongues make the /r/ sound in different phonological environments. From here, your conversation might go to the biology of making speech sounds, or why the /r/ sound can be especially hard to produce for some people, or the linguistics of coarticulation effects. Once people are interested, you have lots of choices for what to talk about.

Figure 6.1 A child using an ultrasound machine at the Tucson Festival of Books

But interest and excitement don't just attract people to your demo. The psychologists Barbara Fredrickson and Christine Branigan found that when college students experienced positive emotions (rather than negative ones), they were more open to exploration and better able to integrate information (Fredrickson & Branigan, 2005). These researchers used nature videos to make people feel good, and even just a few minutes of watching a waddling penguin helped students do better global visual processing and come up with more ideas for activities they would like to do. Making people feel good will help them learn better from you.

What's more, those positive emotions are also part of your long-term strategy. Most conversations in a free-choice learning setting aren't very long. Long chats will probably be no longer than fifteen minutes, and short ones may be under five minutes. There's a real limit to how much people can learn in such a short time, even if you are making them happy. But when people create positive memories of an event, they hold on to those feelings.

Our memories aren't like newsreels: We don't just record our lives and then rewatch key parts when we want. Instead, we hold on to our experiences in bits and pieces, and when we remember something, we have to reassemble the bits and pieces. When you are engaged emotionally by an event, you will remember it more vividly. But it turns out that you're not necessarily remembering all the specific details better. People use the emotional content as an anchor, and they hold on to that firmly, even as the fine-grained details can become hazy. Think of a favorite vacation, or a recent birthday party. You can probably remember whether you liked the event or not, and you might recall the general way things happened. But for most of us, for most events, the moment-to-moment details fade away. Could you ace a test about everything that happened at your last birthday party? The fact that we often forget the specifics doesn't make the experiences unimportant. If you remember that you had a blast at last year's party, you might be inclined to have another such party this year. A positive emotion can encourage us, even if we don't remember all of the exact elements that created it.

If you create positive emotions around language science, it will matter. People may not remember the exact details that you talked about, but if they walk away with the general impression that language science is exciting and interesting, then they are more likely to want to engage with it in the future. Maybe that means they'll notice language phenomena that they missed before interacting with you. Maybe that means they will talk with the next language science expert they encounter at a free-choice location. Maybe it means they will pick up a book on the topic. Maybe it means they will go

Figure 6.2 Ohio State University students having fun at the COSI Science Festival

home and check out language science information on the Internet. Maybe it means they will take a class on linguistics or even end up pursuing an advanced degree in a related science. You never know how big the tree will grow when you plant the seed!

And the reverse is also true. If people walk away from your conversation feeling like your science is boring, judgmental, totally incoherent, or irrelevant, then they will be less likely to want to engage with it going forward. When you're talking with the public, you're representing the field. Represent it as a field that is worthy of their time and attention.

One worry that people new to this kind of work sometimes have is that the activities they design aren't actually fun. So they think that they will be a disappointment to people who are looking for entertainment. Taking a negative attitude like that is probably the best way to make sure that your activity is boring. Instead, try to remember why **you** think the topic of your demo is interesting. If you're having fun with your activity, then you'll dramatically increase the chances that others will have fun with it as well.

So much for why it's important to generate excitement. How exactly do you actually do this? We recommend two main techniques: (1) Give people an Aha! moment about language, and (2) Go back to the basics of how language works.

Aha! Moments

One of the easiest ways to get people interested in a topic is to show them something new or unexpected. Language is complex: It is full of amazing phenomena, and most of them are almost completely unfamiliar to the general public. People may use language all the time, but rarely think about how language actually works, and think about it least of all for the language they themselves speak. You can give an Aha! moment either by showing people something they had absolutely no idea was true, or by showing them something that they absolutely did know was true but had never considered before.

If you've taken an introductory linguistics class, you've probably had many Aha! moments yourself. For example, you may be familiar with this demonstration about allophonic variation. You hold a piece of paper in front of your mouth as you say words containing [p]. (If you had an adventurous instructor, she might have used a lit candle instead of a piece of paper.) First you say words that start with [p] like *pit*, *pot*, and *pat*. The paper (or the flame) will waver for each word. Next, you say words that start with [sp] like *spit*, *spot*, and *spat*. This time, the paper (or the flame) won't move at all. What's going on? When this consonant is at the beginning of the word, we say it differently (with a puff of air) from when it comes after [s] (where we don't really let the air go in the same way). The technical term for that puff of air is aspiration, and in English, whether or not we aspirate a sound depends on its surrounding sounds.

For most language scientists, this phenomenon, and even this specific demonstration, is pretty familiar. But most people have given very little thought to phonetic variability and coarticulation effects, and they tend to think about sounds in terms of the letters we use to represent them. Taken together, that means people are genuinely surprised to find out that they pronounce their [p] differently in different words. Plus, the fact that **you** can predict just how they will shift their pronunciation shows that you know something unexpected.

To show you how broadly you can think about Aha! moments, here's a completely different example drawn from syntax. Ask people to say which of the following mini-conversations is weird:

(1) Did Mary eat a sandwich yet? Yes, she ate already.
(2) Did Susan eat a shoe yet? Yes, she ate already.

This example asks people to make an acceptability judgment of a kind that is common in language science. It's just that most people haven't ever thought

Figure 6.3 Sometimes, you really want to talk about eating a shoe!
Note. This photograph is used with permission of Getty Images. Photo credit: Yoann JEZEQUEL.

about language this way. People don't usually think about how good or how weird a sentence sounds relative to a context, and they don't usually think about how they can change that context to make a sentence sound better (or weirder).

In this case, conversation (2) is weirder than (1) because it breaks a convention about when you're allowed to drop a word in English. Both of these conversations have the same second sentence (the answer to a question), and that sentence has a distinctive property: It leaves out the direct object of the verb. English does let you leave out words like that, but you're not allowed to do it whenever you want. It's OK to leave out the "sandwich" in conversation (1) because sandwiches are things that people often eat. And, in English, missing words usually have to refer to something that would typically belong in that spot in the sentence. You fill in the sandwich with pretty much no thought at all. But in conversation (2), the missing word that you're supposed to fill in refers to an unusual thing to eat. People don't generally eat their shoes. There's nothing wrong about saying the full sentence ("she ate a shoe already"), especially if that's really what Susan did. There's also nothing wrong with leaving out the direct object – after all, conversation (1) sounds just fine. But if you want to talk about something unusual, like eating a shoe, you need to spell it out with all the words. Most people haven't thought about how the rules of linguistic communication (pragmatics) constrains how we interpret missing information. This example shows people that they are bound by rules they didn't even know they were using!

For both the example of aspiration and the example of word dropping, a big part of what creates the Aha! moment is finding out that you're always doing more when you talk than you realized. You're shifting your pronunciations without thinking about it. You're filling in empty words in systematic ways without consciously pondering the alternatives. Our language use is so effortless most of the time that it is easy to overlook just how much goes into every little piece of it. Giving people a glimpse of the complexity that they are pulling off all the time provides just the kind of moment that grabs people's interest and can get them excited about what's going on.

Go Back to Basics

Like any science, language science has its share of theoretical disputes, and if you are doing cutting-edge research, theory is really important for making progress in the field. But, also like any science, there is a large stockpile of facts that all language scientists agree on. For many aspects of language, advanced researchers aren't arguing over the basic facts that need to be explained; they are debating what the right explanation is. If you can describe your topic in a way that is theory-neutral, then you are definitely on the right track. The general public doesn't usually care about academic arguments. What is the phenomenon that is so exciting to researchers that it's worth arguing about? Focus on that phenomenon – that's what the general public will find interesting to talk about!

So, take a step back from the details of any specific science problem and let yourself be awestruck by the big picture. If you're writing a research paper, your goal is to make your question precise enough that you can explain the details and make progress on a tractable problem. But you're not trying to defend a research paper to the general public. The general public wants to understand why someone would bother to look into the topic area in the first place. What are the background assumptions that your detailed question is building on?

In the case of allophonic variation (where blowing on a piece of paper provided an Aha! moment), you can go back to basics by describing some underlying premises of phonology. We change how we pronounce even simple sounds (like [p]) depending on the other sounds around them. But we count the different pronunciations as the same sound so long as they don't change the meaning of the word. You can have people test that part out by asking them to compare a word like *pit* without the puff of air and a word like *spit* with the puff of air. Both of those utterances will sound a little odd, but neither one will create a new English word. And if you want to go further with someone, you can pull out examples from a different language where that difference in pronunciation does create a new word. How remarkable that different languages organize tiny differences in pronunciation in different ways!

In the case of leaving out the direct object from a sentence (where judging a conversation's weirdness provided an Aha! moment), you can go back to basics by describing some underlying premises of pragmatics. Language communicates meaning not only through what we say but also through what we don't say. One of the critical tools we use to understand what's not there is context – sometimes that context comes from other sentences and sometimes it comes from what we know about the world. When you want to talk about very common things, context can do a lot of work. But the more unusual the thing is that you want to talk about, the more you have to say because our background knowledge won't help as much. And if you want to go further with someone, you can again pull out examples from other languages where there are different expectations about what words people will drop. How remarkable that we are able to understand what people don't say!

One big advantage in going back to the basics is that it can help you deal with a common worry about talking with the public, namely that you're not being fully responsible about all the theoretical complexities of the field. (We'll talk more about that in Chapter 9.) The more advanced you are in a science, the more likely you are to have a distinct theoretical point of view about how its focus works. Perhaps you subscribe to a particular theory about where the line between phonology and phonetics should be drawn. Perhaps you are embroiled in debates about the syntactic representation of omitted words. In order for someone to really understand your position, they would need to know a lot of details so they can appreciate your theoretical perspective (and agree with you on its correctness).

But your goal here isn't to convert a colleague to your point of view. And when it comes to most of the basics, pretty much all theoretical positions actually agree with each other. Do you lean toward the nativist or constructivist view of language acquisition? Well, both positions agree that children learn language without explicit instruction. Do you subscribe to the Minimalist program of syntax, or are you more of a Tree Adjoining

Grammar type of person? Well, both positions agree that sentences have hierarchical structure. Do you believe that phonemes emerge from exemplar structures or is Optimality Theory the way to go? Well, both positions agree that different languages have different sound inventories. One way to move yourself toward being theory-neutral is to pretend that your favorite theory is completely wrong. What's left of your phenomenon if your analysis is wrong? If the bare facts of the phenomenon would still be interesting, then you've got something worth talking about.

If you've been working on language for a while, many of these background assumptions may seem so obvious that they're kind of boring. But most people haven't thought about these things before. Once you start viewing language from a somewhat more naïve perspective, all kinds of things will start to seem remarkable. Do you know how fast your tongue has to move in order for you to speak at even a pretty slow speech rate? It's like our tongues are all virtuoso pianists! Do you know that if you change the way you pronounce just a few vowels, people will actually think you're from a different part of the country? How can a tiny acoustic difference reveal where someone was raised? Learning a foreign language is super hard, so how come babies can learn a language without even taking any classes? These are the kinds of fundamental facts about language that keep researchers working for years, and they will help you connect with the public.

CRITICAL TAKE-HOME MESSAGE

To attract people and keep them in a conversation with you, you need to show them why your topic is interesting! Introduce them to core phenomena of language and help them think about language in a new way. If you can get people excited, they will be more likely to talk with you in the short term and more likely to stay interested in language in the long term.

WORKED EXAMPLE BOX

Research journals are full of interesting language phenomena to talk about. But most journals are written for a scholarly audience, and they tend to be full of special terms and fine-grained details. Here, we show how you can take a recent article and find the Aha! moment within it and identify the basics that underlie the latest research.

(cont.)

We went to the flagship journal of the Linguistic Society of America, *Language*. In 2018, the linguists Lauren Clemens and Jessica Coon published an article there titled "Deriving Verb-Initial Word Order in Mayan." This paper was definitely not written for the general public – it's a highly technical piece about the right way to analyze the VSO/VOS word orders common to Mayan languages, and it argues that the VOS word order can be generated in three distinctive ways. How can we turn the core elements of this paper into an engaging demonstration?

In this case, we start by figuring out how to go back to basics. What's the deep language-related fact that underlies this whole paper? Word order. In fact, we find three distinct word order basics here that matter.

The first basic is that languages generally have a dominant word order. For example, in English, most sentences, most of the time, put the subject before the verb and the verb before the direct object. We might even want to introduce a bit of jargon to describe this general fact – the letters S, V, and O are used to stand for subject, verb, and object; and the order we put the letters in represents the order of those three elements in a language's typical sentence. The idea that you can describe a language in this way makes intuitive sense to people, but it isn't necessarily something they've thought of before.

The second basic fact here is that different languages have different dominant word orders. English is SVO, but Japanese is SOV. And, as it happens, Mayan languages (such as Yucatec, Ch'ol, and K'iche') are either VOS or VSO. The *Language* paper itself contains many examples from various Mayan languages, and you can use those to illustrate this second basic fact.

For instance, you could write out these words from the Mayan language Q'anjob'al on different cards along with their English translations (if you're fancy, you might illustrate each word with a picture):

(1) *max y-il* = saw
(2) *no' tx'I'* = dog
(3) *naqLwin* = Pedro

How would you put these pieces together to say "The dog saw Pedro"? The correct answer is 1–2–3, just as they are listed here. You just showed off a word order that is probably very different from what people are familiar with. If your audience is composed of monolingual English speakers, this very well may lead to an Aha! moment for them.

One possible way to develop this activity would simply be to make more examples – either by using more sentences from the Mayan languages

(cont.)

described in the paper or with sentences from other languages. You're helping people appreciate that there's not one right way for all languages to organize their words – different languages do it differently and speakers of those languages understand each other just fine.

But maybe you want to go in a different direction. Another word order basic that is integral to this article is the idea that not every sentence in a language shows off that language's dominant word order. One example from this paper involved the process of leaving out different words in the sentence. In some Mayan languages (e.g., Itzaj), you can either leave out the direct object (as in the English example we discussed in the main text), or leave out the subject of the sentence. So, if you only see a verb and one noun, for example *kill* and *jaguar* the sentence could either be VS ("the jaguar killed [someone]") or VO ("[someone] killed the jaguar"). Ambiguous sentences like this can make it harder to figure out what the dominant word order is overall.

In fact, you can find examples in just about every language that will illustrate nondominant word orders. In English, for example, we can use a different order if we want to emphasize something. This sentence more or less has the order OSV: "It was Italian food I really liked." An example that many people are familiar with is the distinctive way that talks the character Yoda (from the *Star Wars* universe). Yoda uses VOS ordering when he says things like "Killed a jaguar, he did." But because Yoda has some other idiosyncrasies as well, you'd want to choose examples carefully if using him in a demo of VOS sentences.

Depending on how you want to spin these basics, you could be helping people understand what linguists do when they analyze a language (they have to sift through complicated and ambiguous sentences to find dominant patterns). Or you could be helping people appreciate that their own language isn't quite as simple as they might have thought – and it might even share some properties with a language they didn't know much about!

At this point, you may have realized that our activity is barely scratching the surface of what the original paper was really all about. That's OK! Most members of the general public – or even most faculty in a linguistics department – aren't interested enough in the details of word order derivations in Mayan to want to hear about the advanced points in the paper. But for the few people who really are that interested, this back-to-basics approach will help them get there.

CLOSING WORKSHEET

In Chapter 5, we asked you to think about two ways that would allow different kinds of people to engage with your topic, focusing on interactivity and having fun. Review what you wrote for that worksheet.

Do your earlier ideas involve providing people with an Aha! moment? Do they involve going back to basics and helping people appreciate some foundational background? Do they sound like they would be fun to do?

Now revise your interaction! No matter what you thought of before, you can make it better – more interactive, more awe-inspiring, more fun. Write down new and improved versions of your original ideas for interaction.

Further Reading

1 *Science cheerleaders*

Yes, Science Cheerleaders are a real thing! It's a group of former cheerleaders (for sports like the United States National Basketball Association) who have STEM degrees. They aim to break down stereotypes about what a scientist should look like. You can read more about them on their website: https://sciencecheerleaders.org/.

2 *Making /r/ sounds*

Describing experimental research on tongue shape, position, and movement to an academic audience might refer to rhotic misarticulation, biofeedback as treatment, or allophony. For examples of ultrasound imaging in such research, see Byun et al. (2014) and Mielke et al. (2010). For the kind of audience we're describing here, a very different tack will be critical to maintaining their interest.

3 *Making people feel good will help them learn better from you*

There is a large literature on memory and how emotions affect it. For a good review of the basics, we recommend Kensinger (2009). One set of details that we glossed over in the main text is the difference between negative and positive emotions. Both kinds of emotions lead to more vivid memories, but the two differ along other dimensions. One difference is that the cognitive broadening we mentioned in the text as an effect of positive emotions extends from the learning phase into memory recognition and recall. When people recognize positive pictures (Yegiyan & Yonelinas, 2011) or recall positive autobiographical memories (Schaefer & Philpot, 2005), they are more sensitive to peripheral or broader situational properties than when they do the same tasks with negative pictures or negative memories. Negative emotions have the general effect of narrowing people's representations, while positive emotions seem to make them more diffuse and expansive. Another relevant impact of positive emotions is that they improve your prospective memory. That is, people do a better job of remembering to do planned tasks in the future when those tasks evoke positive rather than negative emotions (Rendell et al., 2011). You'll remember to feed the cat but maybe not to clean her litter box.

4 *Yoda's distinctive way of talking*

It's likely that Yoda speaks English. But he does use quite a mix of word orders, possibly because he was scripted by different screenwriters (Kaminsky, 2008; see also http://fd.noneinc.com/secrethistoryofstarwarscom/secrethistoryofstarwars.com/yodaspeak.html). Maybe Hollywood should employ more linguists? ☺ For example, many of his sentences show English constructions that are rare but generally acceptable. As historical linguist George Walkden argues, Yoda 'fronts' his verb phrases more loosely than is typical in modern English (Walkden, 2012). "Stay and help you, I will" is an example of this moving of the verbs *stay* and *help* to the front of the sentence. You can read more about Yoda's syntax in the *Language Log* (e.g., http://itre.cis.upenn.edu/~myl/languagelog/archives/002173.html). Somewhat less technical commentary can be found on *Grammar Girl* (www.quickanddirtytips.com/education/grammar/yoda-grammar) and *The Week* (https://theweek.com/articles/442256/why-strangely-yoda-speaks).

7 Creating Relevance by Making Connections

OPENING WORKSHEET

We've met a lot of different people while working in informal learning settings, including a toddler, a fourth grader, a nurse, a car enthusiast, a math teacher, a devotee of singing shows, a basketball fan, a bookworm, a political junkie, an electrical engineer, an astronaut, a neurosurgeon, and a ninety-year-old Japanese immigrant to the United States.

Think about two kinds of people who you might encounter – you can pick one from the list above of people we've met, or come up with other kinds of people. For each of your two kinds of people, write down the following things:

- Why does language matter to them?
- What aspects of language are likely to be familiar to them?
- Would they be likely to have special knowledge about any dimensions of language?
- Where would they encounter language in their everyday life?

In Chapter 6, we talked about how to make your language phenomenon relevant to people by making it interesting. In that case, the starting point is you: You're trying to attract people by showing off something you care about and putting it in its best (and most interesting) light. You were creating the best sales pitch for a product that you really believe in. In this chapter, we're talking about how to make your work relevant by focusing on the other participants in the conversation. Instead of starting with what you think is interesting, think now about what **other** people find interesting. What matters to them and why? In Chapter 10, we're going to encourage you to really listen to what people say. That's by far the best way to find out what individuals care about. The current chapter offers some useful ways to connect our work for many people.

The Real World Is Relevant

People live in the real world, not on a university campus, and their background context isn't the previous literature, or the history of the field, or academic debates about theory. Their context is what happens in real life. Their real life. As Chapter 5 notes, people's own lives include a lot of language experiences – in school, at the doctor's office, when traveling, when talking to their families. What happens in your own life is relevant to you; if you can connect your topic to something in people's everyday lives, then you instantly make it relevant.

What's more, the real world is something that people know about already. People have funds of knowledge about how it works. Moreover, in Chapters 11 and 12, we'll talk about how to structure information to help people remember it better. The key to doing that well is to provide familiar information before you introduce unfamiliar information. This is because people learn better when they have an established base to work from. Providing a relevant context will make your facts more meaningful. Connecting your work to the real world will therefore not only make it relevant for people; it will also help them understand it better.

The Real World Is Bigger Than You Think

When academics write grant proposals, they are always asked to explain the *broader impacts* or *social relevance* of their work. How will broader society benefit if your proposal is funded? If your topic area has medical or educational applications, you probably feel pretty good about this kind of question. Improving the technology behind hearing aids so that people can understand the speech they hear is a tangible societal benefit. Improving our techniques for teaching individuals with a dyslexia how to read also has broad positive impacts on society. But if your demo is on a more theoretical topic – say, how children learn the meanings of aspectual morphology or how they master the rules of pronoun reference – you have to work a little bit harder to explain why the answer to your research question matters.

But when you're talking with the general public, you don't have to meet the standards of a grant review! The people you're talking with aren't deciding whether or not to fund your research. They are only deciding whether or not to give you a few minutes of their time. Your topic area doesn't have to hold the key to curing cancer or solving world peace; it just has to be relevant enough to justify spending the time to have a conversation with you!

So, how do you link to their real world? The trick is to find someplace – anyplace – where your topic makes contact with people's everyday lives. It isn't actually hard to do this: Remember, language is all around us and people use it and interact with it every day. You just need to be open to how your topic connects with people's everyday experiences. In Chapter 5, we covered a range of life experiences where people connect with language: learning to spell, learning a foreign language, children learning to talk, getting older and losing your hearing, having a speech disorder, having multilingual family members. If you can connect your work to any of these topics, you are well on your way to making it relevant for lots of other people.

But you can think even more broadly than that! Language is something that is interwoven into our everyday lives in a constant, casual way. It's also OK to think about areas where language is playful and fun! We've highlighted three areas below that create great language connections for people – even for people who don't see themselves as "language people."

Advertising

Advertising is often all about language. It is something people encounter regularly as consumers, and some people also produce it as creators. Advertising slogans, company names, company icons, and acronyms are all rich with language content. Anything related to semantics and word combinations will likely have a good advertising link. Thinking about how advertising elements translate from language to language is also a great way to think about cross-linguistic differences. In addition, there's the way that ads play on the social uses of language, using different voices and dialects to evoke different emotions and associations.

For example, suppose you're interested in deverbal nouns and rules that make those productive in English. A quick Google search reveals that the slogan for Bounty paper towels is "the quicker picker-upper." That's a fun turn of phrase and it centers on a verb (*pick up*) turned into a noun; plus, it involves a verb-particle construction (the difference between *pick* and *pick up*). If your audience is from the United States, they will likely have heard the slogan before. Even if they aren't, a native speaker of English will have the intuition that the Bounty slogan is a reasonable – if clever – phrase to say. As a language scientist, you can probe that intuition: What makes the slogan acceptable? What happens if you rearrange the words? If you drop the *-er* on *picker* or on *upper*? How is this phrase noun-y and how is it verb-y? What other phrases work this way? Talking about deverbal nouns is a very academic thing to do. Talking about why the Bounty slogan works is something people can relate to.

In fact, one option is to start with your favorite advertising slogan and then figure out how to describe the language science behind it. For example, how would you explain why calling 7-Up the "Uncola" is effective? How would you explain how we know who is eating something in the Campbell's soup slogan "The soup that eats like a meal"? What kind of conversation might you have based on the old Sara Lee cake slogan "Nobody doesn't like Sara Lee"? The world of advertising covers a wide area and offers a wealth of example sentences that can start interesting conversations.

Cell Phones

Pretty much any topic related to speech perception can be easily connected to your phone. There are the old-fashioned kinds of connections that have been true of phones forever. For example, it's harder to understand people when you can't see them; on the other hand, we do reliably recognize the voices of specific people when they call us. Then there are the newfangled kinds of connections that have arisen from modern cell phones. For example, what are we really communicating with emoji – tone of voice? gestures? something else entirely?

Or think about the way that your phone suggests the next word in your texts – that's a form of predictive parsing. We've done a very simple activity with people where we ask them to start typing into their phones (or into one of our tablets) and see if they agree on what the computer auto-suggests for them. There are some easy ways to trick the programming to offer weird linguistic structures – try inserting lots of adjectives and see what happens, or try using conjoined subjects like "the boy and the girl" and see what it picks for the verb. Or you can demonstrate other kinds of association biases embedded in the program by seeing what pronouns it suggests for different professional titles.

Or consider how you can make your phone do things by talking to it. Automatic speech recognition (ASR) is now fully embedded not only into cell phones, but also many other devices and services. If you are interested in any dimension of speech production or perception, you should be able to make a connection to that kind of technology. And the mistakes these systems make are often as interesting as their successes. Currently (as of 2022, when we are writing this book), ASR systems don't recognize all kinds of speech equally well. For example, in a 2017 study, the computational sociolinguist Rachael Tatman put YouTube's auto-captioning software through a dialect test. She had YouTube caption a series of videos in which individuals who spoke different dialects of English read the same list of words. The individuals came from many different places, including California, New Zealand, and Scotland. So they pronounced the words as you'd expect people from those places to do. Human beings have little trouble understanding all these people, but YouTube did a lot worse at captioning the Scottish English speaker compared to the California English speaker. On top of that, YouTube also

Figure 7.1 Everybody enjoys their phone!
Note. This picture is used with permission from Getty Images. Photo credit: Tim Robberts.

did a lot worse captioning women than it did men. And when the women spoke non-California dialects, YouTube did worst of all. Many people have actually experienced these kinds of problems with ASR for themselves, and it's pretty easy to recreate them: Rachael Tatman's research could be done with just a laptop! If your favorite topic area is differences in linguistic dialect or style or gender, then it is easy to make that relevant by asking people to think about how computers can – and how they should – process those kinds of speech differences.

Popular Songs

Song lyrics would never cut it as a kind of broader impact in a grant, but people do know lots of them! Lyrics are just poetry set to music, and you can connect to both dimensions. On the poetry side, lyrics offer interesting ways to talk about things like alliteration, assonance, and rhyme, as well as just about every kind of wordplay. If you're interested in rap music, try color-coding some rap lyrics to show off what words and phrases are being rhymed and which words are linked by alliteration. This can be a fun way to get people to focus on what language sounds like compared to how it is written.

Or you could think about how the musical element of a song influences how you hear and remember the lyrics. Mishearings of lyrics are common enough to have a name – mondegreens – and they can be pretty funny. Whether it's

Jimi Hendrix kissing this guy or Taylor Swift and her lonely Starbucks lovers, people will have experienced this phenomenon. And if your chosen topic area involves things like phonotactic regularities or coarticulation effects, these misperceptions are great ways to show off your science.

Making Long-Distance Connections: Conversational Digressions

One important feature of the real world is that people are familiar with it and can talk with you about it. Ideally, your conversation is something you're doing with some sense of equality: You're not talking **at** people. You're talking **with** them. But a potential side effect of that equality is that the people you're talking with may take the conversation in a direction that you weren't expecting. What to do?

Here's an example from a conversation one of us (CM) had with a visitor to the USA Science and Engineering Festival back in 2014 who was asking about a demo using spectrograms of people's speech. Before we get to the conversational surprise, you can see in spectrograms a lot of detail about speakers and their speech. People who do a spectrogram demo might sit in front of a laptop that is running a program like Praat to record themselves saying their own names in their own voices. We then show images of their speech. It's easy for them to find vowels in these images when we ask them to consider which sounds last longer; or to find stop consonants (e.g., in a name like *Peter*) when we ask where they see breaks; or to find stressed syllables when we ask which parts of their names are louder. (We adjust our juicy questions to whatever they record.) Conversations about such phonological elements are easy to get going like this, and we often end this demo by printing out wave forms for people to take home. Figure 7.2 illustrates two kinds of images that this demo

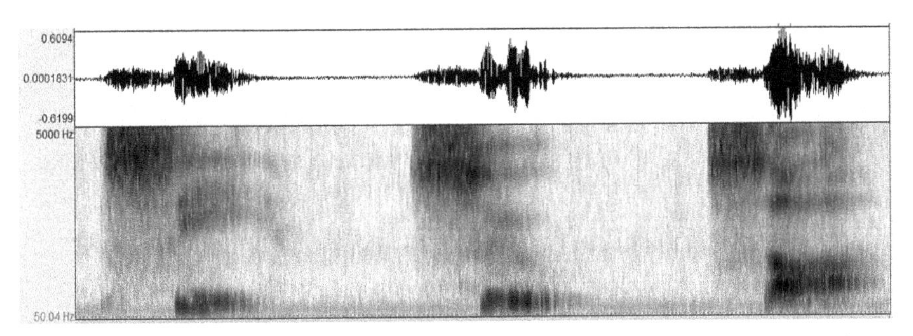

Figure 7.2 A wave form (top) and a spectrogram (bottom) showing the words *see*, *sue*, and *saw*

can show; because we mentioned vowels earlier, this figure shows three words – each starting with the consonant [s] and ending with the consonant [w] and distinguished by the vowels [i], [u], and [ɔ].

Back to our visitor who was unusually inquisitive about spectrograms of speech. It turned out he wanted to know whether spectrographic analyses might have forensic uses. He was animated by the case of the then-owner of the Los Angeles Clippers, Donald Sterling. (The Clippers are a professional basketball team in the United States.) A recording of racist comments had come out, and Sterling was denying that he was the speaker on the recording. The conversation went far beyond the consonants and vowels in the names we were recording – on to what kinds of information spectrographic analyses can show, how one would need some basis for comparison to see whether Sterling was the speaker, and about the use of science in the courts more generally. We hadn't originally thought about this activity as relating to voice recognition for a court case related to racism, but that's the direction the conversation took.

Making a connection to what someone else is interested in requires attending to **their** interests. In this case, we connected a sports fan who cared about sports-related news to the science of speech production and perception. In Chapter 10, we'll add more on the theme of listening to other people. Only through good listening will you be able to make these kinds of unexpected connections.

CRITICAL TAKE-HOME MESSAGE

You can make your topic relevant to other people by connecting it to something that people already care about in the real world. There are many types of real-world connections you can make. Be open to thinking about contexts where your topic matters for people.

WORKED EXAMPLE BOX

In Chapter 6, we talked about some ways to make topics like allophonic variation interesting for people. Here, we want to suggest some ways that you could make that topic relevant as well!

Allophones in song lyrics

Have you ever noticed that singers sometimes pronounce words in weird ways when they sing? Pop stars like Alanis Morissette and Selena Gomez

(cont.)

have gotten some internet attention on this topic: You can hear some clips of this through Reggie Ugwu's 2015 *BuzzFeed* posting, or read about it on Siu-Lan Tan's 2015 posting on *Psychology Today.*

What are they doing? Sometimes they are extending their vowels and turning them into diphthongs. That is, they are pronouncing sounds in a word like *bow* (as in, tie a bow) more like it's *boy.* They also sometimes pronounce consonants at the end of words without fully releasing them. That is, when they say a word like *fight,* they swallow the end of the last [t] sound so the word sounds more like *fie.*

Why are they doing this? One reason seems to be that singing things in a distinctive way helps the singers stand out. And that makes sense from a language science perspective! Regional dialect differences often depend on pronunciation differences similar to the ones these singers are using. For example, in the United States, extending vowels in different ways is a hallmark between Northern and Southern English: Northerners use the diphthong vowel [ai] when they say *pie,* but Southerners just use the single vowel [a] in the same word.

Another reason probably has to do with the fact that lyrics have to fit inside of songs, which have their own rhythms and tempos. It's easy to extend a note over a very long vowel, and swallowing a consonant can help you connect words and stay on beat. A related reason has to do with the fact that lyrics are a form of poetry, and poets have always played around with lengthening and shortening words to fit the poetic structure and to create desired rhyming and timing schemes. So there are lots of good reasons for singers to modify their pronunciations.

What does this all have to do with allophones? An allophone is a variant of a sound that doesn't change the meaning of a word. In Chapter 6, we used the example of the [p] sound – you pronounce it differently at the beginning of a word like *pot* than you do in *spot.* Even though the singers are changing the way they pronounce these sounds, you can still understand the meanings of the lyrics! They usually aren't shifting their pronunciations so much that they cross over into creating new words. We modify our speech sounds all the time so they fit together better in our regular spoken speech; the singers are just doing something a bit more extreme as they are fitting their sounds into a song.

So why do people think these words sound weird? Even though the singers aren't shifting things too far, they are shifting them away from standard spoken pronunciation. And we are so sensitive to even mild variations in how people say things that we notice the singers have done

(cont.)

something unusual. And all of this could be part of the reason that musicologists Nat Condit-Schultze and David Huron have found that it is harder to understand words when they are being sung than when they are being spoken (Condit-Schultze & Huron, 2017).

CLOSING WORKSHEET

Think about the topic area of your doable demo. In Chapters 5 and 6, you worked on turning that topic into an interactive activity. Now think about how you can make your topic area relevant to other people's lives.

Write down two ways that people might encounter your topic area in their everyday life. In addition, see if you can write down one way that the specific activity you came up with can be connected to people's real lives.

Further Reading

1 *Broader impacts in research grants*

Funding agencies across the world have different ways of encouraging researchers to think about how to make their work benefit the broader society. In the United States, for example, the National Science Foundation (NSF) values projects that accomplish what it calls "societally relevant outcomes." These could include results like improving hearing aid technology, broadening the kinds of people who are trained to do some kind of research, or changing the public's understanding of some research – exactly the kind of thing we're talking about in this book. You can read more about NSF's broader vision here: www.nsf.gov/od/oia/special/broaderimpacts/.

Similar considerations matter for other funding agencies, including the Australian Research Council (www.arc.gov.au/engagement-and-impact-assessment) and UK Research and Innovation (www.ukri.org/), which advocates giving "everyone the opportunity to contribute and to benefit, enriching lives locally, nationally, and internationally."

2 *Language is in our everyday lives*

For more examples of how language is woven into our daily lives, we highly recommend Dan Jurafsky's delightful book, *The Language of Food: A Linguist Reads the Menu* (Jurafsky, 2014) (https://web.stanford.edu/~jurafsky/

thelanguageoffood.html). This book is chock-full of interesting cases that could be turned into doable demos. Another great book for source material for demos is *Sold on Language* (Sedivy & Carlson, 2011).

3 *Advertising slogans*

You can find many old commercials featuring classic advertising slogans on YouTube. For the ones we mentioned in the main text, here is a bit of what we found!

- Bounty is the quicker-picker-upper. This article has a brief overview of the classic Bounty ads (including links to videos): www.doitbest.com/resources/manufacturers/bounty-the-quicker-picker-upper.

  It turns out that Bounty isn't completely consistent with its own slogan – if you watch through all the ads, you'll notice that sometimes it's just the "quick" picker-upper. There's a neat activity to be made about comparing these versions!
- 7-up is the Uncola. Here is a classic add from the 1980s: www.youtube.com/watch?v=AXmc7DG4uu8.
- The soup that eats like a meal. Here's an example of this classic Campbell's ad: www.youtube.com/watch?v=JtCds8aQCKY.
- Nobody doesn't like Sara Lee. To see this slogan in action, check out this ad: www.youtube.com/watch?v=YvR9T0rk3go.

  To see just how far Sara Lee is willing to go to play around with unusual quantification, check out this one, which claims that "everybody doesn't like something, but nobody doesn't like Sara Lee": www.youtube.com/watch?v=Iirw147LHkQ.

4 *What are we using emoji to communicate?*

For a wonderful tour of language use in the internet age (including emoji), we recommend Gretchen McCulloch's book, *Because Internet* (McCulloch, 2020). We are also fond of Michelle McSweeney's work in this area: http://michelleamcsweeney.com/.

5 *Research on ASR*

As Tatman (2017) notes, YouTube uses Google's popular ASR. So we can expect these results extend to lots of other domains. But, as she also notes, the fact that captioning is bad in YouTube is particularly frustrating to individuals who are deaf and must rely on these captions frequently.

If you're interested in learning about racial disparities in ASR, see Koenecke et al. (2020). For a popular overview of problems that ASR has with different varieties of speech, this *New York Times* article by Cade Metz is a good starting place (Metz, 2020): www.nytimes.com/2020/03/23/technology/speech-recognition-bias-apple-amazon-google.html. (Fair warning: The *New York Times* has a paywall and only allows you to read a limited number of articles for free.)

6 *Analysis of rap lyrics*

For a crash course in how linguistically interesting rap music is, see this article and video from Estelle Caswell (Caswell, 2016): www.vox.com/2016/5/19/11701976/rapping-deconstructed-best-rhymers-of-all-time.

7 *Mondegreens*

This term for misinterpretations that happen when we mishear lyrics has a lovely back story. Or, as the magnificent *Oxford English Dictionary* (2013) puts it, the word's etymology is thus: "the name *Lady Mondegreen*, a misinterpretation of the phrase *laid him on the green* in the ballad 'The Bonny Earl of Murray.'" Sylvia Wright coined the term as she described this childhood mishearing; apparently, her mother read old English poetry aloud to her, and this ballad was one of her favorites (Wright, 1954). As she and others have noted, mondegreens can be better in some ways than the original wording – funnier, more plausible.

The Taylor Swift mondegreen mentioned in the main text was written about by Melissa Dahl: www.thecut.com/2014/11/why-you-keep-mishearing-that-taylor-swift-lyric.html. And her analysis was augmented by Mark Liberman in the *Language Log*: https://languagelog.ldc.upenn.edu/nll/?p=16169.

Andrew Nevins has put together a series of videos about mondegreens that discuss some great examples: www.youtube.com/watch?v=dBnhkwRmYuQ.

And Nordquist's (2020) piece on mondegreens lists many more examples, including a set of historical mondegreens suggesting intriguing links to language change.

8 *Was Sterling the speaker on the recording?*

Here's an article if you want to read more details about Donald Sterling: www.tmz.com/2014/04/26/donald-sterling-clippers-owner-black-people-racist-audio-magic-johnson/.

9 *Allophones in song lyrics*

Here are the links to these popular articles on song lyrics:

- Reggie Ugwu: www.buzzfeednews.com/article/reggieugwu/what-is-indie-pop-voice#.biXnELLoX
- Siu Lin Tan: www.psychologytoday.com/us/blog/what-shapes-film/201510/six-reasons-pop-singers-pronounce-some-lyrics-in-odd-ways

8 Quality and Credibility

OPENING WORKSHEET

Write down the name of someone who you find to be **trustworthy** and believable. It could be a government official; it could be a teacher; it could be a local authority, such as a zookeeper or a museum docent; it could be someone providing a service to you, such as a mechanic or a nurse; it could be a friend or a family member.

Write down the answers to the following questions:

- What kinds of things does this person know about? What topic areas would you trust this person to explain accurately?
- What makes this person believable about those topic areas? Why do you find this person credible?
- Would you find this person equally believable if they talked to you about a different topic? What are the limits of this person's credibility?

When you engage with people through your doable demo, you will automatically be granted a certain kind of authority: You're the person with the activity that people want to do! In Chapter 2, we encouraged you to think of yourself as a scientist while doing your demo since it is based in real language science. But being a scientific authority carries some special responsibilities. In Chapter 3, we talked about Grice's Maxim of Quality (i.e., tell the truth). Recall that most people tell the truth most of the time; further, most people believe that you are telling the truth most of the time. But in these days of scientific mistrust, not all authorities are automatically granted the grace that we offer a typical conversational partner. You will need to earn people's trust that you are, indeed, telling the truth. So what can you do to strengthen people's belief in you?

Present Yourself as Someone to Believe

If you wanted to know about space travel, who would you rather ask: an astronaut or some guy on the corner who claimed to have been abducted by aliens? What about someone selling tickets for Virgin Galactic? Which of these three people seems most credible as an expert on space travel?

Figure 8.1 Who would you trust about space travel?
Note. Option 1 (left) is used by permission of Getty Images (Photo credit: Marc Dufresne). Option 2 (middle) is used under the Creative Commons Attribution 2.0 Generic license. Option 3 (right) is used by permission of Getty Images (Photo credit: Casper Benson).

It turns out that people have been thinking about credibility for a long time. In fact, this goes all the way back to the ancient Greeks: The philosopher Aristotle argued that a speaker's character affects persuasion (see Rapp, 2010). In *Rhetoric*, Aristotle wrote that a credible person must show (1) practical intelligence, (2) a virtuous character, and (3) goodwill. More recently, educational psychologists Frederike Hendriks, Dorothe Kienhues, and Rainer Bromme studied how we decide whether or not a scientific source is credible (Hendriks et al., 2015). They showed people a collection of scientific snippets (of the sort you would see posted in online blog posts) and asked them to rate a variety of qualities of the person who wrote the snippets. Were they professional or unprofessional? Helpful or hindering? Qualified or unqualified? Fair or unfair? Sincere or insincere? Then the researchers used statistical tools like factor analysis to see how the qualities grouped together. What they found was that Aristotle's broad categories of traits were also contributing to a science writer's credibility. In modern terms, they found that a credible expert is one who has (1) expertise, (2) integrity, and (3) benevolence.

How do you demonstrate your expertise (your practical intelligence)? As we noted in Chapter 2, you don't need to know everything about your topic area in order to support an effective activity. Even so, you should be doing more than just reading words that you yourself can't interpret. One critical component of expertise is competence, so it's a good idea to make sure you know how your activity works: What are the pieces involved? How do you turn things on? What instructions do people need in order to get the central experience? Being able to interact with your materials smoothly – and being able to help others use your materials – will demonstrate your competence.

You should also know the scientific content that you want people to take away from your activity. If you want people to appreciate hierarchical tree structure, you should know what that is! If you're using the IPA, you should know what that abbreviation stands for! (Knowing what an alphabet is will also help.) What's more, it's helpful to be able to describe the core elements in your activity in more than one way. Being able to rephrase your ideas with new words is a good way to show that you understand the ideas and aren't just parroting what you've heard others say.

Yet another way to show your expertise is by being able to link the topic of your activity to people's everyday lives. As we discussed in Chapter 7, connecting your activity to the real world will make it relevant for people. Make sure you have several relevance connections at your fingertips. Like your core scientific points, these should be points that you are well prepared to talk about with people.

How do you demonstrate integrity (your virtuous character)? In the research mentioned above, two of the most important components of integrity were honesty and sincerity. Honesty means that you need to do your homework: When you explain something to someone, make sure that you're drawing on legitimate scholarship. You're not just talking with people about your personal impressions about how language works; instead, you're talking about scientific knowledge that you yourself know to be true. Note, though, that this honesty issue is something that can trip up experts: They sometimes worry that if they aren't covering all the details of their science, then they are dishonest. In Chapter 9, we'll talk more about how incomplete is not the same as incorrect. It is not only possible, but actually desirable, to focus on broad generalizations about your topic area.

One way to demonstrate your honesty about what you know is to admit what you don't know. If somebody asks a question, and you don't know the answer, just say so! We discussed this strategy in Chapter 2, where we pointed out that it won't make you seem foolish to admit you don't know everything. Nobody knows everything. Everybody is aware of that fact. So if (when!) you have to admit that there are limits to your expertise, people will respect your honesty and find you all the more credible.

And you don't have to just leave your "I don't know" hanging out there all alone. You could follow it up with some suggestions about how you'd find out the answer. Is it something that you could explore with the materials you have with you? Is it something that you could look up in a book or on the

Internet? Is it something that nobody knows the answer to and would require a lifetime of study to figure out? Real scientific progress is propelled by what we don't know. That's not at all a bad thing to admit!

As for sincerity, a great way to express this quality is to commit to doing your activity with purpose, respect, and thoughtful preparation. What are you trying to accomplish with your activity? We hope that you're trying to show people who you interact with that your science is a fascinating and exciting area, and that you want to inspire them to learn more about it. If you sincerely try to do these things, people will appreciate that, and it will improve their impression of you. But for you to be truly sincere, you do have to convey that you yourself find your science to be fascinating and exciting. And if you want to inspire people to learn more, then take the core lessons of this book to heart. Seriously listen to people and try to have good conversations with them. Your sincere efforts to connect through listening will also make you more credible.

How do you demonstrate benevolence (your goodwill)? A benevolent expert is not one who is out for personal gain, but is instead trying to share their knowledge for the greater good. The very fact that you are willing to take the time to share what you know in a free-choice environment is a sign of your benevolence. The benefits that you receive from doing your activity are largely intangible (you're getting to see people become interested in language science!), and that lack of explicit reward also enhances your credibility.

But there is another, more moment-to-moment way that you can demonstrate benevolence, and that's by being considerate to the people you are talking with and showing them respect. Respect is important for effective conversations of all sorts, but for conversations about scientific knowledge, it is critical for helping you establish and maintain your credibility.

When it comes to thinking about space travel, we expect you found the astronaut to be more credible than the alternatives: Astronauts have expert knowledge about space travel, they sincerely care about what they do, and they generally aren't trying to sell you a seat on a space flight. So they score highly in terms of expertise, integrity, and benevolence. What about when it comes to thinking about language science?

For many people, the idea of a language expert is someone who wants to correct their grammar and tell them how to talk. We're not so sure that most critics of that sort have genuine expertise (some of what they say about language is patently wrong), but many of them clearly lack integrity and benevolence. These so-called language experts often show a lack of respect for the people they are giving advice to. When you're doing your demo, you should present yourself as a different kind of language expert – you're the kind that is being responsible to the science and can be a credible source for what we know about how language works.

Being Clear Is a Sign of Respect

This book is trying to help you make your science accessible to the general public so that everybody can understand what you have to say. One big reason to be understandable is that it will help you keep people's interest. And another reason to work on being understandable is that it is a sign of respect, and ultimately it will be taken as a sign of your credibility. Imagine taking a class where you don't understand the material well. Now imagine that you go to the teacher to ask for some help. How would you feel if the teacher just kept explaining things exactly the same, confusing way as in class? Being able to explain something in multiple ways is a sign of good teaching, and a marker of someone having genuine expertise (or practical intelligence) about their topic. So when someone can't understand you, you raise the possibility that you lack the expertise to talk about it.

You may also raise the possibility that you lack benevolence (or goodwill). Think again about unhelpful teachers you've met. Maybe they really do know their stuff cold, but they might be unwilling to take their students' needs into consideration – who they are, what they already know, where they are coming from. If a teacher doesn't care about those things, then what do they care about? Are they just engaging in a performance of "I'm the smartest person in the room" with you? That actually doesn't make a person seem particularly credible. Making your activity understandable to the specific people you are talking with demonstrates that you care whether they learn something. That's respectful to them, and it will also reflect well on you.

Credibility and Respect

Would you believe someone who didn't respect you? Would you even want to be in a conversation with that person? People don't have to talk with you in a free-choice environment, so it's up to you to be someone who they want to talk with.

One of the clearest ways to show your respect for your conversational partners is by listening carefully to what they say and responding appropriately. If someone asks you a question, you should answer it. If someone explains their reaction to your materials, you should acknowledge their perspective – even if it wasn't what you were expecting. Just in general, you should treat the other person's contribution to the conversation as relevant and important.

In Chapter 4, we contrasted a deficit model approach with a funds of knowledge approach. One of the major problems with the deficit model is that it fundamentally disrespects others. It treats their personal histories, perspectives, and knowledge base as being inadequate, irrelevant, or unimportant. One of the reasons that people don't respond well to experts who adopt a deficit approach is that people don't like to be disrespected. Moreover, a lack of respect will taint your credibility: If you think little of the people you are talking with, it raises the possibility that you have an ulterior motive for the conversation.

By contrast, the funds of knowledge approach puts respect for the other person front and center. It not only acknowledges that everybody in the conversation has something useful to contribute, but it also actively encourages you to find out what other people already know. You can then draw on their established knowledge to help you improve your message. And, as we mentioned before, language is a topic area where people have ample funds of knowledge! The people you will interact with have lots of experience using language in a variety of contexts – they speak it and write it; they may know more than one; they may have lots of ideas about what it is and how it works. Respect and even celebrate that knowledge when you talk with them!

One worry that you might have is that someone's funds of knowledge may contradict what you see as your core point. For example, one of our activities is about dialects and how they differ across regions of the country. Most of the time, people's personal histories are a huge asset for doing this activity. People have encountered regional dialect differences before and can come up with lots of examples or situations from their own lives where dialect has mattered: They have interesting ideas about how dialect differences come about. There are usually many opportunities to use a person's own experiences to illustrate core dialect findings.

But every now and then – and it is actually an uncommon occurrence – someone will offer up an opinion that embodies an attitude that we don't want to endorse. In the case of dialect, there are some harmful societal attitudes out there about the low character of people who speak in particular ways. In the United States, where we work, many of these opinions are thinly disguised racism, although much of it is also a reflection of sexism and general prejudices against people from certain parts of the country. We don't advocate taking these comments on directly: At best, the person you are talking with will be dismissive of you (and probably of everything else you said); at worst, you might end up making a scene that will not be appreciated by your partners in the venue.

But that doesn't mean that you have to endorse someone's racist (or sexist, or homophobic, or otherwise offensive) point of view. You don't have to be **that** polite! One technique that we have used is to say something like this:

"I know a lot of people think that's true, but actually scientists have found that African American English has a richly structured rule system," or "I know that's something many people believe, but actually, scientists have learned that someone's regional dialect doesn't predict their intelligence." This turn of phrase is also useful for countering language myths that aren't quite as pernicious: "I know a lot of people think that's true, but actually scientists have found that all languages have different regional dialects," or "I've heard people say that before, but actually, scientists have discovered that languages are constantly changing, even in Appalachia."

This technique is helpful in a few different ways. First, by recognizing that the person's point of view is shared by others, you show that person some respect: It isn't crazy for someone to believe this thing – it really is out there in the culture. Second, by explicitly saying that scientists disagree with the view, you are being clear that neither you, nor the field that you represent, agrees with this view (regardless of how common it is). You're unlikely to change somebody's mind with just this technique, but what you can do is lay the groundwork for possible future change. This person now knows that not everybody shares these views. What's more, they know that a credible expert in the field doesn't share these views. In Chapter 9, we'll talk about taking the **long view** and having patience with people: What you're doing isn't about trying to persuade people of any particular position in a single conversation. But it is about paving the way for people to change their minds at some point in the future. And that's part of why it is worth doing the work to be a credible expert: It's a good way to open someone's mind!

CRITICAL TAKE-HOME MESSAGE

Present yourself as a credible expert by being prepared, clear, honest, and respectful of the people you converse with.

WORKED EXAMPLE BOX

One way to give yourself instant credibility is to dress for the part.

Often when we go to festivals, we have everybody on our team wear a T-shirt that advertises our home institution. Colleges and universities are places that people recognize as reputable sources of knowledge. By claiming our school, we are claiming the credibility that comes with the whole institution of higher education.

(cont.)

Figure 8.2 Three Ohio State University students getting ready to engage with visitors at the COSI museum

Note. These students are wearing lab coats in preparation for working with visitors at the local science museum. The logo on their cart represents the lab's organizing sponsor, the Buckeye Language Network. Photo credit: The Ohio State University.

But sometimes we go further. In one of our labs (LW), the students wear lab coats when they interact with people. Lab coats are the stereotypical attire of scientists, and when our students wear them, they encourage people to see them that way. (As we mentioned in Chapter 2, children will often ask them if they are real scientists!)

Some parts of the scientist stereotype are great: Scientists are generally considered to be very smart people who have a lot of expertise in their topic area. These features are important to us for two reasons. First, people don't always think that language is a topic that can be studied scientifically, and we want to emphasize that it is. Second, having expertise is a core element to credibility, and we value that association.

However, there are some stereotypes about scientists that we'd rather not be connected with. We don't want people to think our students are

(cont.)

"mad scientists" who are more interested in getting results than in treating people respectfully. That stereotype doesn't help people perceive us as having integrity or benevolence.

So, as the Spider-Man movies exhort, "With great power comes great responsibility." We want the power that comes from presenting ourselves as experts, but we accept the responsibility that we need to represent ourselves in honest and respectful ways. We work hard to wear our lab coats responsibly!

CLOSING WORKSHEET

One of the most important things you will say during your conversations won't be about your topic. It will be the phrase "I don't know."

For the topic of your own doable demo, write down three things that you **do** know. You can write down very specific pieces of information about how your phenomenon works as well as some more foundational pieces of information that underlie your topic area. But make sure that you feel confident about the three things you write down: What knowledge are you bringing to your conversation?

Now write down three things about your topic area that you do **not** know. What are the limits of the knowledge that you are bringing to your conversation?

Further Reading

1 *Many language critics lack integrity and benevolence*

Language critics are usually cheerleaders for prescriptivism: They are here to tell us what is wrong with our language use. By contrast, language scientists favor descriptivism, which is an approach focused on how language is actually signed, spoken, or written. While we're sure that some language critics really do understand how language works as well as the average language scientist, most of the time, that just doesn't seem to be true. If you're interested in a specific example of where the language critics' approach goes wrong, we recommend Pullum (2014). This article critiques examples of writing advice from prescriptivists who are especially exercised about the English passive. It shows that many of those telling writers to avoid the passive don't even recognize the construction in their own writing. The author reviews and counters their various unsubstantiated 'allegations' against passives (e.g., good writers avoid them). For a broader discussion about the uses and abuses of linguistic prescriptivism, we recommend Anne Curzan's book *Fixing English* (Curzan, 2014).

2 *Linguistic prejudice*

There is ample sociolinguistics scholarship documenting linguistic prejudice. If you want to read a summary of a variety of language myths, including many related to regional prejudice, racism, and sexism, we recommend Bauer and Trudgill (1988) or Kaplan (2016).

3 *Students working at the BLN cart*

This "Buckeye Language Network" or BLN is the cross-college organizing umbrella for language researchers at The Ohio State University, where LW works.

9 Quality vs Quantity

Incomplete ≠ Incorrect

OPENING WORKSHEET

Read through this lentil soup recipe:

(1) Get out a soup pot.

(2) Get out one large yellow onion. You should cut the ends off of the onion and remove the outer layer of the onion (sometimes called the onion skin). Dice the onion into small pieces.

(3) Put 4 tablespoons of extra virgin olive oil in the pot and turn the heat to medium-high.

(4) Once the oil is hot, put the onions in the pot. Cook the onions until they are slightly translucent and very soft.

(5) Sprinkle a teaspoon of salt over the onions.

(6) Add 1 quart of liquid to the pot. You may use vegetable stock (if you want the dish to be vegetarian), or you may use chicken stock. If you use plain water, add some extra salt to the pot.

(7) Add a sprig of thyme to the pot.

(8) Add 1 cup of brown or green lentils. Make sure you have thoroughly cleaned the lentils beforehand! Cover the pot. Cook the lentils in the pot for approximately 45 minutes, or until the lentils are soft.

(9) Peel 2 cloves of garlic and finely dice them. Add the diced garlic to the pot after the lentils have softened.

(10) If you want your soup to be smooth, place it in a blender and puree it briefly. You may puree all of the soup, or just some of it. You can also use a handheld blender and place it in the pot itself to blend the soup.

(11) Add a teaspoon of something slightly acidic, such as lemon juice, apple cider vinegar, or red wine vinegar. Stir the acid into the soup.

(12) Wash a bunch of parsley and finely chop it. Add the chopped parsley to the soup and stir it well.

(13) Ladle the soup into bowls and serve the bowls with soup spoons.

Which steps (or parts of steps) in this recipe are not genuinely needed?

Remove all the steps (or parts of steps) that can be omitted but would still allow you to make a decent soup. How many steps did you modify?

Now remove two more steps (or parts of steps). Can you still follow the recipe? Would it still taste the same? If you answered yes to both those questions, modify two more steps and see what happens!

In earlier chapters, we've encouraged you to have a regular conversation, to make your science broadly interesting, to connect your science with the real world, and to care about your audience's point of view. At this point, you may be feeling like we're recommending that you dump your science in favor of entertainment. We understand where you're coming from – that's a worry that a lot of scientists have when they get this kind of advice.

We like to think about this worry in terms of Grice's theory of cooperative conversation, discussed in Chapter 3. On the one hand, you want your science conversation to respect the Maxim of Quality: You want to tell the truth. On the other hand, you want your science conversation to respect the Maxim of Quantity: You want to provide the right amount of information (channeling Goldilocks: not too little, but also not too much). Scientists often feel like providing a simplified explanation of their work forces them to choose between the maxims. You can be maximally accurate, but then you have to provide way too much information for many people to digest. Or you can provide less information, but then you aren't being as accurate as possible.

The Maxims of Quality and Quantity, however, are not actually in competition with each other. We want to offer an alternative way to think about the problem: INCOMPLETE ≠ INCORRECT. In the rest of this chapter, we'll explain what we mean by that and suggest some ways to approach your explanations that will help you satisfy both maxims.

Am I Dumbing Down My Science?

Real science is complicated. If it were obvious and easy, we wouldn't need experts to do it. And it wouldn't take many years to become an expert. In fact, one of the joys of taking even an introductory course in a science is discovering that there are wonderfully complicated details out there. For example, we have the impression that when we talk, we just "do it" and it doesn't feel hard at all. But as language scientists, we try to understand how talking works, and it turns out to be very complicated. To take one example: Speech sounds can be described along three main dimensions (technically described as place, manner, and voicing) and those dimensions can be described with an alarming level of precision – which is necessary to explain the differences between individual sounds and speech across languages. And another example: A noun turns out to be much more than a "person, place, or thing." It's an abstraction reflecting distributional, syntactic, morphological, semantic, and occasionally phonological properties across languages. When we talk, we are really doing precision mechanics with our mouths and accessing symbols that connect across multiple representational domains. We're not "just" doing anything! Those details are part of what makes our science serious business.

The more you study something, the more conscious you are of all the complicated details that go into it. You also become conscious of the limits of what we know. Evidence can support a claim, but it won't definitively prove it to be true. Most scientific papers are full of qualifications about what has been found – predictions "may" be confirmed, analyses "are consistent" with theories, and data "increases our confidence" in a hypothesis. Scientists are careful because they know that new results might change their minds – theories change when there's enough evidence pointing in another direction. If you want to be accurate about your science, you need to be careful about what you're claiming.

And when you're talking with the general public, you're not actually **doing** your science then and there. Instead, you're **explaining** your science. How much detail should your explanations have in informal learning settings? Not very much. We may move the field forward by being down and dirty in the details, but those details matter because they support generalizations. And while in principle every scientific generalization is open to revision, some of them are so well supported at this point that they're unlikely to be overturned soon. Sometimes it is good to remember that there are a lot of things that scientists agree on. Generalizations about foundational findings can allow you to speak with a lot of confidence that what you're saying is indeed accurate.

Imagine for a moment that you wanted to explain how a traffic stoplight works. The easiest way to put it would be to say: Red means stop and green means go. Of course, as an expert driver, you're likely aware that there are a variety of situations that don't really fit that generalization. In the United States, some intersections allow you to turn right on red; a flashing red light means that you stop briefly and then go if it's clear; you should stop when an emergency vehicle is whizzing by even if the light is green. All of these situations are true, and all go against the simplest generalization about traffic lights. But none of those exceptions are easy to understand unless you already know the simple generalization. "Red means stop and green means go" isn't wrong. It just doesn't cover every situation involving traffic lights. In other words, it's an incomplete description of traffic lights, but it's not an incorrect one.

To put this in terms of language science, imagine that your topic is syntactic bootstrapping. Or, as we would put it when talking with the general public, the fact that you can figure out something about a word's meaning by looking at how it's used in a sentence. You might present people (as we like to do) with the first lines of Lewis Carroll's "Jabberwocky" poem (Carroll, 1871/2010): "'Twas brillig, and the slithy toves did gyre and gimble in the wabe." It's easy to get people to articulate reasonable intuitions about what the noun *toves* means based on its status in the sentence. For people who are shy about offering their intuitions, we often ask them how many toves they think there are here, and they will reliably tell you that they don't know for sure, but there is definitely more than one. Once you can get people to address that one fact, it's pretty easy to get them to think meta-linguistically about what in the sentence helps them guess the meanings of nonsense words.

Now, we could point out that the mere presence of an -*s* at the end of a word (even one that is preceded by a determiner) doesn't necessarily make it plural: Plenty of singular nouns end in -*s* (*asbestos, glass, mess, success).* In fact, not only does the presence of an -*s* at the end of a word not necessarily make it plural, but you can have a plural noun that doesn't have an -*s* at the end (*children, feet, mice).* If you want to get really detailed about how the plural works in English, you really can't just stop by pointing to a word-final -*s.* You might at this point feel obligated to point out that this so-called bootstrapping process of learning from a word's syntactic context involves a lot of probabilistic cue coordination. You might also feel obligated to point out that the field's beliefs about which cues can get coordinated and how that coordination happens has changed over time (and might well change in the future).

But does any of that detail matter **here**? The generalization that you can use the "-s" on *toves* to help you make sense of this poem is a good one and captures the essence of syntactic bootstrapping. All those complications we just noted about plural morphology in English might help you identify situations where syntactic bootstrapping would end up being less effective. They might even be the situations that will force scientists to reconsider how syntactic bootstrapping works. Still, before someone worries about the problem cases for this word learning strategy, they first have to understand what the strategy actually is.

If Chapter 4 convinced you, your goal is to get people engaged enough to learn a little bit about how your science works. They don't have to pass a test on the details of your topic area or be equipped to conduct their own study to investigate the nuanced implications of what you're sharing. Think about the level of description that textbooks provide for those summary statements at the end of each chapter. You aren't reading any whole chapters to people. You want to provide them with enough information that they feel **inspired** to go find out those details for themselves. That's not dumbing down your science: It's opening a door that anyone can walk through.

Three Ways to Balance Quantity with Quality

Finding the right level of generalization to use in talking about your science isn't always easy. To satisfy the Maxim of Quality, you will want to be accurate in your conversation, but to make your conversation accessible to others, you will need to limit the amount of information so that they can take it in. So you will want to say the truth, and nothing but the truth; but you might not always tell the **whole** truth about everything. Here we offer you three suggestions for ways to think about your science so that the concerns of quantity and quality are balanced.

Distinguish Phenomena from Explanation

All scientific fields have theoretical debates about what's going on, and language science is no different. Scientific theories are how we explain what we currently know and predict what will happen in new situations. Theories move science forward, and most scientists are genuinely committed to the elements of their theory. But distinguishing between theoretical positions is rarely an easy task. If one theory predicted that the sun would rise in the east while another one predicted that it would rise in the west, there wouldn't be fights over who was right. Any theory that is worth arguing for is one that can account for a lot of established facts and can make a lot of good predictions about what we should find in the future. The nitty-gritty details that scientists work on are important because they are often the ones that distinguish different theories. If I can find too many exceptions to your generalization, maybe you have the wrong one. And if you really want to be able to explain how something works (and therefore to make good predictions over the long haul), then you really do care about those theoretical differences. Scientists definitely care about them. And people training to become scientists spend a lot of time learning to focus on the cases that matter for the theory.

We, however, don't actually care **what** you believe at the theoretic level because we want you to be focused on the phenomena. Since any decent theory can account for a lot of facts, choose a fact that all decent theories can explain. For example, in our own research on language acquisition, experts debate the extent to which children are innately wired to learn their first language and the extent to which they use domain-general strategies that help them learn lots of things, including language. We certainly have our own opinions on these matters, but they very rarely come up when we're talking with the public. Instead, we talk about striking phenomena in child language development, like the fact that young children are great word learners.

We mentioned before that people can learn new words from a poem like "Jabberwocky" through a process called syntactic bootstrapping. There really isn't a theoretical debate about whether children **can** do syntactic bootstrapping. But there are many debates about how it really works: How do children use sentential context to help them learn word meanings? Which parts of the sentence can they use at different ages? What kinds of meanings can sentence contexts help with? To what extent is the process different across languages? Are children born knowing how to link structures with meanings or do they have to learn them all from experience? There are plenty of highly specific details that matter in this debate. But for most people you'll encounter in a free-choice learning environment, the initial generalization – that children can do it at all – will be news.

Just in general, the phenomena that theories were created to explain are good ones to work with. And it is just fine to focus on the easy and obvious cases that all theories can handle. Those cases might be boring from a theoretical standpoint (because they can't tell you who is right), but they are a perfect starting point for a nonexpert. Before people can care about which theory has the best explanation for something, they need to know that the something even exists. Don't worry about convincing people that something works in a particular way. Instead, start by showing them that it happens at all.

Distinguish Classics from Hot News

The more you know about a topic, the more you are likely to take your basic knowledge for granted. In Chapter 12, we'll talk more about this problem and how knowledge can be a curse. But when you are trying to choose the best phenomenon to share in these public settings, we recommend going with a classic. You're looking for something that has been studied by many people for many years. These phenomena tend to be robust and easy to demonstrate: They have stood the test of time for a reason. Science is a cumulative endeavor and you want facts that are close to the ground floor. Syntactic bootstrapping is just the kind of thing that counts. It has been studied experimentally at least since the 1950s, and as Lewis Carroll showed, it's something that people have known about for a lot longer.

If you've only taken one class about language science, then the classics might be all you know about – good for you! It's going to be easy for you to choose a phenomenon that will work well in a free-choice environment. But the longer you are in a field, the more these bedrock phenomena will feel like old news, or even background noise. The typical focus for advanced courses (or your own research) is what's new in the field. An advanced seminar on syntactic bootstrapping wouldn't be about demonstrating that it happens, it would be about the latest refinement to our understanding. For example, how do preschoolers use function words to define relevant sentential contexts and how quickly can they establish those contexts? The hot news on your topic is what people are talking about at conferences and reading preprints on and presenting in advanced seminars. But remember that the hot news won't make sense to somebody who doesn't already know the basic generalization. Just because you (and lots of other scientists) have known about the classics for a long time doesn't mean the general public knows them at all.

There's no hard and fast rule about what makes something hot news and not a classic. But if the phenomenon was the primary result of a paper published within the last five (or even ten) years, it's probably hot news. And if something gets a half-page or more of description in an introductory textbook, it's probably a classic. You can also think about your phenomenon in terms of what someone needs to know in order to understand it. We'll talk more in Chapter 15 about the process of conscious layering of scaffolding support for learners, but the more details you need in order to explain what your phenomenon is, the more likely it is to be hot news.

Emphasize Process

A common view about science is that it is a body of knowledge – a set of things that experts happen to know. For scientists, though, what makes something a science is the way relevant knowledge builds up. Scientists emphasize the processes of gathering observations, making hypotheses to explain patterns in the observations, testing the hypotheses, and evaluating the evidence that bears on the hypotheses. For scientists – including language scientists – it's the **process** of knowledge creation that really matters. So one way to approach your topic area is to talk about how people figured it out in the first place and how people continue to study it.

You may also recall that experts in the field of informal science learning devoted two of their six strands to talking about scientific process (see Chapter 4). Strand 4 is to get people to think about science as a process and Strand 5 is to get people to use the tools of science. Thinking about how you study your topic can be a great way to help people understand it!

When we want to emphasize process, we focus on two pieces: testing hypotheses and evaluating evidence. Or as we like to put it: guessing what's going to happen and thinking about different ways to explain what we experience. There are lots of ways that you can encourage both of these steps in the scientific process. For example, if you've given people a puzzle to solve or a game to play, an easy way to promote hypothesis testing is to ask them how they could make it easier. One of our activities uses the Stroop task (see Chapter 13) with color words written in ink of different colors (e.g., the word ***yellow*** is written in red ink) . When people are asked to say the color of the **ink**, they get interference from reading the meaning of the word itself, which leads to delays and mistakes. Once people have experienced the phenomenon, we often ask them what we could do to make the game easier. Those are guesses that we can sometimes test right there on the spot. (For example, is it easier to do the game if you take your glasses off? Usually, yes!) Guessing about the different ways to change the task is really a way of hypothesizing about how the phenomenon works – it's the process we use to figure out what's going on.

And we can also talk about how to evaluate the evidence. Is it a fair test of your ability to do this task in a noisy public setting? Was your way of making the task easier really helping or did you improve because it's your fourth time playing the game? Are color words special in some way that creates the effect? Would it work the same if the color words were written in

Figure 9.1 The Stroop task, as seen on the back of a T-shirt
Note. The Stroop task is easy to display. Putting it on a T-shirt makes you a walking demo!

a different language? Talking about how we interpret the evidence we get and whether it is a good way to see if we guessed right is getting at the core of the scientific process. What's more, this kind of approach makes the fact that you might not know something into a real virtue. If someone asks, "What would happen if...," then you have an invitation to ask them how you could figure it out.

When it comes to talking about the tools of science, there are also lots of approaches to take. If you happen to want to work on a topic that has a nifty measurement tool, then this is an easy one. Spectrograms are readily available as tablet apps for very little money, and they are eye-catching, interactive, and show people things they probably haven't seen before. An activity using spectrograms can – like the International Phonetic Alphabet (IPA) names – be individualized as well. (See Chapters 7 and 15 for more examples of how to talk about speech sounds using spectrograms.) But don't overlook the fact that low-tech tools are tools all the same! The IPA is a tool of the language science trade and makes for a great activity (we talk more about using the IPA in Chapters 4 and 11). Another tool that is often used, especially in language development work, is the nonsense word. Lewis Carroll used them for poetic effect, but nonsense words are one of the key ways that language scientists get perfect control over frequency effects: If you have never heard a word before, then its frequency count for you is zero. And if you want to talk about work in a classic theoretical domain, you might talk about how introspection is a tool of language science. Reflecting carefully about what you know has a long history in our field. We appreciate that introspection is a somewhat controversial tool to use within a scientific field, but it is an interesting conversation starter.

Take the Long View

Once you accept that people don't need to learn **everything** about your topic from a brief conversation with you, then you can relax into the idea that your goal is to provide people with an appreciation of your topic. You will only be showing them a piece of your topic – but it will be a real piece. And we hope it will be a piece that is both engaging and understandable all on its own.

One additional worry that you might be having is this: What if people walk away with the wrong idea? What if people misunderstand your point and now believe that your generalization applies more broadly than it does? Or what if they believe they now do know everything about your complex topic when in fact they have just been introduced to a very small part? Or worse: What if people misunderstand what you say and walk away believing something that is genuinely **wrong**. What can you do about that?

The short answer to that is, "Nothing!" You can't control what people believe. If you have ever taught a group of amateurs – whether they are students in an intro class, knitters in a club, visitors to a historic site, or girl scouts at a demonstration – then you know full well that not everyone is going to learn from you equally well. No amount of detail or technique on your part will guarantee that what you say will stick in the way that you intend it to for everyone.

What's more, when it comes to language, people may have entered the conversation with you having some prior misconceptions. They will likely be trying to connect whatever you say to their own understanding of language, and that understanding might be flawed. For example, syntactic bootstrapping is supposed to help people appreciate one way people learn new words. But some people really don't like the idea that new words enter the language all the time and might walk away with the idea that you have to watch what kids read or they will learn bad slang. (This example is not as far-fetched as you might believe.) It's OK to feel a little bit sad about the state of the universe when something like this happens, but then you just have to let it go and move on.

The very best thing you can do to stop this from happening is to help people be interested in and excited about your science. If you accomplish that, you increase the odds that they will be inspired to learn more about your topic – including learning about the details that you skipped over, but also including information that may override their misconceptions. Education does not succeed or fail because of one individual conversation. It is a process that happens over many encounters which may take many years to happen. Your goal is to help people with a lifelong project of improved understanding of scientific facts and processes. Your conversation is just one piece in a very large puzzle.

CRITICAL TAKE-HOME MESSAGE

In order to make your science accessible for others, you will not be able to cover all its details. Providing an incomplete description is not the same as providing an inaccurate one! Focusing on well-established phenomena and emphasizing how our science works can help you balance quality and quantity in your conversation.

WORKED EXAMPLE BOX

Mayan glyphs

One of our activities is about the writing system used by the ancient Mayan people. As can be seen in the image in Figure 9.2, this system looks very different from modern alphabetic systems, whether you're thinking of the Roman alphabet, or Cyrillic, or Devenagri, or Hangul.

We offer images like this as puzzles to be solved. People get a set of cards with the component parts of this image (along with some extras) labeled with syllables. Their job is to try and recreate the whole picture and then figure out how to pronounce it. The puzzle works because it turns out that these complex pictures are composed of syllable units organized in a regular order that goes roughly from left to right. The image in Figure 9.3 shows the same glyph meaning *jaguar*, but with each syllable labeled. The pronunciation for this word is /balam/.

We have two main messages that this demo supports. The first one is about how languages work in general: Letters are not the same thing as sounds. Writing systems are cultural artifacts that can capture what a language sounds like, but language itself isn't the same as that representation. This point is true of Mayan, and it's also true of every writing system out there (see the description of the ghoti demo in Chapter 17 for another approach to this core point).

Our second message is aimed at de-exoticizing unfamiliar languages. Even though the Mayan writing system is ancient, and even though it

Figure 9.2 This image shows the word for *jaguar*

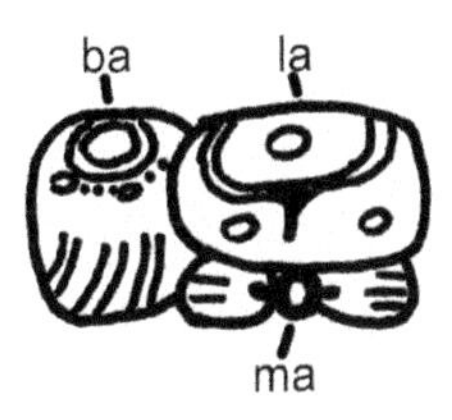

Figure 9.3 This image shows the syllabic breakdown for *jaguar*

(cont.)

Figure 9.4 This image shows the glyph for *jaguar*

Figure 9.5 Here's an example of a logo-phonetic symbol (it also means *jaguar*)
Note. All the Mayan glyph images were used with permission of Andreas Fuls (Fuls, 2019).

looks a lot like pictures, it actually works a lot like alphabets people are familiar with. It breaks down the words into component sounds, which are then ordered in a systematic way. Once you know what those individual components are, you can figure out what a brand-new word is. We turn this process into a matching game with cards.

Of course, the actual Mayan writing system is more complicated than we've described it so far. For example, it turns out that Mayan does have a parallel system of logographic symbols – that is, some glyphs can't be broken down into individual sounds but really do stand for a whole word. In fact, the word *jaguar* has such a glyph, and it's shown in Figure 9.4.

What's more, sometimes the logographic glyph would be combined with some of the symbols representing phonetic syllables to form a combination system that contained both, and it's illustrated in Figure 9.5.

At this point, it's worth mentioning that we're not experts on ancient Mayan, or any modern Mayan language. We certainly don't know everything about this writing system! In fact, one thing that we do know is that there are many, many more complications to this system than what we've presented here. Our demo doesn't come close to providing a complete explanation for how this Mayan writing system worked.

And that's OK. What our demo does do is provide people with a glimpse of how another language organizes its writing system. We hope that

(cont.)

people have an Aha! moment when they realize that something that looks so different from their own alphabet and was used by an ancient culture nevertheless works a lot like how their own language does. We hope that people appreciate that the sounds of a language can be represented by all sorts of different looking symbols. We hope that we have made this topic interesting enough to inspire some people to want to learn more about the complexities of how Mayan worked.

CLOSING WORKSHEET

Review your notes about your doable demo from all the previous worksheets.

What is your core phenomenon? That is, what is creating an Aha! moment for you? (See Chapter 6.)

What is your explanation of that phenomenon? Try to get your explanation to the level you would see in a textbook summary. What's the larger generalization that you are illustrating with your phenomenon? Write your explanation down now if you haven't already done so.

Now go through your explanation and see if you can reduce it by 10 percent. Count the words if you want to be precise, but make your explanation shorter. Is your reduced explanation still understandable and reasonably accurate? Great! Now cut out another 10 percent! Keep repeating this process until your explanation is no longer a reasonable description of your phenomenon. Only once you've reached that point should you restore 10 percent of the content.

If your explanation is more than one sentence, you now have a second task: Make a one-sentence version of it. This sentence is going to be your *Critical Take-Home Message* for your doable demo. If someone were only going to remember one scientific fact from their conversation with you, this is the one you want it to be!

Further Reading

1 *Real science is complicated*

Objectivity is one concept that is often invoked as being a necessary complication for science. We can unpack objectivity in several ways – engaging in certain agreed-on practices when finding and reporting facts, being true to the established facts, and avoiding social and individual values and biases (Reiss & Sprenger, 2020). Other angles on such philosophical points include asking whether any factual observation can be entirely atheoretical (Wikipedia article: https://en.wikipedia.org/wiki/Philosophy_of_science), or whether objectivity is actually desirable, or whether theories can ever be falsified (Singham, 2020). One reason to think about such debates from science studies and philosophy of science is that they keep us humble, and that is valuable in the conversations that this book encourages. As this chapter emphasizes, we believe that it is fine to talk more casually about the facts and theories that we use to engage the public. After all, these conversations are short and aimed at generating excitement and interest.

2 *Syntactic bootstrapping*

The term *syntactic bootstrapping* shows how jargon develops in a field. First, consider the word *bootstrapping*. English has this idiom: *I lifted myself up by my bootstraps*. Literally, this isn't possible because your bootstraps are attached to your boots; as an idiom, it means that you succeeded without help from others. Philosophers (and computer scientists and statisticians) took up this idea of success without help to refer to processes where one gradually and iteratively improves by leveraging what one already has to gain something greater.

In the domain of language, Steven Pinker used the term *semantic bootstrapping* to refer to the idea that children are innately endowed with links between a word's meanings and its syntactic categorization (en.wikipedia.org/wiki/Semantic_bootstrapping). For example, children will expect that a word referring to an object (like *table*) will be a noun, while a word referring to an action (like *devour*) will be a verb. For Pinker, meaning was the information that allowed the child to bootstrap her way into grammar. Then, Barbara Landau and Lila Gleitman (1985) showed that children need more to learn many kinds of words. By studying how blind children learn sight-related words like *look* and *red*, they showed that the entry to learning a word must sometimes be through its syntactic properties. They used the term *syntactic bootstrapping* as a clever way to highlight the reverse of what semantic bootstrapping describes.

However, bootstrapping came to be used much more broadly than this one contrast suggests. Currently, it refers to any situation where learners leverage one kind of information to help them identify another kind of information. And in fact, the *X bootstrapping* phrase itself is now used productively by researchers to refer to many such situations: for example, *prosodic bootstrapping*, *aspectual bootstrapping*, *morphological bootstrapping*. For scientists in the field, the jargon phrase *syntactic bootstrapping* is useful, productive, and a reminder of the history of the field. But for people outside the field, it is just two difficult words combined to make a difficult phrase. One of the fun things about learning about a science is that these kinds of phrases become linked to people and debates that you care about. But those details are best left for people who are purposefully going deeper into a field.

3 *First line of Carroll's "Jabberwocky" poem*

You can read the full text of the poem in Carroll (1871/2010) or here: www.poetryfoundation.org/poems/42916/jabberwocky. And you can read a nice analysis of it by Oliver Tearle (including some relevant links to language science) on this website: https://interestingliterature.com/2016/01/a-short-analysis-of-jabberwocky-by-lewis-carroll/.

"Jabberwocky" has also been translated into dozens of languages. You can find some of these efforts here: www76.pair.com/keithlim/jabberwocky/index.html.

4 *Using function words to define contexts for syntactic bootstrapping*

If this hot news topic about syntactic bootstrapping interests you, we recommend reading Babineau et al. (2021).

5 *Emphasize process*

Of course, science teachers are very aware of the importance of process for explaining science! You can read about the importance of process in the Next Generation Science Standards (www.nextgenscience.org/). It's also central for teachers at the National Science Teaching Association (www.nsta.org/nstas-official-positions/nature-science).

6 *Stroop effect*

A relatively common question we get about the Stroop effect is about the weird name. In fact, it is named after John Ridley Stroop, who was the first person to publish a paper demonstrating it (Stroop, 1935).

7 *Mayan glyphs demo*

The Mayan glyphs demo was created, evaluated, and refined by former Ohio State University student, Abigail Sarver-Verhey, who has gone on to become a designer of museum exhibits: www.abigailsarververhey.com/. Much of the information for this demo comes from Houston (1988).

10 Learn to Listen

OPENING WORKSHEET

Think about different kinds of people you might encounter when you are doing your demo in a free-choice learning environment. For example:

- A young child, a teenager, a middle-aged parent, a grandparent;
- A teacher, a college student from a related discipline, an architect, a car mechanic, a nurse;
- A person who is multilingual, a person who has traveled widely, a person with hearing loss.

Pick two people from our list above. Write down your answers to the following questions about each of those two people.

What questions do you think each person would have about the topic of your doable demo? What questions do you think they would have about the specific activity you are working on?

Conversations are not monologues, lectures, or performances! As we saw from Chapter 3, a good conversation is fundamentally cooperative, and cooperative conversation requires contributions from everyone involved. What does that mean for you? It means you have to let other people talk, too. What else? You don't just wait until the other people finish talking and then keep going with what you started. You listen to those people and respond to what they say.

Ask Questions

The easiest way to guarantee that other people talk is to ask them questions! But not any kind of question will do. You're trying to encourage successful conversational interaction, so don't make it easy for someone to answer you with a single word. Make your own questions open-ended, so that their answers have to involve real substance. And don't worry if your first question doesn't get things going – you can always ask more! You can even ask people two or three questions at once. This gives them choices about which to answer. Also, some people need a little extra encouragement, so feel free to push people gently to contribute more: "Can you say more about what you mean?" or "Why do you think so?" Not all questions will work equally well with all people, so have more than one prepared so that you can always ask another one.

There are plenty of ways to ask a good question. For example, you can try to make the topic relevant by asking people to connect your topic to elements in their own lives. Can they describe a time when they noticed your phenomenon in their daily life? What are their ideas about why it happens? One of the great features about language is that everybody has experience with it. Asking about those experiences engages people and will help them see why your topic matters. Encouraging people to tell you anecdotes from their own lives and opinions based on their funds of knowledge will engage them and may even give you new ideas about how to make the topic relevant.

Another great approach is to ask people to reflect on what you're doing with them in the moment and to encourage them to explore its possibilities. If you begin your conversation by trying to spark excitement with a specific example (see Chapter 6 for why this matters and Chapter 13 for some practical suggestions), then you can use that example as a base for your questions. Ask people to think about the experience you're giving them: What are they thinking when they do it? What makes it hard or easy, or puzzling, or funny? As linguists have long known, introspection can be a powerful tool of scientific investigation. Ask people questions that help them introspect about the piece of language you are focusing on.

You can even invite people to engage in a bit of scientific reasoning. Is there a way for people to manipulate your materials to create a different effect? Even if it's not possible to change things in this moment, you can always engage in a thought experiment. What would happen if you spoke a different language? Or if you were a child? Or if you ran the audio backward?

The key to these questions is to foster a conversation about your topic where the nonexpert can have something real to contribute. Museum professionals Sue Allen and Joshua Gutwill have called these kinds of questions "juicy," as they are intended to be "satisfying, enjoyable, and full of possibilities" just like a perfectly ripe piece of fruit (Allen & Gutwill, 2009). Juicy questions are ones that nonexperts can talk about and can use your materials/examples to gain some real insight about. Critically, a juicy question isn't one that requires a base of expert knowledge to answer. The answer to a juicy question isn't something you just know; it's something that you can figure out by working with what you've got. In fact, one sign that your conversation is going extremely well is that people will not only figure out the answers to your questions but will even ask some juicy questions of their own.

For example, we've used an activity with a set of blocks to show people how historical linguists see connections across languages. Each block has a different word on it (like *father* or *three*); each side of a block shows the word in a different color; each color corresponds to a different language (e.g., *père* in red, *pater* in green, *fader* in blue). We ask people to find the patterns across the words and the languages (colors). We encourage them to play around with the blocks to see different groupings, or to say the words out loud to help them notice the relationships between the letters and the sounds. Our juicy questions explore what people notice about the different sounds (or even letters) that are common within one color and different across the colors. We ask them to suggest different ways to describe the relationships across the words to help them discover connections. These questions engage people with the materials. People don't always recreate Grimm's laws with our materials, but they usually notice some of the systematic ways that the languages are different from each other.

We have also – unfortunately – found that some questions can stop a conversation cold. Unless you've had the right coursework, you may not know the actual identities of the languages we used in this demo, or how they are related to each other. You also may not be able to come up with examples outside of our set: Asking people to think of another Germanic language or to translate each word into Portuguese isn't fair because the demo doesn't include the tools to answer them. Those kinds of questions turn the conversation back into a lecture, or worse, into a test that few people can pass. Instead, we want juicy questions that are full of possibilities rather than being focused on one correct answer.

Part of being in an informal learning setting is that you don't need to worry about tests or grades. And that's true even if you are using juicy questions. No matter how good your question is, it won't work for all people. If your question falls flat, it's OK to give hints! It's fantastic if you can get people to spontaneously come up with an analysis of your phenomenon, but it's also fine if you just get people to reflect your own analysis back at you. Asking people to put something into their own words is a fair and useful question (if a little obvious for many people). Alternatively, ask people to consider how your phenomenon connects with their own experiences. Remember, it's more important to get people interested in what you're doing than for them to be able to conduct a proper scientific analysis of it.

Listen to the Answers

Questions will get people talking, but they also help you create a conversation if you actually listen to the answers. Your questions shouldn't be rhetorical props that give the illusion of interaction but really are just ways for you to say what's next on your cue card. You need to be flexible enough that your part of the conversation can be influenced by what the other person says!

The first step to being a good listener is to provide the time for the other person to answer. Many people will want time to think about what you're asking, so you need to give that to them. How much time should you give them? More than you think. You already know what you want this conversation to be about; in fact, if you're working in a free-choice environment, you may have already had this conversation dozens of times before with other people. But for the person you're talking with **right now**, it's probably the very first time they have talked about this topic. You came with a set of prepared juicy questions, but they didn't come with a set of prepared answers! They need time to figure out what they think.

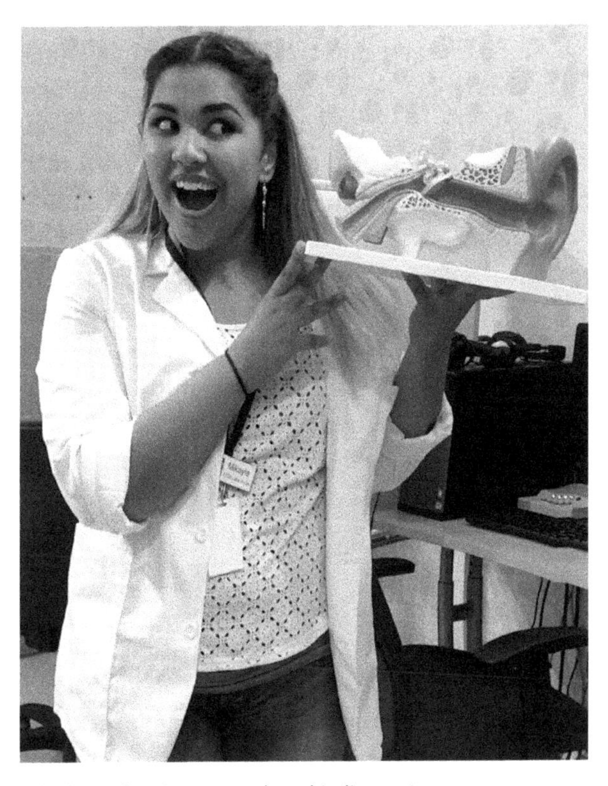

Figure 10.1 You don't need a giant ear to be a big listener!

There's an old trick that teachers use in classrooms, and it will work in this context too. After you've asked a question, count to ten slowly (silently, inside your head). Breathe deeply (but quietly). Just keep looking at the person with an open, slightly expectant expression on your face. The first few times you do this, those ten seconds will last forever, and in our experience, most people will respond to you long before you reach ten! But your patience will pay off with many more people being willing, and able, to interact with you.

The second step to being a good listener is to actually, for real, hear what the other person says. It is critical that you are open to the possibility that people won't say what you were expecting, or hoping, that they would. If you're not sure whether you're really paying attention, try echoing back what the person's answer was. If you're having trouble doing that, you might want to ask people to repeat, or to clarify, what they said. To make the conversation a good one, you need to respond to what people are saying. If you don't know what that is, your conversation won't go well.

Sometimes people will express their confusion. This could be a small thing (maybe they didn't hear you well). Or it could concern terminology (see Chapter 14 for a judicious approach to technical terms). Or it could reflect larger concepts (maybe they don't see the point of what you're saying). Take a confused response for the helpful feedback that it is! This is your chance to solve a problem, whether that means speaking up, defining terms, or explaining examples in a different way. You might end up talking more about foundational concepts than you expected, or you might end up talking more about real-world applications. But it's better for you to talk about fewer things in a more understandable way than for you to talk about a lot of things in a way that nobody follows.

Sometimes people will surprise you. They bring their own funds of knowledge to the conversation – their life histories and personal agendas. What's important to them may not be what you had planned on at all. If this happens, have some faith in the cooperative nature of conversations. Most likely, the person you're talking with is trying to be relevant to what they perceive as your topic. But if their starting place differs a bit from yours, it may take you some effort to figure out the connections. You can always ask people to tell you more! And if you do, they'll love it and you'll learn something from the exchange.

It could be that the person has misunderstood you in some way that will hinder downstream communication. Maybe they think you're asking about their personal history with language when you bring up historical linguistics. If that happens, you can gently correct them and move the conversation back to where you want it. It is always important in these cases to acknowledge what the person did bring up. For example, you might say something like "I can see what you mean – we all have histories. Some linguists study the histories of whole languages too, like English or Spanish. How do you think the history of a language might be like the history of a person?" Don't assume they made a mistake because they aren't smart or well educated or interested. Instead, assume that they were making a sensible connection, even if it wasn't what you expected. If you don't see the connection right away, ask them to say a bit more so that **you** can figure it out.

In fact, sometimes, they may be making a sensible connection that you actually do want to talk about! Maybe the differences across languages reminds them of spelling errors that they have made. That's a connection that you could use to talk about how mishearings and misanalyses actually are a factor in historical change. For example, the word *apron* was actually *napron* in Middle English (spoken some five hundred years ago or so). But apparently *a napron* got reanalyzed as *an apron* at some point, and so the word changed. Or maybe the person you're talking with just saw a documentary about how scholars use differences in languages to track the migration of people over time, so they want to talk with you about how language informs our understanding of how cultures and societies have interacted over history. That conversation would take you away from classic analyses of sound change, but it surely is an exciting one to have on the topic of historical linguistics! Most importantly, the person you've been having this conversation with will leave it satisfied with the conversation itself and likely intrigued about the idea of a language's history.

Try to resist thinking of surprises as problems. Instead, think of them as opportunities to learn about what's on other people's minds. Conversational surprises are an opportunity for you to learn new ways to stay relevant!

Don't Be Defensive

We mentioned above how important it is that we avoid making the people you're talking with feel like they are being tested. But it's possible that **you** will feel like you are the one being tested. If you're used to formal classrooms, then you're used to being graded on your performance. That's not what's going on here!

You don't have to prove that you did your homework, or that you've got all the answers, or that you're the smartest person there. The people you're talking with aren't going to give you gold stars or demerits. When they ask you questions, they aren't trying to catch you out in a mistake or create a "gotcha" moment. When they tell you about a personal experience, they aren't trying to teach you a lesson or imply that what you're doing isn't valuable. People are talking with you because they want to have a conversation with you about the topic you introduced. They are asking questions because they want to know answers. They are telling you about themselves because they think their experiences are relevant to the topic. They are trying to cooperate with you! Please take their questions and comments in that spirit, and be as straightforward and cooperative as you can be.

In fact, pretending people are being cooperative even in the rare cases where they are not can be a great strategy for dealing with them. It demonstrates your confidence. You know that what you're doing is worthwhile and that you're doing it well. If it doesn't seem like the person you're talking with agrees, you can assume (or if you need to, pretend) that they are just socially awkward. A great way to deal with a socially awkward person is to be especially socially appropriate yourself.

We mentioned another way to demonstrate your confidence in Chapter 8: It is OK to say "I don't know" when someone asks a question that you don't know the answer to. It is also OK for you to ask people for more information. If you aren't understanding the direction they want to take the conversation, go ahead and ask them to clarify. Why are they bringing that new information up? What do they see as the connection? Of course, when you ask these questions, be sure that you are doing it in a respectful way! You don't want to sound accusatory, as if you are unhappy that they aren't sticking to your script. Getting people to talk with you requires a certain amount of trust – in this case, trust that you will respect their perspective and are interested in what they have to say. And if you take the funds of knowledge approach seriously, you will be interested in what they have to say!

But what if you feel like you're getting a lot of difficult questions and a lot of off-the-wall comments not just from one person, but from lots of the people who you talk with? Think of those as data points: You're learning something about how you're presenting yourself and your topic. As we mentioned in Chapter 5, audience design is **your** responsibility. It's up to you to figure out who your audience is and what they already know that is relevant to understanding your topic. If you aren't sure whether people are following you, try asking them! It's up to you to make your topic interesting and your demonstrations engaging and relevant. If you're not connecting with people, don't blame your audience. Instead, learn to listen.

CRITICAL TAKE-HOME MESSAGE

A good conversation requires give and take from everyone involved. To get people talking, ask lots of questions that you prepared in advance. Try to make your questions "juicy" so that they engage rather than test people. To keep up your end of the conversation, really listen and respond to what people are saying in a respectful and connected way.

WORKED EXAMPLE BOX

One demo we like to do concerns regional dialects. Everybody knows that people in different parts of the country (or the world) use different words for the same things, even when they speak the same language. English speakers in the United Kingdom say *lift* while English speakers in the United States say *elevator.* Within the United States, there is a famous beverage divide: Carbonated drinks are called *soda, pop,* or *coke,* depending on where people live. And the phenomenon is not, of course, unique to English! For example, Spanish speakers in Venezuela call a carbonated beverage *fresca* while those in Argentina call it *gaseosa.*

For our demo, we rely on the hard work of the sociolinguistics community who have produced lots of fun resources that allow you to show maps where different words are more commonly used. We present people with an image (a refreshing looking drink, perhaps, as shown in Figure 10.2) and ask what they call it. Then we show them the geographic breakdown for the different words people use for the same item, as shown in the map in Figure 10.3.

Figure 10.2 Picture used to elicit a term for a carbonated beverage
Note. Used with permission of Getty Images. Photo credit: Surasak Pumdontri/EyeEm.

(cont.)

Here's what it looks like for our Spanish soda example:

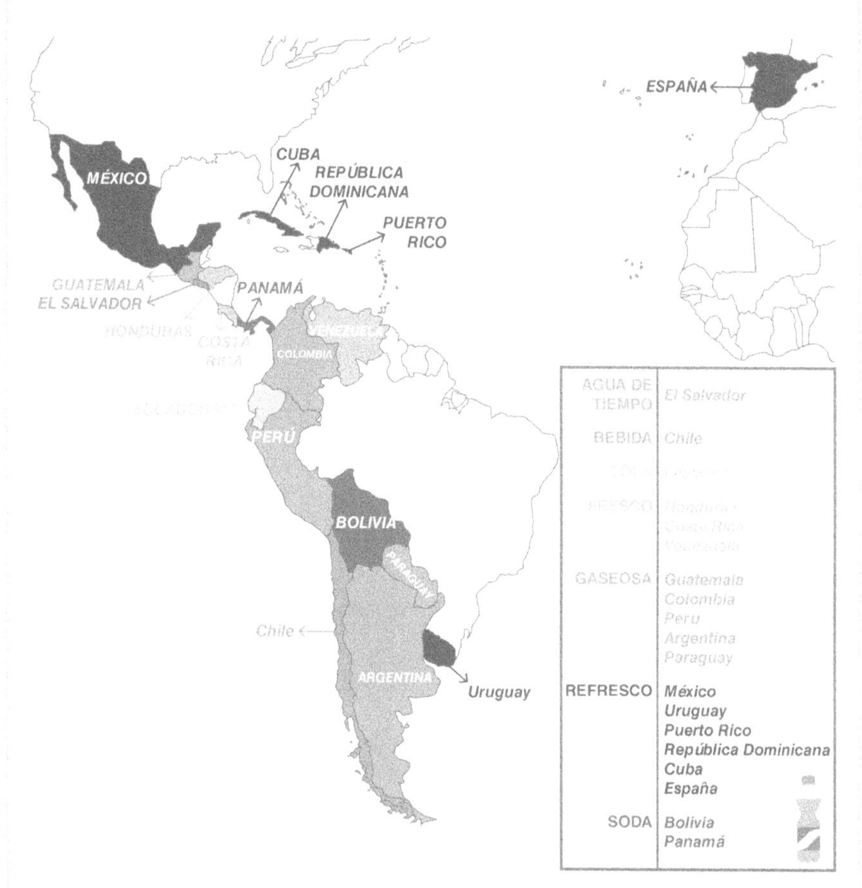

Figure 10.3 Map showing what different dialects of Spanish around the world call a carbonated beverage

This demo is all about the questions! We try to make these questions juicy, in order to get people to think about what these differences mean, where they come from, what they tell us in general, and especially what they tell us about language! Here are some examples of questions we've tried. They are grouped into categories. In each category are a few different versions/phrasings of a key question as well as different ways of approaching that category of question.

Opening questions (needed to make the example work)

What do you call this item?

(cont.)

Questions encouraging people to notice things in our materials

When you look at this map, what do you notice about where people use different words for this item? Does it fit with your own experience? How is the map for this word similar to / different from the map for the last word? Why do you think that would be?

Questions about extending the phenomenon

Do you know anybody who uses a different word for this item? Where are they from? Can you think of any examples of words that help you figure out where people are from? Do you ever use different words for the same item? Why do you do that?

Questions about social relevance

Why do you think people use these different words? What do you think about people who use a different word from you?

CLOSING WORKSHEET

For your demo activity, think of three juicy questions that you can ask people.

Do your questions have clear right and wrong answers? If so, they probably aren't juicy! Try again!

What kind of answers would you like people to give to your questions? How do those answers draw on the other person's funds of knowledge?

How do your questions encourage people to explore your materials?

How can you follow up each of your questions to encourage yet more engagement?

Further Reading

1 *You have to let the other person talk*

Of course, in some contexts, we don't care what other people have to say and we really don't listen to them. Here's a clip from the movie *His Girl Friday*, where neither character is really listening to what the other one is saying: www.youtube.com/watch?v=vTut0y3EebE#t=3m10s.

2 *Juicy questions*

Some years ago, San Francisco's Exploratorium (www.exploratorium.edu/) began developing programs that would enhance science inquiry skills in students aged ten to thirteen years during museum field trips. An important consideration was to have the programs work without requiring earlier preparation on the part of teachers or chaperones (Allen & Gutwill, 2009; Gutwill & Allen, 2012). For our purposes here, it's interesting that the original game designers found no need to regiment an exploration phase. Exploration should come naturally for people who we interact with too if we – like museum exhibit designers – spark interest through the observations, experiences, and tools that we share. What mattered for real inquiry was getting visitors to ask a "juicy" question – one that "nobody in their group knew the answer to, yet was realistically answerable at the exhibit" (Allen & Gutwill, 2009, p. 293). The "answerable at the exhibit" part helped keep adults from becoming "teachers" who relayed stock answers to the rest of the group. So, questions like "what happens if" are juicier than "why" questions; many of the latter can't be answered then and there. These considerations show us the importance of helping our conversational partners ask and answer their own questions about language.

3 *The words* père, pater, fader

Describing what makes two words "similar" or "different" from each other requires the technical tools of phonology, but nonexperts can still find the right pieces. For example, if you use two words that start with an [f] sound in English (*father, fish*), people can notice that this sound changes to [p] in French (*père, poisson*) but remains an [f] in Norwegian (*far, fisk*). There is a similar pattern if you look at words that start with [t] in English: *Two* and *ten* are translated as *deux* and *dix* in French and *to* and *ti* in Norwegian. Just these few examples suggest that English is more similar to Norwegian than to French, which is in fact the case. Of course, English isn't the same as Norwegian, and there are also opportunities here to look at places where those words don't line up (focusing on the ends of the words helps a lot with that part). Our demo focuses on a few European languages, but it could easily be done with any languages that are related to each other.

4 *Grimm's laws*

One of the great discoveries of language science is how to use the relationship among the sounds across related words in different languages to trace their historical ancestry. These relationships can even be used to reconstruct a language no longer spoken, such as Proto-Indo-European. Jacob Grimm was not the first linguist who identified these kinds of relationships, but his particular formulation of the rules of sound changes was very influential, and they are frequently called Grimm's laws. And yes, this Jacob Grimm is one of the brothers who documented and popularized many folk/fairy tales. You can read the basics about Grimm's life and work here: https://en.wikipedia.org/wiki/Jacob_Grimm.

5 *Have some faith in the cooperative nature of conversations*

Although perhaps most famous for her research on gendered communication and communication within families, Deborah Tannen has published a lot that is relevant to this point (e.g., Tannen, 1986). For example, she's shown that "enthusiastic listenership" takes different forms. This includes devices that some speakers perceive as interruptions, but that the 'interrupters' use to show how well they're actually listening. Tannen also illuminates cross-cultural communication of the kind we discussed in Chapter 3's Heathrow-based example (e.g., Tannen, 1984). Here is a list of her articles for general audiences, which is an easy way to benefit from her insights into conversations: www.deborahtannen.com/general-audience-articles.

6 *Classroom trick: Count to ten after asking a question*

Classroom teachers aren't the only people who have noticed that pausing after asking questions is a good idea. It's also a very popular idea in the business world. To read about how a professor in a business school approaches the idea, we recommend James G. Clawson's work (e.g., Clawson, 2008). But if you want a more popular business approach, you can try this blog post: www.briantracy.com/blog/sales-success/the-power-of-pausing/.

7 *Pretending people are being cooperative*

When it comes to the question of dealing with noncooperative people, we know that some are on the receiving end of this kind of behavior more than others. We are both older white women with PhDs, and people in free-choice learning environments very rarely treat us like we aren't qualified to be doing demos. But we are keenly aware that some of our students, especially younger women of color, encounter less cooperativeness than we do. We still find that the strategy of willfully pretending that the other person is being cooperative is pretty effective, largely because it keeps the situation from escalating. Generally, we try to publicly grant as much authority to our students as possible. As we note in Chapter 8, wearing lab coats is one tactic that we sometimes use. But on a more interpersonal level, we don't step on our students' authority in front of their audience. We trust them to handle themselves and their demos in public, and we don't interrupt them (except occasionally to compliment them in front of people) or take over the interaction from them. We can't control the rest of the universe, but we can, ourselves, treat our students with the respect they deserve.

8 *Demos on regional dialects in English and Spanish*

Our English version of this activity uses lots of materials that we got from Jeff Reaser at North Carolina State University: https://chass.ncsu.edu/people/jlreaser/. He and his colleagues have an extensive program of research on regional dialects, including exciting work on how to promote tolerance for people who speak nonstandard dialects. Our Spanish version of this activity was developed by several students from The Ohio State University, most notably Shasteny Cabrera and Luana Lamberti.

Some people may already be familiar with these kinds of maps from a popular dialect quiz that was published in the *New York Times*: www.nytimes.com/inter

active/2014/upshot/dialect-quiz-map.html. (Fair warning: The *New York Times* has a paywall and only allows you to read a limited number of articles for free.) And this quiz is also now available in a handy book form from Josh Katz: *Speaking American: How Y'all, Youse, and You Guys Talk: A Visual Guide* (www.amazon.com/dp/0544703391/). If you'd like to go back to the original sociolinguists whose work inspired the *New York Times* quiz, see this website from Bert Vaux and Scott Golder: www.tekstlab.uio.no/cambridge_survey.

11 Information Structure

OPENING WORKSHEET

Imagine a conversation with each of the following kinds of people:

- Someone who is about your age;
- Someone who is from the same country as you;
- Someone who has almost nothing in common with you – someone who is much older (or much younger) and who is from a country halfway around the globe where English is not prominent.

For each of these people, write down three things that both of you know.

Now write down three things that **you** know, but the other person probably doesn't know.

You might want to consider things related to popular culture, food customs, social etiquette, knowledge of the local area, world history, or the current weather.

In Chapter 3, we laid out four principles from Grice's theory about cooperative conversation. The fourth one was the Maxim of Manner. This maxim emphasizes the value of brevity, clarity, and orderliness. As we have noted, being clear is not easy to do. But since clarity is an important part of any good conversation, and an absolutely critical part of any good conversation about science, we're going to use the next few chapters to give suggestions about how to address the Maxim of Manner. And lucky for us, the field of language science has a lot to contribute on this topic! We'll focus on one of the most central distinctions that language science has given us about how to be clear.

The Heart of Clarity: GIVEN BEFORE NEW

If you want your public engagement to be clear, talk about familiar things (GIVEN) before moving to unfamiliar things (NEW). GIVEN BEFORE NEW is a nice, short mantra, but there are actually two big ideas inside of it. The first idea concerns the difference between given information and new information. The second idea concerns the ideal ordering for these two kinds of information.

Let's start with the difference between given and new information. As we discussed in Chapter 3, in order to have a successful conversation, you and your audience create that conversation together. But as we discussed in Chapter 5, you and your audience are going to come into that conversation from different places – you'll have different backgrounds, reference points, and expectations. In short, your funds of knowledge will differ. What you need to do together is to define a space that includes the information that you share with each other. The technical term for this space is the COMMON GROUND. Given information is what is already in the common ground. New information is what you're introducing into your shared space in order to make it part of the common ground.

In principle, this is an easy distinction to make, but in practice it can be hard to know if something in a particular conversation is given or new. Things that we say explicitly should move seamlessly from new to given information. If someone announces, "I enjoy reading books by George Eliot," that's new information for the conversation. But now that this has been said, the information becomes part of the common ground and all participants in the conversation can assume it as a given.

Or can we? What if you don't know who Eliot was or what any of her books are about? Or what if you didn't exactly catch the way that name was pronounced? We all have a lot of assumptions about the common ground – what everybody knows – and what is a distinctive addition into it. The more similar you are to the person you're talking with, the more information you share. With members of your own family, you can assume that people will know all sorts of things: Your family knows the name of your childhood pet (if you had one), whether or not you like broccoli, and maybe even your shoe size. The givens within a family can be so extensive that family members can often speak with each other in a kind of shorthand since everybody knows so much about each other.

With people who are outside your family but still from your general community, you take less for granted. Even so, there are still many things that you can assume as givens in your common ground: Students at the same university know about their school's sports teams, the basic layout of their campus, and what good test-taking etiquette is. Some of these pieces of information are specific to each university (like the campus layout), and others are shared by just about all college students (test-taking etiquette). But probably none of these items could be assumed to be given in the common ground if you were talking to an elderly Tibetan monk. Just about the only things that can always be assumed as given are things that everybody knows by virtue of being a human on Earth (things fall when you drop them, the sun rises daily) or things that are happening right in front of you (it's snowing, we're inside a building).

When you start thinking about given and new information in terms of language science, you will almost certainly overestimate the given information. In Chapter 12, we'll talk a little about why that's true; and in Chapters 13 and 14, we'll talk about ways to ensure that you've established what's given before you provide new information. But as you probably already know, one of the most important ways to make sure that you and your conversational partners are in the same common ground is to listen to what they say! In Chapter 10, we talked about how important paying attention to your partner is. Tracking the common ground and what information is given in it is one more critical reason to listen!

Which brings us to the second big idea inside of GIVEN BEFORE NEW: The order that you talk about things matters. A conversation isn't a painting in a museum where you are looking at a finished product. With paintings, you may not have any idea which part was painted first or last – you get some effect of the painting all at once. But a conversation unfolds over time, and that means that its success depends on what order people say things. It's more like a TV series where you need to understand the earlier episodes in order for the later ones to make sense. Imagine that you started watching a new TV program but the first three episodes were missing and you had to start in the middle. You wouldn't know who the characters are, or what they want, or where they're going. By the time you get to the middle of a series, there's a lot of information that is being treated as given. And, if that information is new for you, you have to work really hard to try and piece together how the common ground got set up in the first place.

The general idea is really just plain common sense: You build on what you already know. There's a reason college students don't start their coursework with advanced seminars. Those seminars assume that students have already mastered the information in the introductory courses. This idea is also connected to the funds of knowledge approach discussed in Chapter 4: People will connect with you better if you build on the knowledge that they are bringing to your conversation. Given information is what you and your conversational partner already know – it's the common ground. The new information isn't going to make sense unless you have that shared foundation of knowledge in place. You need to build these conversations from the bottom up.

We Understand Language as We Listen to It

One of the reasons that order is so important is because we listen to language in real time. When we listen to people talking, we don't wait until the end of each sentence to compute that sentence's meaning. We actively engage with what we're hearing (or reading), and we are making meaning even as each sentence unfolds.

Seriously – you aren't waiting for anything! As soon as you hear even a single sound of a word, you automatically start trying to predict what the word will be. Psycholinguists Paul Allopenna, James Magnuson, and Michael Tanenhaus showed that as soon as you hear the /k/ sound, you will start looking around for objects that start that way – a can, a candle, a koala bear, a chameleon, and so on (Allopenna et al., 1998). We are eager to know what people are talking about and we have no reservations about trying to jump ahead whenever possible.

Of course, sometimes you will guess wrong about where the sentence is going and when that happens, you will slow down and may even get genuinely confused. In fact, language science researchers are experts at creating sentences that will encourage you to go down the wrong structural path and predict the wrong things – that's how they figure out the kind of guesses people like to make. The technical term for sentences that mislead you is a fun one: They are called *garden-path* sentences because they lead you down a garden path and right into a dead end.

For example, check out the start of this sentence:

(1) The scientist examined . . .

What do you think will come next? Examining is something that scientists are likely to do, and most people start imagining things that a scientist might examine (maybe data? maybe specimens? maybe the literature?). Now see what happens when we continue the sentence in an unexpected direction: *The scientist examined by the prosecutor was easy to understand.* Most people are surprised when they hit the word *by* – it's just not what they were guessing would come next. In this particular sentence, the scientist isn't doing the examining; instead, she's getting examined!

What actually happens when a sentence takes a surprising turn? It depends on the specific sentence and how badly it violated people's expectations. But it can get bad. In some cases, people simply slow down. If they were reading the sentence (and not listening to it), they might go back and reread the first part and figure out where they went wrong. In some cases, people misunderstand the sentence as meaning something closer to their expectations: For instance, they might think the scientist examined the prosecutor. And in some cases, people reject the sentence entirely and report that it was nonsense or badly formed.

Sentence (1) is a classic garden-path sentence because it works against your natural expectations. But it turns out that those expectations can be changed. Think about how this sentence will continue:

(2) The specimen examined...

Sentence (2) has the same form as sentence (1), but changing the subject from *scientist* to *specimen* changes your expectations. If this sentence continued like the last one, most people wouldn't find it very surprising: *The specimen examined by the prosecutor was easy to see.* This sentence doesn't slow people down, or confuse them, or make them throw their hands up.

So what are people basing their sentence interpretation guesses on? As these examples show us, one thing people care about is what they already know. We use what we already know about scientists and specimens to guess what someone else is going to say about them.

And what works for the word level, and for the sentence level, also works for the level of a whole conversation. People will come into a conversation with previous knowledge, and they will start using that knowledge to guess where you're going next. So where you start is going to make a big difference for people's expectations.

One way to think about it is that we are trying to create a movie in our heads that corresponds to what people are saying. These movies (or mental models, to use a bit of jargon) are built out of what people tell us, combined with lots of other information that we already know about the general topic. If we tell you that we're going to show you something about Mayan glyphs (see the Worked Example Box in Chapter 9), you will create a mental model that starts with what we just said and whatever else you know about the topic. Maybe you know that the Maya lived in Central America. Maybe you think about Egyptian writing when you hear the term *hieroglyphics*. Maybe these words don't mean much to you at all. But you will use whatever you've got to start creating a mental idea that helps you guess where our conversation is going to go.

Here's where all the pieces start to come together! You will start building your mental model with the things you heard first. If what you hear first is something that is familiar to you – it's given information – then you will start building a rich mental model with a firm foundation. This foundation will allow you to start thinking usefully about the topic, and so when you hear something new about Mayan hieroglyphics, you will have something solid to connect that information to. But what happens if what you hear first isn't given? What if instead it is unfamiliar information and therefore for you, it is new information? You'll have a harder time laying down the initial foundation for starting the conversation with new information. You won't know what kind of information to be thinking about, so you won't have ideas on your mind that can connect to what's coming. You also won't be able to guess where things are going, so you won't have that sense that following the conversation is easy. It won't be like watching a romantic comedy or an action movie where you know roughly where events are going. It will be more like watching one of those avant-garde movies where you have to stay on your toes the whole time and you are occasionally uncomfortable. Now ask yourself this: Which kind of movie do you think most people might want to see?

By orienting people with given information first, you lay the groundwork to make the new information easier to digest. Of course, you also raise the possibility that you'll create a garden path in your conversation. If people have a lot of unexpected associations to your topic area, then the conversation may not go at all where you want to (maybe mentioning the Maya makes people think about the death metal band MaYaN). If that happens, we remind you of the advice from Chapter 10, that it is really important that you listen to people! The only way you'll know if people's guesses have taken them too far afield is if you pay attention to what they say to you.

CRITICAL TAKE-HOME MESSAGE

People are expecting you to provide given information before new information, and they will understand you better if you do that.

WORKED EXAMPLE BOX

A favorite activity that we've mentioned in a variety of places is making name tags in the International Phonetic Alphabet (IPA). The core of the activity is very straightforward (you use the IPA to write a name tag for a person), and the language science education comes in while you talk through how those symbols represent their name.

(cont.)

Here's one potential way to do that:

Did you know that language scientists have a special system, called the International Phonetic Alphabet, or IPA, that lets them write down sounds from languages around the world? Sometimes the IPA letters will be the same ones you use when you spell your name, but other times they will be different. Let's try it! Your name is Cecile! Great – I'm going to write that like this: [səsil]. In the IPA you can see that you've got the same sibilant consonant in there twice – those are the two things that look like S's. But when you *spell your name, you use two Cs instead. Have you heard about "hard Cs" and "soft Cs" in English? Which one do you use in your name? What do those Cs really sound like? English spelling doesn't have just one letter for one sound – that's why the letter C can be pronounced different ways. But in the IPA, each symbol goes to just one sound.*

We've heard many students give an explanation that works basically like the one above. The way the student is thinking about it is this: I start with a nice quick summary of what I want to explain, and then I break it down for people in a more specific way. My summary orients people and helps them stay patient through the longer explanation.

But we do **not** recommend that you present information in that order! Why not? Because that quick overview is full of new information. The specific breakdown can feel like it's long-winded, and students worry that they need to get to their main point more quickly because otherwise people might leave. But people need that familiar or given information first in order to make sense of the quick summary. The given information is what people can readily understand – it won't feel like a distraction. Instead, it will help people get oriented. Starting with information that people **do not** understand is more likely to make them stop listening and so leave. If they didn't understand where you started, why would they think they can understand where you're headed?

In this example, it's pretty easy to reorder things to get the given information before the new info. We'd prefer this way:

Your name is Cecile! Great – I'm going to write that like this: [səsil]. I'm using an alphabet especially made to write any sound from any spoken language. It lets me write down the sounds of your name exactly as you *say them. Did you notice that you've got two Cs in the spelling of your name but that I didn't write them down? What did I use instead? Have you heard about "hard Cs" and "soft Cs" in English? Which one do you use in your name? What do those Cs really*

(cont.)

sound like? Since the sound you say in your name is an S sound, that's what I wrote. Language scientists call this alphabet the International Phonetic Alphabet because it lets them write down the sounds of languages from around the world.

CLOSING WORKSHEET

Review the interaction that you have planned for your doable demo. You'll want to especially remind yourself of what you wrote for Chapter 6 (where you identified an Aha! moment to provide), and for Chapter 7 (where you came up with ways that your topic is relevant to people's lives), and for Chapter 9 (where you identified your Critical Take-Home Message), and for Chapter 10 (where you came up with some juicy questions).

Write down the ideal interaction that you want to have with most people. Try to write this as a series of steps. How will you invite people to your table or cart or booth? What will you show them first? What questions will you ask them? When and how will you try to connect your activity to people's lives? What do you have to explain to help people enjoy your activity? When will you mention your Critical Take-Home Message?

Once you have a reasonable order for all your pieces, try moving things around. What happens if you move the last thing to the beginning? What happens if you start in the middle?

Try identifying what elements of common ground are needed to understand each one of your steps. You should need the least common ground for the early points, and as your common ground grows you can need more. Is this reflected in your ordering? If not, try a new order.

Further Reading

1 *The heart of clarity: Given before New*

The study of discourse organization is a vast field with a long tradition. We've adopted one set of technical terms from this field (i.e., given, new, common ground), but other researchers have used other terms. For example, theme/rheme and topic/comment are commonly used alternatives to given/new, and some researchers refer to mutual knowledge rather than common ground. The differences in terminology reflect different academic traditions, but also some theoretical differences in exactly what matters for structuring information. Our choice of terms is not intended to be a statement about our theoretical commitments in this area: We use given/new because we find the terms transparent and punchy. Moreover, we are taking our own advice from Chapter 9 seriously. Pretty much all theoretical perspectives agree on the basics of the distinction and the role of common ground for navigating it. The details that distinguish between different perspectives don't matter for the purposes of accessible science communication.

2 *Report that [the sentence] was nonsense or badly formed*

Many jokes put garden-path sentences to good use, or at least, they use them to make people smirk and groan. To see a nice collection of such jokes, we recommend the website put together by the linguist Beatrice Santorini: www.ling.upenn.edu/~beatrice/humor/. The section on syntax jokes has lots of examples based on structural ambiguities of the kind discussed in the main text.

3 *Mental models*

There is a large literature on mental models and how they organize text comprehension. Our use of mental models here extrapolates from psycholinguistics research by Zwaan (2008) and Gernsbacher (1990).

4 *Death metal band MaYaN*

You can read more about this band on Wikipedia: https://en.wikipedia.org/wiki/Mayan_(band).

And you can watch a music video of their song "War on Terror" here: www.youtube.com/watch?v=BhBeb3ZMyow.

12 The Curse of Knowledge

OPENING WORKSHEET

Pick something you don't know much about (a piece of linguistics would work, but so would making an origami model, or the ingredients in a hot sauce, or a historical event, or the chemical structure of alcohol).

Write down what you **do** know about this topic. Also write down three questions you have about this topic. Label what you just wrote "Before." Put it away and don't look at it until you have finished the rest of this worksheet. It's fine (even desirable) if you wait a day or two before doing the next part.

Go learn about your topic. You don't have to learn everything, but do spend at least half an hour to an hour reading about it.

Write down what you learned. Also write down three questions that you still have about the topic. Label what you just wrote "After."

Now, go back to what you wrote originally, and compare your before and after versions of what you know. How much of what you knew in the After part was included in the Before part? How much is new? Did you find answers to your original questions?

In Chapter 11, we laid out the key for how to present information in an understandable way: Start the conversation with given (known, familiar) information before you move to new information. In principle, it's easy to follow this advice. In practice, it can be hard to know what counts as given and what counts as new. In conversations in informal learning settings, given and new need to be defined in a cooperative way – given information has to be familiar information for **everybody** in the conversation; information counts as new if it is new for **anybody** in the conversation.

The problem is that it's not always easy to keep track of the difference between what everybody knows and what just one person knows, especially when that one person is yourself. Once you know something, you can't unknow it. The most you can do is imagine what it feels like (what it felt like) to not know it. That imaginative leap is a skill, and not an easy one to master. Your own knowledge – which is probably just the thing that makes you want to talk to other people – will follow you like a curse. It will constantly interfere with your ability to accurately guess what other people know, and therefore, it will interfere with your ability to organize your information from given to new.

Kids Are Hilariously Cursed

The idea that what you already know interferes with your figuring out what other people know has been studied extensively in the field of developmental psychology. One term for this idea is the CURSE OF KNOWLEDGE, which is just one piece of a research area known as THEORY OF MIND. The way we understand other people – why they do what they do – is by assuming that they have minds that are filled with mental objects like desires, goals, emotions, and beliefs. Minds aren't something you can see or touch, so what we have is a theory about someone else's mind. We use that theory to predict what people will do. If we hypothesize that in your mind you desire to go home, and you believe the bus stops on the corner, and you think that you have exact change in your pocket, then we can predict that you'll go to the corner to wait for the bus. What could be viewed as a weird random act (Why in the world would someone stand on a street corner for twenty minutes?) becomes a very sensible activity – even one that can be predicted fairly reliably.

It turns out that this ability to think about other people's minds is a complex and difficult skill. And it's one that research has shown will trip kids up for years. In a classic task designed to study theory of mind in children, a three-year-old child is shown a box that the child knows well. In the original (British) version of the task, it was a box for the popular candy Smarties; other researchers have used boxes for all kinds of products that kids know very well: crayons, Cheerios, Graham Crackers. The key is that the child has opened boxes like this one before and knows what is typically inside of them. The researcher asks three-year-olds what is in the box, and they always say it's what you'd expect to find.

Then the researcher opens the box up and – surprise! – there's something else inside. Maybe it's pencils, or cotton balls, or toy dinosaurs. Whatever it is, it is something the child can label, but not what is usually in the box. Then the researcher closes up the box and asks some variants of the critical questions: *When you first saw this box, what did you think was in it? If I showed this box to your friend now, what would they say was in the box?*

And here's where the curse comes in. The child knows what's in the box now, and that interferes with their ability to say what a naïve person would guess is in the box. Children frequently say that their friend would guess there are toy dinosaurs in the box. They even frequently say that they themselves **did** guess that there would be toy dinosaurs in the box. The children cannot make the imaginative leap from what they know to be true now (there are toy dinosaurs in the box) to what someone less knowledgeable would believe about the contents of the box. Their knowledge curses them.

The Smarties task, as it is commonly known, has been done with thousands of children in many different variations. The good news is that children do overcome this extreme version of the curse. There are ways to make the task easier for young children so that their knowledge doesn't interfere as much. But the most reliable way to get children to pass the task is to wait for them to grow up: Four-year-old children generally get it right (particularly if they are middle-class Western children), and by the time children are six years old, most are great at the task.

But just because we get better at separating what we know from what someone else knows doesn't mean that we ever fully grow out of the curse.

Adults Are Cursed Too!

Generally speaking, adults don't fail the Smarties task. In fact, the right answer usually seems so obvious to adults that parents are often shocked to hear their three-year-old children's responses. But it turns out it's not that hard to trip adults up either.

Sometimes the curse plays itself out in small ways. The psychologists Boaz Keysar, Shuhong Lin, and Dale Barr designed a situation where adults had to remember that they knew something that their partner didn't know – a classic theory of mind situation. Here's the setup: One adult (the "director") has to tell another adult (the "mover") to move around a bunch of objects on a table. The catch? The mover hides one of the objects in a paper bag before the director even walks in the door. So during the game, the mover knows something that the director doesn't, namely, what's in the bag.

How can we tell if the mover is cursed with their secret knowledge about the bag's contents? The experimenters compared two conditions to get at this question. In their control condition, the mover put some batteries in the bag, and the director never saw anything like batteries during the game. But in the cursed condition, the mover put a roll of tape inside the bag. And critically, during the game, there was a cassette music tape on the table as part of the moving game.

The sketch in Figure 12.1 shows what's going on inside each person's head when they look at the paper bag in the cursed condition: The director only sees a bag without knowing its contents, and the mover sees a bag that she knows has a roll of tape inside.

Figure 12.1 The mover sees a bag that has a roll of tape in it, but the director just sees a bag
Note. Image from Keysar et al. (2003) used with permission.

In the critical trials, the director told the mover to move "the tape." From the director's point of view, there's only one tape in the game – the cassette tape on the table. But for the mover, there's one kind of tape on the table and a different kind of tape in the bag. What happens then?

Figure 12.2 The director mentions the tape, and the mover thinks about what's in the bag
Note. Image from Keysar et al. (2003) used with permission.

The mover really shouldn't think about what's in the bag when the director mentions tape. After all, the director doesn't know that there is tape in there; but the mover does know that, since she helped hide the tape. What's fascinating is that the mover just can't stop herself from knowing about the hidden tape. And that knowledge affects her behavior in the task.

When the experimenters compared how the movers behaved in the cursed condition to the control condition (when there were irrelevant batteries in the bag), they found that the movers who were cursed by their own knowledge looked at the paper bag holding the hidden roll of tape five times more often. But wait – there's more: 82 percent of the movers were slower to reach for the visible cassette tape, and 71 percent of them actually reached at least once for the paper bag containing the hidden tape! The movers were truly cursed. Just like little children, they treated the directors like they had the same knowledge about what was in the bag that they had themselves.

One big place that adults have a blind spot is when they think about things they used to believe – or rather, about things they used to be unsure of. We often make predictions about how things are going to turn out: who will win the election, what the final score of the game will be, when the meeting will end. Some predictions are easier (or harder) to make, but they all have an element of uncertainty to them since you can never really know the future. But if you talk to people after they know an outcome, they tend to remember being a lot more certain about how things would turn out, and they also tend to think the actual outcome was more obvious than it probably was. There's an old adage that "hindsight is 20/20," and researchers have called this the "hindsight bias."

At its core, this bias reflects the curse of knowledge: Once you know how something turned out, it is hard to unknow it. It is also apparently very hard to make the imaginative leap to how it felt to be unsure about what would happen. We remember seeing the handwriting clearly written on the wall when in fact if you ask people before they know an outcome, they are a lot more hazy about how things will go.

From the perspective of talking with the general public about new material, it is worth dwelling for a moment on the fact that hindsight bias means that we usually overestimate how certain and how knowledgeable we were in the past. We view the past cursed by our present state of understanding. It may be very human to think we always knew better, but it isn't helpful for talking with people who are still in what was your past state.

The Curse of Language Knowledge

When you're talking with people about language, there's an extra factor to consider, and that's the fact that people really do know their native language.

One of the reasons that language is so fun to talk about with everybody is that they do use language all the time, often in creative and sophisticated ways. People have strong funds of knowledge concerning language, and there is a sense in which all participants in these conversations are experts. In fact, one of the core findings of language science is that people implicitly know the rules, structures, and components of their language. For example, everyone who speaks English will automatically use the SVO order for their basic sentences. At this implicit level, just about all of language can be taken as a given – it is well known and familiar to them and to you.

But don't think that because people are implicit experts at language, they also have an explicit understanding of how language works. For example, you can ask any English speaker – from a grandmother to a child in the first grade – how to make a plural form of a noun using the wug test. (In fact, we do this task as a demo activity.) You just introduce a nonsense word ("here is a wug") and ask people what you call two of them. They usually say that *wugs* is the plural form. So clearly there is a real and important sense in which people **know** the rule for the English plural. But just because you can **do** the plural, doesn't mean that you can also explain it. If you ask people what the plural rule is, they will almost certainly tell you that you "add an s" to the word. But language scientists know the rule is more complicated than that! At a minimum, the English plural rule also requires you to know something about the sound system of the language – the plural of wug, after all, doesn't add an /s/ sound; it's really a /z/ sound. And people do in fact produce the correct sound. So they really don't have the explicit knowledge to explain the actual rule that they themselves are following!

Consider a related example. Most people you'll be talking with not only use language well but can also move their legs in various ways – they can walk, run, hop, skip, and jump. Just because they can **do** those things, though, doesn't mean that they can explain **how** their legs work. In fact, mechanical descriptions of different types of motions can get pretty complicated! Being able to do something and being able to explain it are very different things.

You probably do have some explicit analyses of language if you're planning on talking about language science. But it is the curse of knowledge that makes you feel like your explicit understanding trickles down to your implicit knowledge. People can use language outstandingly well without having any scientific analysis for why it works as it does. Don't let your language science savvy lead you to overinterpret what people know about language.

One way to find out what people know, and to create some common ground, is to invite them to share an experience with you. Ideally, to share a fascinating and even puzzling experience. In Chapter 13, we'll talk about how to create some experiences that will anchor this conversation, and which can help you keep the curse of knowledge at bay.

CRITICAL TAKE-HOME MESSAGE

You need to be able to tell the difference between what is given information and what is new information for the people you are talking with. And unfortunately, human psychology is not going to make that easy: Once you know something yourself, it is very hard to imagine what it felt like to not know it. Learning to take this imaginative leap is an important skill for effectively communicating with the public because it will help you appreciate your audience's starting place.

WORKED EXAMPLE BOX

Suppose you have an activity that shows off our implicit knowledge about reference. You want to impress on people that without any explicit instruction, they already know that a reflexive pronoun like *herself* can and usually must find its referent within the same clause (rule A) but that a nonreflexive pronoun like *her* cannot find its referent within the same clause (rule B).

For example, here is a (very) brief story that illustrates the rules:

Mary and Jane went to the store.
Mary bought herself a popsicle.
Then Jane got her a napkin.

There are two different pronouns there – *herself* and *her* – but they refer to the very same person! The reflexive pronoun *herself* links up with the woman in its own sentence (Mary), while *her* links up with someone outside its own sentence. Since the only woman outside the Jane sentence is Mary, she is the referent for *her* as well.

It's pretty easy to guess that the average person on the street hasn't heard of these rules or what linguists call Binding Theory since they are part of a specific linguistic theory, which not everybody is trained in. If you were trained in it, you probably remember the class where the rules were first covered. If you weren't trained in it, you may be busily looking them up on the Internet at this very moment! So binding rules are definitely new information.

(cont.)

But which pieces of these rules about reference are new for that person on the street, and which ones are given? Should you expect that this person knows what a reflexive pronoun is? Do they know what a pronoun is? Do they know what a noun is? What about a clause?

If you're the kind of person who thinks it would be fun to explain these rules in an informal setting, you're probably the kind of person who doesn't actually remember learning what a pronoun is. Was that something they covered in fourth grade language arts? Or is that one of those Intro to Linguistics concepts? It's knowledge that you may have had for a while and know well, and it's connected to lots of other things that you know. But thinking about pronouns just might be a new thing for the person you're talking with.

You should assume that everything involving explicit knowledge is new. Anything that would be in the main text (not an example sentence) in a linguistics textbook should be treated as new. Why? Because if it's in the main text, then that means that it is how you talk **about** language. And anything that's meta like that should be treated as new. Basically, only example sentences can be treated as given.

And if this whole example seemed like it was full of new information to you, then you know what we mean. Try to channel that feeling when you're working on your own demo and make sure you're providing all the background context people need to understand whatever you want to talk about.

CLOSING WORKSHEET

Review what you've put together so far for your doable demo. Focus especially on what you wrote for Chapter 8 (where you identified things that you did and didn't know about your topic), as well as for Chapter 9 (where you wrote your Critical Take-Home Message).

Identify a few key concepts that are central for your demo activity. You're looking for words or phrases that describe important elements of your topic area. They can refer to very specific elements of your activity (*prepositional phrase attachment*) or to foundational concepts (*hierarchical structure* or even *sentence*).

Use your favorite web browser to find out how that phrase is used by people in the world at large. You might also try entering your phrase into Google Images. Is the dominant use the same as the one you have in mind? Is it similar? Is it completely different?

Further Reading

1 *Theory of mind*

Theory of mind is a large area of research involving adults, children, infants, and nonhuman animals. You can get some sense of its breadth through Wikipedia: https://en.wikipedia.org/wiki/Theory_of_mind. See also Birch and Bloom (2007), which links the curse of knowledge to this theory of mind research with children.

2 *Hindsight bias*

Research on the hindsight bias goes back at least to the 1970s, and it is associated with economists and psychologists such as Robin Hogarth, Daniel Kahneman, Amos Tversky, and Baruch Fischoff.

3 *The wug test*

Originally published in Berko (1958), this task has been used a great deal by many researchers. The wug is also the unofficial mascot for many language science groups and events.

4. *Explicit descriptions of motion*

One way to get a sense of how hard it is to be explicit about mechanical motion is by seeing how people build robots that move. For example, read more about MIT's Biomimetic Robotics Laboratory (https://biomimetics.mit.edu/) after enjoying this video showing off their robot cheetah: www.youtube.com/watch?v=QZ1DaQgg3lE.

5 *Binding Theory*

Binding Theory was introduced in Noam Chomsky's book *Lectures on Government and Binding* (Chomsky, 1981/1993). The theory represented at the time sweeping changes to his earlier work (e.g., Chomsky, 1957, 1965). Being a theory, it has of course been further revised in more recent years.

13 Start with Examples

OPENING WORKSHEET

A picture can be worth a thousand words. Consider this diagram:

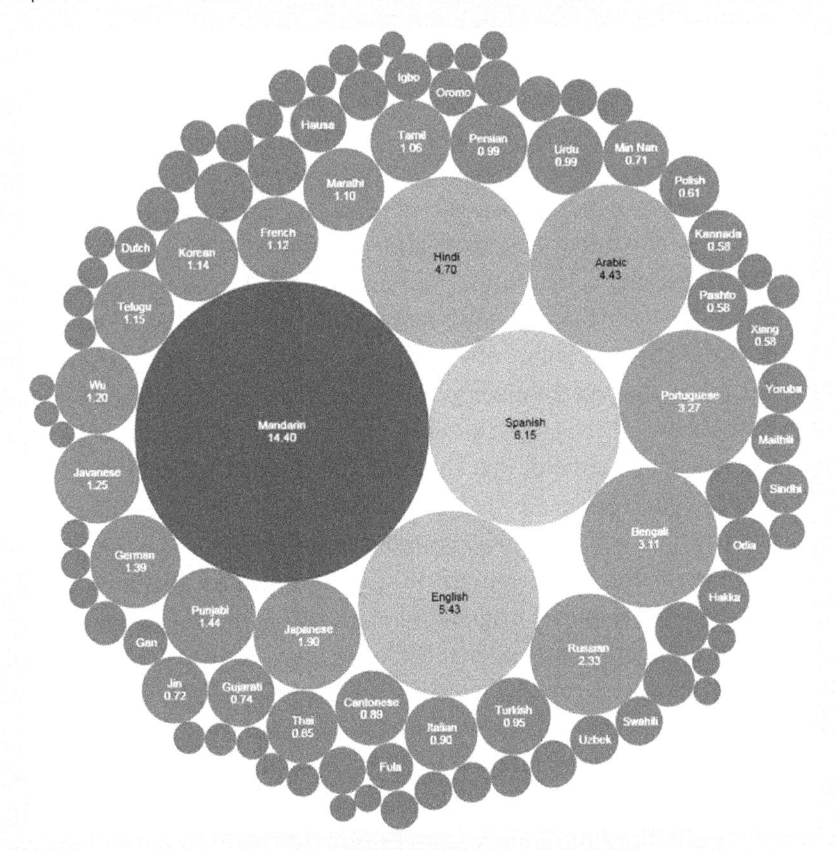

Figure 13.1 Number of native speakers of different languages around the world
Note. This image is used under the Creative Commons Attribution – ShareAlike 4.0 International license.

Write down the main point of this figure in words. How many words did that take? What does the figure convey that goes beyond that main point? What does it convey that is harder to get across with your words (or that takes a lot of words to accomplish)?

First impressions matter, so it's good to start by really impressing people! You know from Chapter 11 that you want to begin your conversation with given information. In this chapter, we're going to encourage you to introduce that given information in memorable and fun ways.

Good Research Is Full of Good Examples

If you read an academic paper about a topic, it often starts with an introduction that situates the topic in terms of the past literature. It might review various theoretical positions that aim to explain relevant phenomena. That's part of the standard convention that scientists use when writing their ideas down for other experts, and it's the general convention that students use when trying to prove that they have understood a complex topic.

But in a free-choice learning environment, you're rarely talking with experts. So don't start with a long story about all the different ways that scientists from different points of views have investigated your phenomenon. Instead, start by sharing the phenomenon itself with the other people in your conversation! One of the easiest ways to create common ground is by giving your audience an experience that they can talk about with you.

Choosing a good example to illustrate your phenomenon isn't all that hard: Most people without formal training in a science are unfamiliar with the classic examples that you'll see in any introductory textbook on that science. Don't worry about originality when using those examples. Enjoy standing on the shoulders of giants! Or, as we show in the Worked Example Box in Chapter 6, you can always tap a more advanced source – such as a recent academic paper – and use one of its examples.

You should also feel free to freshen up some of those old examples. Some of the classics in the language sciences are actually a bit sexist (and sometimes a bit violent), so you'll want to make sure that your examples work well with any public audience.

One place to find good phenomena is in research articles. If you're looking at a theoretical linguistics paper, then check out the example words or sentences that are used to illustrate the core arguments. If you're looking at a more experimentally oriented paper, then check out the task that the researchers presented to their participants. Either way, just remember that you're not trying to accomplish the same thing that the paper did – you don't need to show all the nuances of the theoretical position, and you definitely aren't running an experiment. You get to skip the hard parts – the exceptions that require extra explanation, the control items and counterbalancing setups, and so on. You can just jump right in and share the fun stuff with people.

For example, we do an activity that is about the process of word learning. Our goal is to help people understand the various learning strategies that child and adult learners use. To help people experience the core problem, we show them a cluttered picture, tell them that it shows *gavagai*, and ask them what they think that new word means. This conversation starter is just an implementation of a thought experiment that the philosopher W. V. O. Quine devised in 1960. We even use his nonsense word! Even though this example is featured in countless textbooks as well as by countless researchers in academic papers, it's new for most people you'll encounter. And the reason that the example has been used by so many scientists is because it really is a great illustration of the problem: Without any other cues, it is impossible to know what *gavagai* means!

Figure 13.2 An Ohio State University student engaging a COSI museum visitor with the word learning demo
Note. The student is asking what the word *gavagai* might mean.

Our activity continues by running people through very short and very easy versions of classic word learning tasks that have been done with children. We didn't make these tasks from scratch; we borrowed them from the literature. But as soon as someone does each task, we have created another experience to talk about.

If you are basing your activity on an experimental study, one thing that it is important to be clear about – both for yourself and for the people you talk with – is that even though the activity is based on real studies, you aren't trying to collect new data on the topic when you use it. The people you are talking with are **not** research participants! There won't be any new results to add to the word learning literature based on what people guess in our word learning demo. In fact, we chose our tasks precisely because there have been so many studies on word learning using them already that we're pretty confident in how well they work. The results are already in! But if you do get a person who likes thinking about the experimental process more generally, feel free to go with it. Such people can often provide the very reasons that this setting would mess up the results, if it were actual research. As we discussed in Chapter 10, it can be really helpful to let the conversation shift over to something that interests an individual visitor!

Give Them Something to Talk About

Your goal is to create a conversation starter, so you want to make your examples as striking as possible. You are using your phenomenon to draw people in, so don't be afraid to make it big and bold. Also don't be afraid to make your examples a little bit silly and fun. You want people to be interested enough in what you're doing that they want to stay and talk with you about it. There are many ways that you create such an experience for your audience – what works best will depend a lot on the specific phenomenon you have in mind. Here are a few ideas for how to get started talking about many common language science topics.

Use Your Body!

We all carry around our very own speech production apparatus with us everywhere we go! If you want to talk about any aspect of phonetics or phonology, why not let people play with the apparatus they came with. Obviously, you can't touch all of your articulators, but the lips, teeth, nose, and tongue are pretty easy to get to. And you can feel your vocal cords vibrate if you put your hand to your throat. You can also feel a puff of air on

Figure 13.3 You can feel your vocal cords vibrate!
Note. An Ohio State University student doing a demo about speech production. Here, she is showing how voicing works. Photo credit: The Ohio State University.

aspirated stops if you put your hand in front of your mouth. One simple activity we've used to explain how speech sounds work just involves having people hold on to their lips, front teeth, tongue, or nose while they say "apples and bananas." Try it yourself and see what happens!

Special Hardware or Software

Some people associate complicated machinery with the sciences. Since many language scientists use such tools, hardware and software are another way to start conversations. For example, activities that encourage people to use their own speech production apparatus could be paired with ultrasound imaging as we mentioned in Chapter 6. A group watching images of one person's moving tongue can easily be tied to some juicy questions, which your tools give them ways to answer then and there. Another example involves having a laptop running Praat or a similar program that can show wave forms and spectrograms of sound that you record on the spot. People can record their own names and see how a language scientist would analyze their speech! Or you can pair this tool with an fMRI video of opera arias (very vowel-y) and beatboxing (very consonant-y). (See the link in the Resource List.) These videos illustrate differences between consonants and vowels from an articulatory perspective, but if someone enjoying your demo is willing to produce either type of music, Praat will also illustrate the difference from the acoustic perspective. Remember that showing off the tools of science is one of the core goals of informal science learning (it's Strand 5!).

Videos

There are plenty of great videos freely available on the web that will show off a wonderful range of phenomena: X-rays or endoscopy of the vocal tract, tongue twisters in different languages, kids performing classic language tasks, animations for how sound moves through the ear, movie stars singing in Pig Latin (seriously!). Many of these videos are funny, or gross, or visually and auditorily striking. Videos with unusual sounds will bring people in as well, some just to see what's making the noise and then staying for the science conversation. For example, one of our favorite vocal tract videos provides a larynx-eye-view of people singing the "Kyrie" from Tomás Luis de Victoria's *Missa O Magnum Mysterium*; and as mentioned above, another favorite contrasts fMRI footage of an operatic aria with some beatboxing. We provide a few of our favorites in the Resource List in this chapter, but new videos are added all the time – just search for the topic you're interested in and see what you can find!

One thing to be aware of is that many of the videos may contain elements that you don't want. Some videos are just too long, and asking people to watch them in their entirety won't leave any time for conversation. Other videos contain mini-lectures about your topic along with the examples. These are great for getting ideas and learning about things for yourself, but the full video rarely works well for free-choice learning. We encourage you to pare things down by editing the video to the specific experience that you want to share. By now, we hope we've convinced you that you want to have a conversation with people, not give a lecture. Letting a video give a lecture for you isn't a conversation either! You want to stick to the video clips – or parts of video clips – that illustrate your phenomenon so you can engage people in a conversation.

RESOURCE LIST: ONLINE VIDEOS

Here is a list of some of our favorite videos. But there are many more out there!

Your body doing speech (good search terms: larynx, vocal cords, X-ray):

- "The Diva and the Emcee": www.youtube.com/watch?v=M2OdAp7MJAI

- "What Happens in Your Throat When You Beatbox?" (Tom Thum): www.youtube.com/watch?v=LqdFL0u2HLY&t=253s
- "Cords: Hear Us and Have Mercy": www.youtube.com/watch?v=5rJ8nCTgZ2Q

Pig Latin (good search terms: Pig Latin, language games):

- "*The Simpsons* Gibberish/Pig Latin": www.youtube.com/watch?v=t_sWPz1CS0g
- "*Gold Diggers of 1933*: We're in the Money": www.youtube.com/watch?v=UJOjTNuuEVw

Tongue twisters (good search terms: tongue twisters):

- "Moses Supposes": www.youtube.com/watch?v=tciT9bmCMq8
- Xhosa tongue twister: www.youtube.com/watch?v=KZlp-croVYw
- "Lion-Eating Poet . . .": www.youtube.com/watch?v=vExjnn_3ep4
- More tongue twisters to use: https://clearingcustoms.net/2018/06/10/if-peter-piper-picked-a-peck-of-global-tongue-twisters/
- "70 People Try 70 Tongue-Twisters from 70 Languages": www.youtube.com/watch?v=SI1J2bbbOt4
- Various tongue twisters on Omniglot, including some audio files: www.omniglot.com/language/tonguetwisters/index.htm

Just a few more:

- Broca's patient who says only "tono": www.youtube.com/watch?v=6CJWo5TDHLE&t=1s
- Categorical perception: www.youtube.com/watch?v=4V5pQyKsgg4

Pictures and Objects

No matter what you're talking about, adding something visual or tactile will help. Pictures attract attention, you can point to things in them, and people can find things in them on their own as well. If your core phenomenon is a contrast between two sentences, write those sentences on giant cards so people can see them and point to their parts. If you care about a meaning difference between two sentences, illustrate those meanings with pictures. Or consider asking people to place stickers on a picture to vote on their preferred interpretation. Want to talk about how the ear processes sound waves? Consider getting a giant model of the ear that can be taken apart. Maps are great if you want to talk about dialects or endangered languages, and they also open up opportunities for people to mark things with crayons or stickers.

If you're interested in discussing writing systems, you could use a small whiteboard and some markers. One of our activities is about syntactic ambiguity, and we present sentence trees on a giant piece of felt that is attached to a wall or on a stand (see Chapter 14 for more on that demo!). Many phenomena of language are very abstract, and visual aids can provide a good anchor that will help keep your topic the focus of the conversation.

Games and Puzzles

Anything that has ever been on a linguistic problem set can be turned into a puzzle. Anything that has ever been made into a psychological experiment can be turned into some kind of game. People like getting scores, and they have fun getting tricked. If you're looking for a ready store of relatively concise language problems, you can check out the website for the North American Computational Linguistics Open (NACLO) competition at www.nacloweb.org. NACLO posts practice problems on a variety of topics using a variety of languages. (Just be sure to give credit to the people who created those problems!)

Plus, games and puzzles lend themselves naturally to incorporating various kinds of objects into the experience – cards that need to be flipped over, blocks that need to be rearranged, buttons that need to be pressed, wheels that need to be spun. Also, many puzzles work well with crowds. If you can pose a clever juicy question, you can help a whole group of people have a conversation about it! And what's more, puzzles provide a great opportunity to give people something they can take away with them. We often have stacks of paper-based puzzles that include information about how to contact us later or suggestions for teachers to use in their own classrooms.

The trick with approaching your core experience through games and puzzles is to make the experience challenging enough for people to be interested, but not so hard that it frustrates them. It is often a good idea to have different versions of your game/puzzle – one that is easier to do and therefore more appropriate for kids, and one that is harder to do and would be a bit more fun for adults. But even more important is realizing that you don't want people to feel like you're administering a test. If people can't solve the puzzle, or if they get a low score in the game, you should make sure that you know how to focus the conversation on the experience itself, and not on the final result. After all, the point is to get people talking, not to see how well they do on a brain teaser!

The More the Merrier

When you're first thinking about your demo activity, it can be helpful to center it around a single interesting example. But most phenomena can be illustrated in multiple ways, and most topic areas are rich enough to support several related examples. In Chapter 10, we suggested that you prepare multiple juicy questions for your activity so that you can tailor questions for your audience and to help people engage with your materials in different ways. The same thing is true for examples. Having multiple access points to your topic will help you be flexible with different audiences: Some people will really love the gross-out dimension of the larynx-eye view of the vocal cords, while others will be more intrigued by seeing an actual tool like Praat at work. Moreover, by illustrating your topic in different ways, you'll help people create connections across the examples and reach a richer understanding. There is no reason why you can't use your own body, and show a video, and have people do a puzzle all as part of the same demo!

First Steps, Not Last Steps

Your visual aids and interactive demonstrations are only to get the ball rolling: They are what starts the conversation, not what ends it! You're creating a conversational common ground. The given information there will support what comes next. You're also designing an experience that should be fun for lots of different audiences. One great way to help people connect with your phenomenon right from the beginning is by asking them questions about it! In Chapter 10, we emphasized the importance of encouraging people to engage with your materials with a sense of exploration. Think of your materials as a launchpad for asking juicy questions: What do people notice? What can they figure out? What do they find unexpected or confusing? People learn best when they discover things on their own. You just need to give them something that is worth investigating!

CRITICAL TAKE-HOME MESSAGE

Begin your conversation by giving your audience an experience that they can talk about with you (and maybe also with each other).

WORKED EXAMPLE BOX

When you're thinking about how to illustrate your phenomenon, we encourage you to think broadly and creatively! One of our most popular activities uses the Stroop effect. In the spirit of this chapter, we'll start by showing you what it is! So get out your crayons and markers and channel your inner child.

Write down the word ***blue*** in red ink, the word ***green*** in purple ink, and the word ***yellow*** in green ink. Now for each word, say the color that the letters are written in.

How did that feel? Did you "get Strooped," as we like to say?

This phenomenon depends on the fact that reading is an automatic process for expert readers (which you likely are). So even though the task asks you to focus on the colors, you can't stop yourself from reading the words – and of course, the meanings of those words directly conflict with the colors you're supposed to name.

The Stroop effect can be demonstrated in many different ways. We just did it with three words on a printed page, and you can do that, too.

Or, you could print out dozens and dozens of words on a giant poster. That's a great way to get whole groups of people doing the task at one time.

Or, you could use an online iPad app that implements this effect. There are many such apps available (and new ones get posted all the time). Some of the apps are long and boring, but some are set up to work much like a game. Using an iPad gives the activity a slightly more high-tech flavor, and if you use one of the game-type apps (that give you a score!), it can encourage friendly competition.

Or, you could present people with a piece of paper that allows someone to color in each of the color words. Of course, you have to tell people to color in the words with the 'wrong' color (e.g., use a red crayon to color in the word "blue"), and that turns out to be part of the fun. This approach has the added bonus that people can take the cards home with them and do the activity with their own friends and family.

Or, if you like the bonus of giving things away, you could print out the key words on a small object to give away – a keyring, a zipper pull, a highlighter pen. It really only takes three words for people to understand what's going on, and many cheap giveaway objects can handle three words!

(cont.)

Or, you could print the words on the back of a T-shirt so that everywhere you go, you are giving new people the opportunity to do the task. (We don't give those away to the general public, but we do give them away to our students!)

Or, you could take advantage of your language science depth and create any of these items using a different language! If you're working in a space where there are people who speak another language, then this is a terrific opportunity to include them. And for the people who don't know that language, they can feel what it's like to have reading not be automatic! We often choose a language that uses a different alphabet from English (Korean, Russian, Arabic) to really block people's ability to read.

Or, maybe you're worried that children who can't yet read won't understand the effect. We encourage you to include those children as part of your activity anyway – they won't experience the interference that

Figure 13.4 A partial collection of different ways that we engage people with the Stroop demo. And see also Figure 9.1 for another example.

(cont.)

expert readers do, and it can be lots of fun for them to be the ones who do best by not getting Strooped while the adults around do get Strooped!

But you can also give nonreaders the core experience: Use a picture of a sun and a moon and ask people to say "day" to the moon and "night" to the sun. They will experience the interference there, even without written language!

You don't need to do **all** of these things with your demo activity. But we invite you to consider the possibility that there are many different ways to implement your own demo so that the phenomenon at its heart excites interest.

CLOSING WORKSHEET

It's time to get more concrete about how your doable demo is going to work: Plan out the materials that you would like to actually use, and focus on how your materials invite interactions with others.

What can people do with your materials? Are they just looking at something? Does that something change? Are they listening to something? Are they listening to themselves? Can they touch something? Can they move something? What or who are they interacting with?

How attention-grabbing are your materials? Are they big? Colorful? Do they move around? Are they loud? Can you be silly while using them?

What kind of reaction are you hoping for? Do you want people to gasp in surprise? Do you want them to say, "Oh gross!" Do you want them to laugh? Do you want them to talk to each other (if you're talking with a group)?

Is there any component of your materials that people could take away with them? Can they (or you) create something that they take home? Is there a relevant image that you could put on a sticker or other small object?

Further Reading

1 *Academic papers*

In fact, academic papers are so formulaic that it's easy to make fun of them. One comic from XKCD makes the point very well, and has spawned a fun meme so you

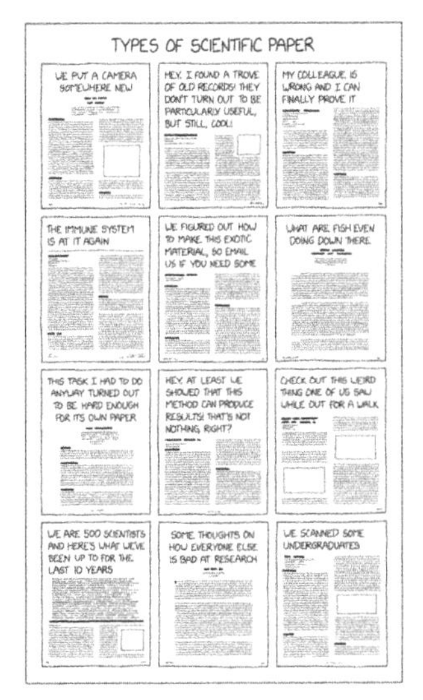

Figure 13.5 XKCD comic #2456: Types of Scientific Paper (https://xkcd.com/2456/)
Note. Reprinted with permission from Randall Munroe.

can generate versions of this for yourself. You can read about the meme here: www.theatlantic.com/science/archive/2021/05/xkcd-science-paper-meme-nails-academic-publishing/618810/

But we couldn't resist showing the original XKCD version in Figure 13.5.

2 *Make your examples work well with a public audience*

You can read more about the unfortunate history that the field of linguistics has with using examples that are not particularly inclusive or appropriate in Cépeda et al. (2021). Sadly, the point of this very recent article is that the field hasn't taken the lessons of respect all that much to heart in the last thirty-plus years.

3 *Word learning demo*

If you want to know more about this demo, LW has posted the materials and guidelines from her lab, as well as a video version of it online: https://u.osu.edu/thebln/language-outreach/.

4 *You aren't trying to collect data with the demo*

Of course, there are many researchers who actually **do** collect data in informal learning locations. For example, LW collects research data on-site at the COSI museum (https://u.osu.edu/thebln/language-pod/), as do many other language scientists and psychologists. And the Museum of Science in Boston has pioneered the Living Labs program, which creates partnerships between museums and university researchers for data collection purposes (www.mos.org/living-laboratory). For discussion about this practice among developmental psychologists, see David Sobel and Jennifer Jipson's book *Cognitive Development in Museum Settings* (Sobel & Jipson, 2015). And to be extra clear – all of the researchers who do data collection (and not just engagement) in these settings always get official ethical clearance from their home institutions before they do it!

5 *Larynx-eye view of people singing*

You'll find a link to the video we mention (the "gross" one that shows the larynx in detail) in a box in the main text. But if you discover that you love the music itself, you might enjoy hearing it in a more traditional format, along with seeing the musical score instead of the vocal cords: www.youtube.com/watch?v=RDC96uZIvYM.

6 *Maps are great if you want to talk about dialects*

There are many (many!) dialect maps out there for different parts of the world. These maps work great on their own, but it can be particularly interesting to combine maps about language with maps about other things. For example, in *The Language of Food* (Jurafsky, 2014), Dan Jurafsky discusses the different pronunciations of the word *pecan* in the United States. Depending on where people live, they might pronounce this word PEE-can, pee-CAN, peeKAHN or pickAHN (to use Jurafsky's phonetic spellings). The word itself is a borrowing from Illinois, a language in the Algonquin family of Native American languages. The Illinois word was pronounced something like paKAHni. In his book, Jurafsky places two maps side-by-side. One shows the places in the United States where the current pronunciation of *pecan* is closest to the original Illinois word (pickAHN). The other map shows the places in the United States where the pecan tree is indigenous – that is, where the Illinois speakers would have been most likely to gather pecans. The overlap between the two maps is striking! As Jurafsky notes, the people who are currently living closest to the original Illinois territory are the people who pronounce the word most like the original Illinois people that the word was borrowed from in the first place. Language is connected to many different things – history, culture, food, trade. It can deepen people's perspective about how language is interwoven into our lives to illustrate the ways that language intersects with other things we care about.

7 *The Stroop effect can be demonstrated in many different ways*

One example of an alternate to the original Stroop tests uses figures that people can easily label and the names for those figures. A series of figures can be presented, with each one labeled with the name of a different figure, as shown in Figure 13.6. Readers who are asked to name the figures will be slower and less accurate in this case.

But if the same figures are labeled correctly, readers will be faster and more accurate in naming the figures.

You can imagine something similar with line drawings of animals like an elephant, a giraffe, and a gorilla. You could also use easily recognizable and nameable foods or any other such category.

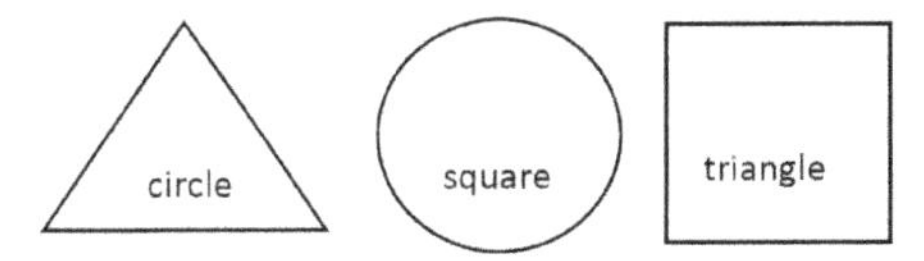

Figure 13.6 Name the shape outline

14 What's New?

Jargon

OPENING WORKSHEET

What would you call the item pictured in Figure 14.1? Write down at least five different nouns that label it.

Figure 14.1 What is this?
Note. Used with permission of Getty Images. Photo credit: Chris Stein.

Maybe you called this a banana, a patch of grass, an anomaly, or food. Or maybe you came up with an innovation, compost, a problem, or a genetic experiment. Each of those words and phrases means something – some are more or less specific ways of getting at roughly the same thing, some focus on different attributes, some have different emotional valences. But none of them are wrong. They do different work for you, and each would be appropriate in some context (or with some audience).

Now think about your doable demo. What words could you use to describe your demo activity? Write down at least five different ways to describe it. What does each of the different descriptions focus on? Which ones make the activity sound more exciting, interesting, and fun? Which ones make it sound harder and more challenging?

Chapter 11 laid out the principle of Given before New, and Chapter 13 focused on ways to provide given information. Now we turn to some special problems involving the introduction of new information. As you'll see, our advice hasn't changed: It is still critical to save the new information for later.

Concepts First!

Every subgroup of people, including subgroups of scientists, has their own special set of words they like to use. These are jargon terms. Jargon is the ultimate in new information. For people outside of the group that uses those terms, these words are often unfamiliar, and they often mark new ideas. They should never ever start your conversation. In fact, it is totally fine if they never show up in your conversation at all. Deciding whether or not to use any jargon should depend on how the conversation unfolds. Make sure that the person you're talking with is both ready and interested in hearing some.

So where should you start? With given information. You must make your key concept part of the conversational common ground first. Only once that has been done successfully will your new terms have something solid to attach to. This idea, that new terms stick better after you understand something about the concepts they are supposed to stick to, isn't unique to informal science learning. It applies just as well to formal classroom-based learning.

Consider, for example, a study that was done in 2008 by education researchers Bryan Brown and Kihyun Ryoo with children in fifth-grade science classes. They developed two different web-based lesson plans to teach the children about plants. In the concepts-first lesson plan, the children first learned the core concepts with everyday language describing things with easy-to-understand words like *food* and *green pigments*. In the jargon-first lesson plan, the concepts were introduced from the very beginning with their scientific terms (*glucose* and *chlorophylls*). Then both groups of children got practice with the scientific terms and their definitions, followed by examples of several plant experiments using the scientific terms.

Now, the overall lesson plans were pretty good, and all the kids learned about plants from these lessons. Figure 14.2 shows how well the children did

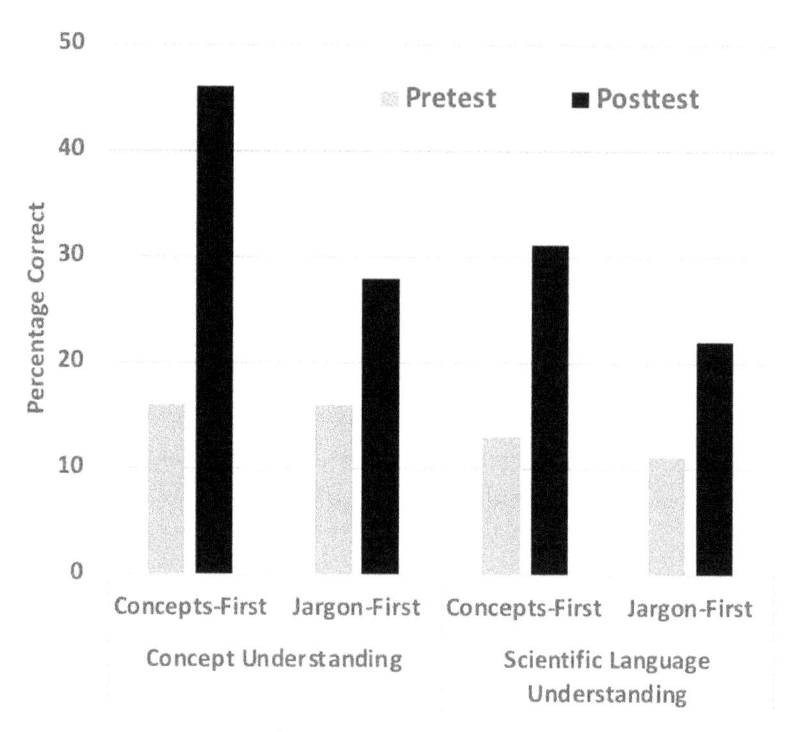

Figure 14.2 Learning concepts before jargon helps in the classroom
Note. Our adaptation of Figure 1 in Brown and Ryoo (2008). Students understood both scientific terms and scientific concepts better when the concepts were first introduced without jargon terms.

on a plant test before the lesson (the pretest scores are shown in the lighter bars) and after the lesson (the posttest scores are shown in the darker bars). As you can see, everybody did better on the posttest! But the children who were taught with the concepts-first lesson improved more than the children who started off with the jargon. And not only did the concepts-first group of children learn more about the concepts, but they also learned more about the specialized scientific vocabulary.

So, even when you're in a classroom environment, where students are often required to learn the specialized vocabulary, it still helps to ground them with concepts before laying the jargon on them. Given before New isn't a specialized feature of informal science learning, or even of general conversations. It is how people are built to process information, and giving information to them in that order helps them learn!

How to Spot Jargon

Before we worry about how to get rid of jargon terms, it's good to know how to find them in the first place. Because of the curse of knowledge (Chapter 12), it can be hard to identify all the terms that you use comfortably that are actually jargon. If you've known what a word means for a while, it will feel like everyday vocabulary that everyone knows. But remember that not everybody has read textbooks and papers on your science before; most people won't know what your specialized vocabulary means. To make matters even more confusing, sometimes people will think those words mean something different from what you think they mean! If you have any doubts at all that you're using jargon, or that you're using an everyday term in a technical way, then assume that you're using jargon. You will need to rephrase what you're talking about to avoid that term!

Some jargon is very easy to spot. The language sciences, like all sciences, are littered with words that sound "fancy" because they are often multisyllabic and have Latin or Greek origins. Words like *telicity*, *pharyngealization*, and *syntax* are relevant examples of such influence on the English language. The incomparable *Oxford English Dictionary* notes that *telic* is from Greek, *pharyngeal* is from Latin, and *syntax* has both Greek and Latin origins.

It is also easy to spot terms that involve proper names, acronyms, or weird arrangements of words that you really can't imagine ever reading outside of an academic article. Some examples from linguistics are *Grimm's Law*, *SVO*, *V2 languages*, *X-bar theory*, and *do-support*. These terms are all very specialized, and – assuming you know what all of them mean yourself! – you likely remember the class in which you first encountered them.

But some jargon is much harder to spot. Again, like all other sciences, the language sciences repurpose many common words to refer to technical concepts. These are words that everybody knows, but they have a technical meaning inside of language science that is different from their common usage. Words like *ambiguity*, *argument*, *aspect*, *binding*, *click*, *control*, *scope*, *stress*, and *tree* are some examples. There is obviously a connection between how language scientists use these words and how they are used in everyday speech, but that connection is really only apparent after you understand how the words are used in the science that makes the technical terms. It's impossible to make the link if you don't already know the concepts involved.

A closely related set of words involves specialized relationships. Language science uses common relational terms when talking about theoretical structures. For example, the terms *high*, *low*, *front*, and *back* are all common words, but they have very specific meanings in the context of talking about the vowel space. If you are familiar with how your vowel space can be described, these terms will seem very intuitive – what could possibly be confusing about a *high-front vowel* (like the [i] sound in *feet*)? Actually, a lot! For people who are unfamiliar with the science behind vowels, it's not at all clear what kind of space you're talking about. And even for language scientists, these relational terms refer to somewhat different things depending on whether you're talking about articulatory phonetics (in which case they refer to places in the mouth) or acoustic phonetics (in which case they refer to places on a chart of formant values). The simplicity of the words is hiding a lot of information.

The last class of specialized vocabulary that is worth watching out for is popular grammar terms – both from school and from headlines. Some examples would be *passive construction, parsing, uptalk, creaky voice, preposition*, and *(split) infinitives*. These are terms that are linked to popular ideas about how language works, and many of them are prescriptivist bugaboos about what is bad/ugly/confusing in how some people talk. We hope that you, as a representative of language science, are not planning on endorsing any of those prescriptivist points of view! But from the perspective of jargon usage, what you need to be aware of is that many people use these terms a little bit differently from language scientists. What you think a passive construction is, and what a member of the general public thinks a passive construction is, could very well be different things. Even if someone is spontaneously using one of your jargon terms, don't assume that they mean the same thing by it as you do!

But I Can't Explain Anything without These Words! Actually, You Can. Si, *Se Puede!*

One of the most common complaints from students who are just starting to do demos in free-choice locations is that they **have** to use specialized vocabulary terms. They claim they simply **cannot** explain what their favorite topic is without them. This is not true.

Keep in mind that your jargon terms are names for things. Instead of worrying about the label for the thing, try just talking about the thing itself. In Chapter 13, we discussed different ways that you can show people a phenomenon. Just letting people talk about that experience is a great way to get them to appreciate the thing that you care about.

Consider next what level of detail your audience needs to really appreciate your phenomenon. You're not trying to train new colleagues here, so it doesn't matter if they won't be able to understand an academic article on the topic. It's fine to rephrase jargon terms into everyday language. That shift may make your description a bit less scientifically modern from a terminological standpoint, but it will allow you to share your core points with anyone. For example, one activity we've done looks at syntactic ambiguity with prepositional phrases (PPs). Or, to put it another way: *Who's got the banana?*

The activity starts with this sentence: *The man touched the monkey with a banana*. We then ask people whether they can think of meanings for the sentence. As they describe each meaning, we bring out a picture to go with

Figure 14.3 The syntactic ambiguity demo
Note. A University of Arizona student at the AAAS Family Science Days festival showing pictures of meanings for *The man touched the monkey with the banana*. She is pointing to one representation of what we mean by mentally linking "with the banana" to different words.

that meaning. We ask how the exact same words in the same order can mean two different things. The demo shows how these meaning differences depend on whether we mentally link *with the banana* (a PP) to *touched* or to *the monkey*. The activity can be used to show that language scientists have a special way of describing those different mental links. We can do the whole activity without ever saying the phrases *PP attachment* or *syntactic ambiguity* even though that's precisely what the demo is about.

Rephrasing jargon terms will often mean that you will need a lot more words to describe your topic than you would in academic writing. One thing that jargon buys scientists is a great shorthand way to talk about their work with each other. But your audience can keep better track of a lot of easy-to-understand words than if you use a few brand-new terms. And for the record, using less jargon actually helps scientists too. An investigation from 2021 by two biologists, Alejandro Martínez and Stefano Mammola, looked at which scientific papers get cited by other scientists. They found that the more jargon used in the title and abstract of a paper, the less likely it was to be cited by other researchers. Even scientists are turned off by jargon!

You might also notice that the less technical rephrasing makes it harder to see which scientific theories you are committed to and which scientific debates you are part of. But the audience in an informal learning setting doesn't care if you are an advocate of Minimalist syntax or Categorial Grammar. The central goal of this activity is not to advocate for one theory of syntax over another; it is just to show people that we can, and do, mentally make different links among the words in a sentence. What's more, those different mental links lead directly to different interpretations of the sentence.

The nontechnical rephrasing in the syntactic ambiguity demo also helps us identify the critical components of the sentence that people need to attend to in order to understand the underlying phenomenon, namely, the phrase that gets linked to different places in the sentence (*with the banana*) and the two phrases that it can get linked to (*the man* and *the monkey*). If you can get your audience to understand how those three pieces are related, then you basically did teach them how PP-attachment options explain syntactic ambiguity. Or at least, you have taught them enough that they are in a good position to learn more.

One final advantage to using less jargon is that people will be more interested in what you're talking about. Biology education researchers Tobias Dorfner, Christian Förtsch, and Birgit J. Neuhaus analyzed how secondary school teachers in a German school used jargon in a biology class (Dorfner et al., 2020). The researchers found that there was a negative link between the amount of jargon that the teachers used and how interested the students were in the class. Specifically, the more jargon the teachers used, the less interested the students were. One of the perks of interactions in an informal venue is that people are there to explore their natural curiosity and have some fun. Jargon is a wet blanket on people's interest. Everyday language (and perhaps a monkey or two) keeps the mood positive.

Jargon can also be used to show that language scientists know how to have fun with their science (trust us, monkeys are a fun way to talk about syntactic ambiguity). We also often wear a banana suit for this demo (as you can see in Figure 14.3 and many people come over to the demo just to learn why someone is dressed as a bright yellow banana. Plus, we offer banana candies at the end of this activity so people can take away a little fun with them.

Another critical lesson to remember is that an incomplete explanation is not an incorrect one (Chapter 9)! Just because you're not using all the technical jargon you could to explain your demo doesn't mean you're explaining it wrong. Getting people to understand the main concepts – even if they don't understand **all** the fancy words that scientists use to describe those concepts – is still correct. In Chapter 15, we will expand on this idea by discussing how you might consider breaking down your topic area so that you are trying to explain the piece of it that your audience is most likely to really profit from.

But . . . Jargon Is Part of Science

The general public doesn't need the precision or the distinctions that the scientist does. However, that specialized vocabulary does have a role to play when you're talking with the public: Those terms mark you as a scientist and as an expert more generally. People **know** that scientists need jargon and that being able to use such terms fluently is a sign that you know the details.

But more than that, people know that part of learning about something scientific is learning new words. In Chapter 4, we laid out the six strands of science learning. You may recall that Strand 5 was about showing people the tools of science – the specialized items that we use to make science happen. The National Research Council's original framing of this strand referred explicitly to the language of science, and as language scientists, we're aware of the fact that words are themselves a kind of tool. Further, philosophers have argued that jargon is also an important tool of science. Understanding new words can help people understand how the science is working.

A new term might help people label and remember an idea that is new for them. For example, an activity that we've used before highlights the McGurk effect during speech perception. The name of the effect is a jargon term for something that most people are unaware happens. (This jargon is fairly easy to spot since it involves a proper name.) If you search online for the term itself, you'll find lots of videos showing it off, and we've put links to a few of our favorites in the Resource List below. If you've never experienced the McGurk effect before, we do recommend that you go and try one out before you continue reading.

RESOURCE LIST: SEE THE MCGURK EFFECT

Here are a few videos showing the McGurk effect:

- This one is super basic and short: www.youtube.com/watch?v=aFPtc8BVdJk
- This one comes with some surrounding explanation: www.youtube.com/watch?v=ypd5txtGdGw
- And here's one from some of our students: https://drive.google.com/file/d/1HkdaTXllUenbi1st63XARxL_iXl5_eSH/view

The effect shows how we combine auditory and visual information when perceiving speech. Listen to one of the McGurk effect videos with your eyes closed and write down the sound you hear. Now turn the sound off and just watch. What sound does it look like the person is making? It will be a different sound! The videos are set up so that there's a mismatch between the auditory and visual channels: What is coming to your ears and what is coming to your eyes are different. Round out the experience by watching and listening at the same time. People resolve the mismatching information in different ways. Some people are very audio dominant and will perceive the sound coming to their ears; some people are very visual dominant and, even with the sound on, will 'hear' the sound that they see; most people do something in the middle. That usually means perceiving a sound that is between the audio and visual information. So if the audio has a /ba/ (which is pronounced by closing the lips at the front of your mouth) and the video has a /ga/ (which is pronounced by making a closure at the back of your mouth with the back of your tongue), you might hear a /da/ (which is pronounced by making a closure in the middle of your mouth with the front of your tongue). The McGurk effect shows that your naïve ideas about how we hear things just aren't right: It's not all about the ears! It's our brain that perceives speech, and the brain integrates information from lots of places.

You don't need to use the term *McGurk effect* to explain the core idea that our hearing is influenced by our vision. But the term labels an experience that people have probably never had before. It tells people that this experience is scientifically important, and it allows them to refer to it in an easy, shorthand way – just the way language scientists refer to it!

Keep It Simple

So far, we've just been talking about jargon – words that are technical for a specific field of study. But there is another kind of word (and sentence) that we recommend avoiding as well: big fancy words and long, complex constructions. One of our former English teachers used to say, "Never use a five-dollar word when a ten-cent one will do." There's a misconception out there that using big words makes you sound smart. In fact, the smartest people out there do most of their work with ten-cent words. What makes you sound **really** smart is saying things that people understand! This lesson is one that definitely applies when you're talking with people in a free-choice setting, but it is also one that applies in more contexts than most people realize –

your academic writing will probably also be better if you rely more on ten-cent words as well.

And in addition to those five-dollar words, there are also five-dollar sentences out there. These are constructions with multiple clauses and lots of connectives like *whereas* and *heretofore*. You're going to want to avoid those too. Take your ten-cent words and put them inside simple sentences that anyone can easily follow.

Keeping your words and sentences simple and clear is the best way to achieve the goals related to knowing your audience that we laid out in Chapter 5. One of the fastest and easiest ways to lose your audience is to be hard to understand. You've probably experienced this yourself. Have you ever dropped a class because you went on the first day and couldn't understand a thing that the teacher said? Have you ever stopped reading a newspaper article or a blog post because you couldn't follow it? If people find you hard to understand, then they will do the equivalent of dropping the class or surfing away from a blog: They will walk away from you. Most people are pretty polite, so they may suddenly discover they need to go to the bathroom or remember that their bus is coming soon. While the ideal time will vary with the venue, it's generally a good idea to aim for getting people to stick with you long enough for you to show them something interesting and for you to come out with your Critical Take-Home Message (see Chapter 16).

Not only is being hard to understand a turnoff for people in general; it is also going to keep the people who do engage with you from learning much. To put this in terms of the strands of science learning, if you're hard to understand, you will fail to spark anyone's interest. And people who are bored (or just being polite) aren't going to be very receptive to the content of your science. So even if you feel like focusing on your manner is all about the form and not the substance, remember that if you don't have decent form, nobody will ever learn the substance.

CRITICAL TAKE-HOME MESSAGE

Jargon is the ultimate in new information, and you should avoid using it. Instead, present a phenomenon for people to experience, and use everyday language to talk about it. You might want to include a jargon term (but really just one, or at **most** two) to show how technical terms are part of your science. But in that case, be sure to present the concept first so that people have something for the specialized label to attach to. Given before New!

WORKED EXAMPLE BOX

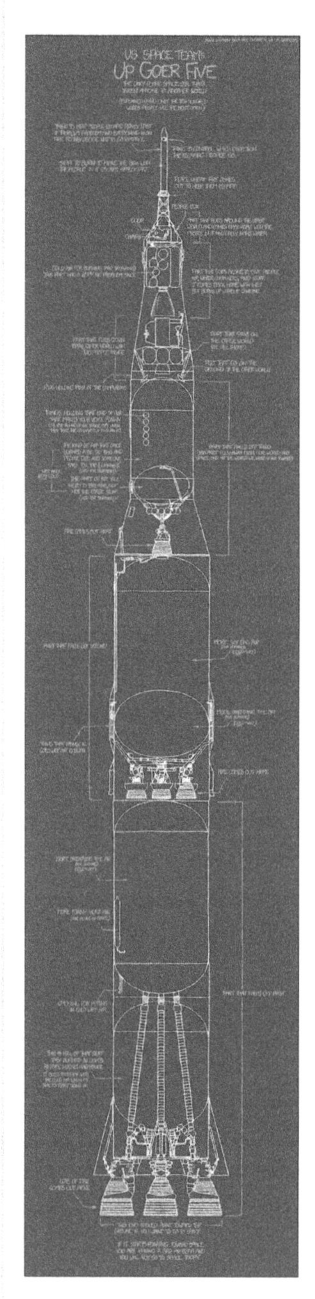

Figure 14.4 XKCD comic 1133: Up Goer Five (https://xkcd.com/1133/)

Note. Used with permission of Randall Munroe.

There are lots of online tools that can help you identify jargon, and the Closing Worksheet is going to ask you to pick one and use it on your own work. But before you do this yourself, we wanted to show you a bit about how one of these works!

We're going to use what is (by far!) the strictest of all such editors – the Up-Goer Five Text Editor (https://splasho.com/upgoer5/).

This editor was inspired by a strip from the XKCD comic created by Randall Munroe (see Figure 14.4). If you've never read the strip before (https://xkcd.com), we recommend it! In one of Munroe's most famous posts, he described the NASA Saturn V rocket using the thousand most frequent words of English. And since words like *NASA* and *rocket* aren't among those thousand words, he called it "US Space Team's Up Goer Five." For that matter, the word *thousand* isn't among the thousand most frequent words, so as the author says, he really uses the "ten hundred words people use most often." You can read more of Munroe's stripped down explanations in his book *Thing Explainer.*

The Up-Goer Five Text Editor website was created by Theo Sanderson, and it lets you see if your writing meets the very strict Up-Goer Five standard: Every word you enter that doesn't meet the super high-frequency standard will get marked in red. In case you're wondering how Sanderson decided what the thousand allowable words were, he used the Spell Checker Oriented Wordlist (SCOWL) to determine his frequencies.

To show how this works, we'll see just how well we were doing at avoiding

(cont.)

jargon as we wrote this book! So here's a sentence that used to live in this chapter:

> *For the uninitiated, jargon terms are unfamiliar and functionally denote new concepts.*

The Up-Goer Five Text Editor flagged seven out of the twelve words – that's 58 percent of the sentence! One of the flagged words is clearly jargon: *jargon.* Given what this chapter is about, you can understand why we might want to keep that word. But what about the rest? The word *denote* also raises a flag: It's Latin based. It's a word that philosophers of language use a lot but isn't one that is used much outside of the academic literature. This word needs to be changed, and the word *mean* will serve us just as well here.

Some of the words that the Up-Goer Five editor flagged are words that feel like everyday words, but we might be using them in a somewhat jargon-y way: *unfamiliar, functionally, concepts.* These are words it's worth thinking about. Do we really need each of them? In this case, we might argue that the word *functionally* is just providing a level of nuance that doesn't really matter here. So we could leave it out. The word *concept* means something pretty specific in the world of semantics, but maybe we don't need to be **that** specific. A word like *idea* means something similar and is much more understandable.

Another word that the editor flagged is us showing off our fancy vocabularies – *uninitiated.* This one is a classic five-dollar word, and there are plenty of ten-cent substitutes that we could use instead.

The last two words that the editor flagged are ones we wouldn't normally worry about too much – *unfamiliar* and *terms.* Neither of these words is really a jargon term in our science, and they don't seem like five-dollar words. But it is useful to be reminded about just how many words you regularly use that aren't super frequent in the language.

Now for the hard part: rewriting our sentence so that it passes the Up-Goer Five Text Editor! Here's a new version of the sentence that does pass the editor:

> *For people outside the group, new words that most people do not use are often not well known, and they show off new ideas.*

One thing you might notice is that the new version of the sentence is twice as long. (As Grice might put it, we solved the clarity problem at the cost of prolixity.) That is almost always true: One of the things that jargon buys you is the ability to package ideas efficiently. It often takes a

(cont.)

full sentence or phrase to cover one nice noun: *jargon* became *new words that most people do not use.*

You might feel like it's overkill to have to figure out how to rephrase a fairly common word like *unfamiliar.* But there is real value to going through this exercise. First, it will help you get more mentally flexible in how you phrase things. Our students sometimes tell us that there is just "no other possible way" to describe something. But there is **always** another possible way. This exercise will force you to start thinking about some of those ways. And you'll notice that some of the changes could be pretty helpful. For example, the word *words* would probably be far more understandable to most people than *terms*, and the difference in meaning between the two is very slight.

Another reason to value this exercise is that if you're planning on talking with children, it really will help you get things to a better place. *Unfamiliar* may be an easy word for an adult but a five-year-old will genuinely benefit from a simpler word. It's a very good idea to know how to make your activity accessible for everybody! (Of course, if you go back to the beginning of this chapter, you'll see that we didn't listen to all of the advice from the Up-Goer Five Text Editor, and we definitely kept the word *unfamiliar.*)

Last, we're not the only people who like this editor! The bloggers Chris Rowan and Anne Jefferson at *Scientific American* have written about it and challenged all kinds of scientists to describe their work in a way that meets the Up-Goer Five Text Editor's standard. You can read the results in their Tumblr "The Ten Hundred Words of Science" here: https://tenhundredwordsofscience.tumblr.com/.

CLOSING WORKSHEET

Review some of the key messages you came up with for your activity. In Chapter 9, you wrote down your Critical Take-Home Message, and in Chapter 7, you wrote down some ways to link your activity to people's real lives.

Now, write down two of the main messages. Does either one contain any jargon? Circle every word that might be jargon. Which ones were easy to spot? Which ones were more difficult (and why?). How can you rephrase each of those terms so that you get your point across without it?

Now enter your messages into one of the online editors designed to help you avoid jargon. Here are our favorites:

- Up-Goer Five Text Editor: https://splasho.com/upgoer5/
  See the Worked Example Box for a full description!
- Hemingway Editor: https://hemingwayapp.com/
  This editor will mark words that have simpler alternatives. It also marks long sentences that have complex structures. And it gets very exercised about the passive construction (for better or worse).
- De-Jargonizer: http://scienceandpublic.com/
  This editor will tag your words in red if they are rare, and in orange if they are moderately infrequent. It will also give you a score for how suitable your writing is for a general audience.

How many of your words get marked by one of these editors? Were they the same words that you identified as likely jargon? How can you rephrase your main points so that you can 'pass' these online tools?

Further Reading

1 *Influence on the English language*

The geography and history of English speakers explains many such influences on the English language. Here's an example: As the Roman Empire extended across what we now call Europe, Latin became useful for doing business with the Romans. It was the language of the church, as well as a lingua franca for scholars. A little later, when French speakers ruled Britain, the French language – itself influenced by Latin – became useful for government, law, and religion. In the computer sciences, you can see something similar happening with English now. English terms for computational concepts and tools and so on are being borrowed into other languages. In those languages then, words that came from English are prevalent in the computer sciences.

2 *Use of common relational terms as jargon*

The domain of syntax also has its share of relational jargon. Sentence trees look a lot like family trees, and syntacticians have imported common family relationships to describe relations between nodes on a tree: A mother node has daughter nodes, for instance. When you're comfortable with hierarchical tree structures, having these friendly words to describe how pieces of the tree are connected to each other is very helpful. But people who are unfamiliar with syntax do not find them nearly as obvious. One place that the connection falls down hard is the fact that syntax only uses a very small set of kinship terms to describe relations. The most obvious omission is that there are no male nodes – no fathers, sons, or brothers. There are also no nodes related to marriage – no wives, or sisters-in-law, or stepdaughters. And relations that require connections across multiple people are infrequent (aunts) or missing entirely (nieces, grandmothers, granddaughters). If you know how a syntactic tree works, it's kind of fun to link the positions to kinship terms; but knowing how kinship works won't really explain how a syntactic tree works!

3 *What the general public thinks the passive construction is*

In fact, the linguist Geoff Pullum has written extensively about how people, including many who like to write about language, have very odd ideas about the passive construction. You can read the text of one of his famous papers here: www.lel.ed.ac.uk/~gpullum/passive_loathing.html. If you want to read more from linguists (including Pullum but also lots of others), here is a long list of blog posts on the topic from the *Language Log* site: www.lel.ed.ac.uk/grammar/passives.html#passivepostlist.

4 *The man touched the monkey with a banana*

The syntactic ambiguity demo reflects research in a University of Arizona dissertation (Zimmer, 2016). Elly Zimmer, who has gone on to develop linguistics-based curricula for K-12 students, helped refine a number of our demos.

5 *PP attachment and syntactic ambiguity*

PP attachment is in-house talk for how a prepositional phrase (PP) associates with words preceding it. If a PP has more than one option for this association, this is a standing syntactic ambiguity. In other words, it's a word string that has more than one structural analysis, and this has consequences for our interpretation of the sentence. The ambiguity doesn't depend on a single word such as *bank* or *buffalo*. Instead, it shows different options for connecting the words. In addition, the ambiguity is not resolved by words later in the sentence, as in a garden-path sentence. As we discussed in Chapter 11, garden-path sentences are temporarily ambiguous ("The scientist examined . . ." can go in different directions), but those sentences do resolve into a single interpretation by the end ("The scientist examined by the prosecutor" is not ambiguous).

A favorite illustration of PP-attachment ambiguity comes from Groucho Marx. In the hilarious 1930 movie *Animal Crackers* (directed by Victor Heerman), Groucho's character says, "I shot an elephant in my pajamas." He pauses, and then follows up with "How he got in my pajamas, I don't know" (you can hear the joke here: www.youtube.com/watch?v=NfN_gcjGoJo). The PP *in my pajamas* can either be attached to the verb *shot*, or to the object noun phrase *an elephant*. When the PP associates with the verb, *I shot an elephant in my pajamas* is interpreted to mean that the speaker was wearing pajamas when he shot an elephant. When the PP associates with the object *an elephant*, the sentence is interpreted to mean that the elephant was inside the speaker's pajamas. The ambiguity is where exactly in the sentence the phrase *in my pajamas* attaches. And different attachments support different meanings.

6 *Jargon is a tool of science*

Highlighting the tools of science is one of the core goals of informal science learning (it's Strand 5). But terminological tools can be particularly tricky ones to use and explain. A central point that philosophers make is that scientific terms don't stand on their own: They are mutually interdependent, and collectively they create what's known as a "web of belief." When scientific revolutions happen, words can be cut off from this web and they stop meaning anything at all (*phlogiston* is a famous example). This shows that:

(1) Terms are critical for creating a coherent science.
(2) You can't really understand a scientific theory unless you know a **lot** of terms. You have to know enough to support a whole web.

These points should make us wary about using technical terms – an extension of the curse of knowledge. Once you're inside the web, all the words make sense because they are all mutually defined. In short, they are interconnected. But if you're new to a web, each term can feel like it's just pulling a loose string in a sweater and the whole thing always feels like it's unraveling. For more on this, see Thomas Kuhn's classic philosophy book *The Structure of Scientific Revolutions* (Kuhn, 1962); or try a more psychological approach with a more recent book, Carey (2009).

7 *The McGurk effect*

First reported by McGurk and MacDonald (1976), what is now called the McGurk effect is a perceptual illusion that can be described as an integration of auditory and visual cues. This description is too simple though, as much depends on the specific cues that are used as well as their order. For example, if the auditory signal relays [g] and the visual signal relays [b], people most typically perceive a [bg] sequence rather than a fusion of [b] and [g] (Tiippana, 2014).

8 *De-Jargonizer*

This tagger was created as a tool to help scientists be more aware of how much jargon they are using. It depends primarily on word frequency counts, but its assessment of a word as jargon has been validated by comparison to other kinds of word taggers, as well as by seeing how it analyzes both technical and nontechnical writing (as well as oral presentations like Ted Talks). The details can be found in Rakedzon et al. (2017).

15 From Given to New

Scaffolding

OPENING WORKSHEET

All the sciences include complex problems. The first time you look at almost any of these, it can feel like everything matters all at once and you can't find a good starting point. But all these complex problems can be broken down into component parts. Human genetics is complicated, but it can be decomposed into four bases (ACGT). Chemical molecules are complicated, but they are all made of atoms.

The same is true of our favorite science. In fact, a classic type of problem set in linguistics involves showing people some sentences in an unfamiliar language and asking them to figure out how to make new sentences in that language. At first glance, the unfamiliar language looks impenetrable: How could you ever figure out its component parts? The standard method is to look for pieces that repeat and see how they compare to the translations in the language that people do know. Once you figure out one piece, you can use it to find more and more pieces until you've broken everything down into its component parts.

We would add that it's important to begin by taking a deep breath and believing that the problem really is solvable. It's easier to find the component parts in this kind of linguistics problem if you believe that they are there to be found.

So give it a try! Here's a language analysis problem that we adapted from one that Rachel Nordlinger made for the Australian Computational and Linguistics Olympiad in 2008. You can find the full version through the International Linguistics Olympiad website (https://ioling.org/).

Lalana Chinantec is a language spoken by approximately ten thousand people who live in the Oaxaca region of Mexico. For the record, we've adjusted the orthography a little bit to make this easier to read, but it won't change the way that you solve the problem.

Here are a few phrases in Lalana Chinantec and their English translations.

kalakwaa kwee liiuh	The beautiful corn grew.
kaladʒö kwee	The corn turned out well.
liiuh kalane kwee kwaa kya	My tall corn yellowed beautifully.
meelakwaa kwee	The corn has grown.

Can you figure out the meaning of this word?	*Kwee*
How about this word?	*Liuh*
What do you think this sentence means?	*Meelakwaa kweee liiuh*

Now try thinking about your doable demo in the same way! Take a deep breath and believe that you can break your complex science down into smaller pieces. What are the component parts of your demo? Write those down. How can you put them together in different ways?

In previous chapters, we laid out how to start with given information and we cautioned you to save the new information until the end. In Chapter 13, we encouraged you to start your interaction by putting some striking given information on the table for people. In other words, start with compelling examples or a phenomenon that people can experience for themselves. In Chapter 14, we discouraged technical terms in general and suggested that very new information like jargon should come only after you've explained or demonstrated your concepts in super accessible ways.

But there's more to the idea that given comes before new than just saying "examples before jargon." There is also the question of how you organize your concepts so that they build in a natural way from given to new. And you will probably have already realized that audience matters here too. In this chapter, we're going to show you how to break down a complex concept in a way that will allow you to reconstruct it for people from the bottom up. One of the key lessons for this chapter is that combining information is a form of new knowledge because it depends on understanding the pieces that are coming together. With that point in mind, we're going to first review some things you already know.

Building Up to More

Every audience you work with will benefit from getting given information before new information. But just how much new information can you give someone? It depends! Informal learning venues like museums and festivals gather a very broad range of people. In Chapter 5, we talked about how different people come with different motivations: Explorers want to learn about new things, Hobbyists want to build on knowledge they have, Facilitators want to help others learn something, and Spiritual Pilgrims and Experience Seekers are generally more interested in the experience itself. Each of these kinds of people brings a different level of background knowledge to your demo. That means that you need to take extra care to make sure that all the given information you care about is firmly in place before introducing anything new. And if you're working with young children, you should assume that **nothing** is given information!

Think about your topic like it's a big building. On the ground floor of the building are the foundational ideas of your topic, and as you go up the floors, the information gets more and more detailed. You've been working on this building for a while now, and maybe you're comfortable on the top floors, near the roof. But the people you're talking with have to build this building for themselves. You're going to help them do this by providing SCAFFOLDING that will support their efforts. But any building project, including your scaffolding, needs to start from the bottom. You can't start by supporting people on the seventh floor; your support scaffolding needs to begin with the foundations. If you don't provide the scaffolding from the bottom up, you will leave people hanging out of a high story window – and that is never a comfortable place to be.

Figure 15.1 It's no fun to be left hanging with no scaffolding to support you!
Note. This image is used with permission from Getty Images. Photo credit: Hulton Archive/ Stringer.

Audience Design

Recall that speakers who consciously accommodate to those they are addressing start by finding shared knowledge and then work to share more knowledge that is based on that common ground. Scaffolding is one way to instantiate this kind of partner-specific approach.

One useful way to think about building your scaffolding is to imagine talking to a young child, then an older child, then a teenager, then a college student, and then someone who is an expert in your field. Each level of scaffolding will provide true information, but each higher level will add more detail and more nuance.

Another good reason to imagine starting with your youngest potential audience is that, if you're in a free-choice learning environment, you may well be talking with an actual young child! Older members of your audience will surely understand your explanation to a younger member of their group, and they will appreciate that you made the demo interesting for the youngest members of their group. Further, the older members may get interested themselves, which will allow you to move further up your building.

In practice, approaching people this way means that you will very rarely get all the way to the top of your building. You may spend all your time talking with someone about what you consider to be a very basic part of the topic – maybe even something you consider such deep background that you never intended to talk about it at all. But remember the curse of knowledge from Chapter 12. Just because you've known something for a long time doesn't mean that everyone else knows it, and it doesn't mean that it's not worth talking about!

So think about Chapter 4 and remember your goals! You want people to get excited about your topic, and you want them to enjoy learning about it. That's the very first strand of informal science learning. If all they are ready to learn is at the foundational level of your topic, then so be it! Working with people where they are will get them more excited about what you're doing and will actually lead to more real learning.

Break It Down, Then Build It Up

One of the hardest parts about building scaffolding is figuring out what information really goes on which floor of your building. When you're trying to break down a problem that you already understand, it is often easier to start at the top and move down. Sometimes it helps to start by letting yourself describe your topic using language that is as technical as you want.

Let's imagine that you want to explain why formants are critical to defining the vowel space. You might describe your core point something like this:

> *You can describe most individual vowels and distinguish among them by looking at their first two formants. In fact, the classic vowel chart plots each vowel as a function of its F1 (Y-axis) and F2 (X-axis) values.*

There are several easy-to-identify jargon terms in this description (*F1*, *F2*, *formant*, *Y-axis*, *X-axis*), and one jargon term you might not immediately spot: *vowel*. One clue that *vowel* is a technical term within the field is the fact that linguists have specialized charts that we use to describe them. Nonlinguists also use the word *vowel*, but often they don't mean the same thing that you do. What do most people think about first when you say *vowel*? If you're not sure, go and ask someone (a nonlinguist!) in your family. Or try googling it. You will find is that the most common association people have to vowels is the letters a, e, i, o, u (and sometimes y).

Now we have our first clue about what needs to go on the ground floor of our building. If nonexperts are thinking about letters, and you are thinking about speech sounds, then you need to make sure that **sounds** are the first

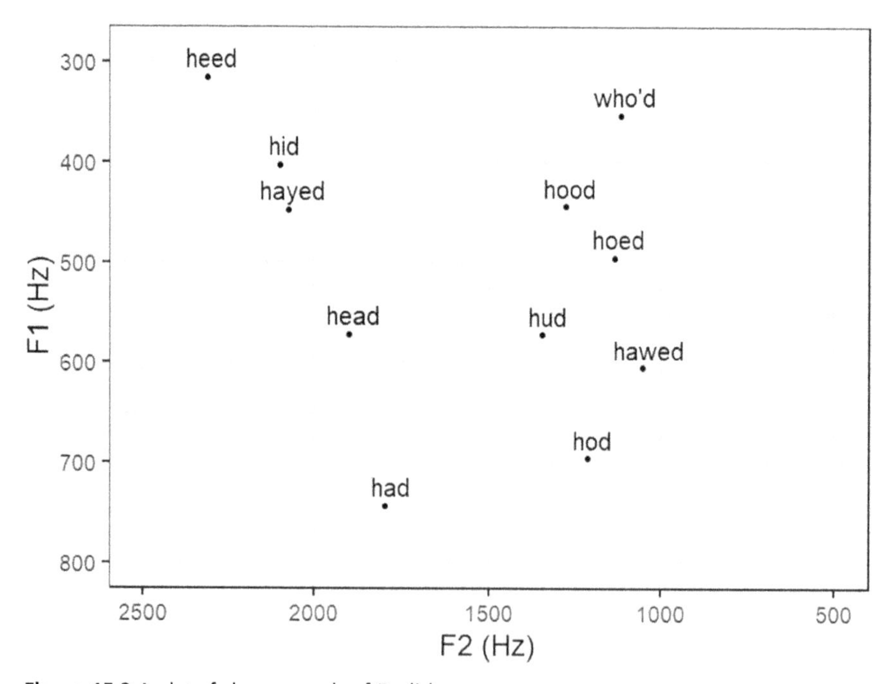

Figure 15.2 A plot of eleven vowels of English
Note. In this graph, each vowel is shown inside the same pair of consonants, [h] and [d]. This figure was created by Jory Ross, a graduate student at The Ohio State University.

given in your interaction. How do you do that? Make some noise!! Speech sounds are fun for the whole family to produce! (And check out some ways to encourage people to produce sounds in the Worked Example Box.)

Once you get people to focus on sounds and not letters, where do you go next? To figure that out, head back up to the top floor and work your way down! In this activity, we want the top of our building to be about formants, so think about what you're going to need to get up there. What do we mean by *formant*? It has to do with the frequencies in the sound wave. The vocal cords vibrate at one frequency (called the *fundamental frequency*), but the sound wave that the vocal cords make has to pass through the rest of the vocal tract before it gets out to where people hear it. We use our speech articulators – things like our tongues, lips, and that little flap at the very back of your throat – to modify the shape of our vocal tracts, which causes the sound wave to change shape as well. These changes result in lots of distinctive patterns. And these distinctive patterns that we make in the sound wave correspond to vowel formants. This description is still pretty technical, but it contains several concepts that aren't too hard to rephrase and use on earlier levels. Let's take a look!

What do we mean by *frequency*? Start by thinking about what the difference is between a high-frequency sound and a low-frequency sound. That difference corresponds to pitch. So what you're really talking about is the fact that we can make high- and low-pitched sounds. And the fundamental frequency is really about the fact that some people have characteristically lower or higher voices. Great! This distinction is also easy to get people – even very young people – to make for themselves. Just ask people to make high and low sounds. We are still on a low floor of the building.

What about *vocal cords*, *vocal tract*, and *articulators*? These terms refer to actual parts of a person's body, and that means you can ask people to touch the ones they brought with them! Well, it's actually a little unsanitary to really touch most such things directly, but you can definitely ask people to touch their throats to feel their vocal cords vibrating. And it is pleasantly gross for most kids to touch their fingers on their teeth, lips, and tongue. Alternatively, there are loads of great pictures out there of all these things as well as anatomical models you can buy that will show what these look like. (There are also great videos, such as the ones we mentioned in Chapter 13.) These body parts aren't all that exotic, so we're still relatively low in our building.

Finally, what do we mean by *sound wave*? This phrase actually describes a genuine physical entity, although one that is hard to see. But it's not impossible to see (see our suggestions in the Worked Example Box), and it is definitely not impossible to describe what a sound wave is and connect it to other kinds of waves that people may know about. A very young child might not have the patience for this concept, but you could talk about it with an older child. So we've moved up the building, but we're still not on a high floor yet.

The whole point was to use formants to describe vowels, so let's not lose sight of those! What do we mean by *vowel*? We mean a speech sound that is made with little or no obstruction of the airflow. How can you explain what that means? Better yet, just show what it means! Try asking people to sing a few syllables (like *tra la la*) and see which parts they can hold on to for the longest. You can hold a note on a vowel pretty easily but not as easily on a consonant. This difference is one that is easy for people to produce and easy to reflect on. As a rough-and-ready rule, almost anything involving speech sounds is going to be something that you can get people to **do**. Plus, there are some great videos out there showing what the vocal tract looks like when you say both vowel and consonant sounds (see our suggestions in the Worked Example Box). But vowels go on a slightly higher floor than the general category of speech sounds – vowels are a type of speech sound, and more specific things belong on higher floors.

By now we've got all the basic pieces in place, and what we need to do next is combine them to really explain how formant frequencies connect to different vowels. Typically, combining information will be on a higher floor of your structure. But until the component pieces have been established as given information, there's no point in trying to combine them. You want the combination itself to be the only news. Don't try to introduce a new concept and also combine it with an old one at the same time.

In terms of how you actually accomplish the combination, we recommend that you provide some kind of visual aid to help you and your conversational partners. These aids will help people keep track of all the component parts and make it easier to focus on how the different pieces add up to something more. If you're talking about something like vowel formants, using images of spectrograms or wave forms can be helpful (see Figure 7.2 for examples). Better still, use software that will allow you to see spectrograms in real time (there are lots of cheap or free spectrogram programs out there). Just because you're near the top of your building doesn't mean you should stop trying to provide striking examples and experiences for people. Those are powerful learning tools for every level.

Be Careful with Your Jargon

The lower you are in the building, the less jargon you should use. If you're talking to a preschooler, you should stay on the ground floor of the building the whole time, using absolutely **no** technical terms at all. The higher you go in the building, the older the person you're likely to be talking with, and the more jargon you might introduce.

But remember the core lessons from Chapter 14: Never introduce a jargon term until after you've introduced the concept for it. And never introduce more than one (or, at most, two) jargon terms during the course of your activity. If you are feeling like you really need more technical terms than that, you should think more seriously about what your main points are and how you're building up to them. If you need more than two jargon terms, you might be trying to go too high too fast.

One way to be sure that your scaffolding is providing enough support is to do knowledge checks. See if you can get people to articulate your concept in their own words before you offer them a technical description, and before you move to a higher floor. And don't be afraid to go back down if you realize that someone is confused!

Incomplete ≠ Incorrect

You may not be satisfied with providing scaffolding from the bottom up. After all, if what you really want to talk about is vowel formants, you might feel like encouraging preschoolers to make high and low sounds isn't really what you came for. It's fine if your deep motivation is to share your passion for an abstract, technical element of your own language expertise. Just remember that you may need to inspire people at a more general level if you want them to appreciate your favorite piece of language. Before someone can be impressed by vowel formants, they need to understand how language scientists describe speech sounds. And if you want people to learn about speech sounds, then you'll also want to encourage them to develop an interest in language science itself. Revisit your core goals and remember what you're doing in this informal free-choice learning environment!

The closest that a preschooler is likely to come to formants is learning that they can make different speech sounds and that a language science expert can make cool pictures of those sounds. That truly is step one for learning about formants, and you should feel successful if you are able to do that.

As you work with older children, teenagers, and adults, you may still feel like you're not **really** explaining the nuances of formants or how the vowel space works. From the perspective of working professionals in language science, that may be true. But your goal isn't to create new language scientists; your goal is to get the general public interested in language and to give people some insight into what a language scientist is an expert in. And it's also worth keeping those relevance connections in mind! Who cares about vowel formants? Clinicians who treat children with speech impairments do. Forensic experts who work on voice identification do. Dialect coaches who help actors sound like they are from different regions do. You're helping people understand some of the science that makes these things possible. Measure your success not from the heights of what a linguist knows, but from what that person knew before they talked with you. Helping people move to a higher floor in your building is progress, even when that means just moving from the first to the second floor.

CRITICAL TAKE-HOME MESSAGE

Moving from given to new information needs to be done in a structured way. Break your topic down into component parts and introduce the foundations first. And don't worry if you don't get all the way to the top!

WORKED EXAMPLE BOX

In the main text, we talked in general about how to structure your explanations from the bottom up to go from basic speech production all the way to vowel formants. Here, we provide some detailed ideas about five different levels of explanation. For these interactions, we're going to assume that you have access to a few resources – a few apps for an iPad, a vowel chart diagram, and the ability to play a few videos. Here's how each level might work.

For a young child

[Technical terms: none]
[Tools: something that shows a spectrogram. There are many inexpensive apps available that display spectrograms in many colors. If you want something very simple, the Singing Fingers app works well with young children. If you want something a bit more technical, the program Praat will show you both spectrograms and wave forms.]

Did you know you can make different kinds of sounds with your mouth? Let's try! Let's make a sound like we're giant monsters [you're encouraging sounds that are loud and low in pitch]. Now let's make a sound like we're

(cont.)

tiny fairies [you're encouraging sounds that are quieter and higher in pitch]. My app lets us see what sounds **look** like. Do you see – those sounds look different on my program! Different sounds look different! What other kind of sounds can we make? I wonder what those look like?

For an older child

[Technical terms: high/low; loud/soft]
[Tools: something that shows a spectrogram]

What ways are monster and fairy sounds different? Which one is higher than the other? Which one is louder than the other? Can you make a really high sound? And a really low one? What do you see that's different on my program when you do that? [If you're showing a spectrogram, point to frequency bands that differ.] Can you think of any other ways that sounds can be different?

For a teenager

[Technical terms: sound wave; vowel]
[Tools: something that shows a spectrogram;
"The Diva and the Emcee" video (www.youtube.com/watch?v=M2OdAp7MJAI);
video of guitar strings making sound waves (www.youtube.com/watch?v=SoAv8E86Ifo)]

Let's try making some language sounds! Can you say ah, ee, ooo, and oh? Those sounds are all vowels! [If your audience seems unsure about what vowels are, show them "The Diva and the Emcee" video and point out how they differ – mouth open for vowels in an aria and more closed for consonants (and other percussive sounds) in beatboxing. You can also ask people to sing a word or short phrase and extend it in time. It's easy to extend vowels but not so easy to extend most consonants!] My program lets you see what sounds look like. Do you notice any differences between them? When you make these sounds, you make waves in the air. Do you want to see what sound waves look like? [Show guitar video.] Do you notice anything about how the strings move differently? Now let's look at a program that shows properties of those sound waves. The sounds we make when we talk sound different because they have different properties in their sound waves. Let's look at the patterns you get from two different vowels (pick two that have very different spectrogram profiles, like /a/ and /i/). What differences do you see?

(cont.)

For a college student

[Technical terms: spectrogram; frequency]
[Tools: something that shows a spectrogram;
video of guitar strings making sound waves (www.youtube.com/watch?v=SoAv8E86Ifo)]

Can you say two different vowel sounds, like aah and eee? I've got a special program that makes spectrograms, and it will show you what those sounds look like. What do you notice about how they are different? What this spectrogram measures is the frequencies in a sound wave. Waves go up and down, and if they do that really fast, we say the wave is high frequency; it changes very frequently between going up and down and back again. When the waves go up and down more slowly, they change less frequently and we call them low frequency. You can see what this looks like for guitar strings that make different frequencies [show guitar video]. When you say a real language sound, you're actually making really complicated waves that have peaks at different frequencies. Let's try saying a whole bunch of vowels to see how the patterns are different! What do you notice on the spectrogram that is different for each vowel?

For an expert in a language-related field

[Technical terms: formant]
[Tools: Something that shows a spectrogram;
vowel space diagram, such as this: https://en.wikipedia.org/wiki/Vowel_diagram#/media/File:California_English_vowel_chart.svg]

We can describe vowels in terms of a few core properties of how they are produced in the mouth, such as whether they are high or low, or front or back. Can you think of vowels of these different types? [Show the vowel chart and work with the person to fill in four or five vowels from different parts of the chart.] We can also describe these different vowels in terms of the kinds of sound waves that produce them. Each vowel sound is made up of a complex sound wave that has different components, and we can control the intensity of those components by the way we use our speech articulators to change the shape of our vocal tract. Different vowels have intensity peaks at different frequencies. The first formant roughly corresponds to vowel height. Try saying a high and a low vowel and see if you can see the difference on the spectrogram. The second formant links to another frequency component in the sound wave. It is related to whether a

(cont.)

vowel is front or back. That one is a little hard to see on a spectrogram, but it's basically there in the way the lines are clustered together for some vowels and spread apart more for others.

Figure 15.3 A look at Praat windows showing sound files, spectrograms, and wave forms
Note. Praat is a program that lets you visualize sound in a variety of ways. It's fun to have people record their names so you can show them their personal formants, or voiceless stops, or stressed syllables. Praat makes it easy to select, label, and print a wave form for some unusual name tags.

CLOSING WORKSHEET

Review the Critical Take-Home Message for your doable demo. You should find that in your Closing Worksheet from Chapter 9. Break down your core message into its component parts: What foundational information does it depend on? What dimensions of it are likely to be given for other people and what parts are likely to be new?

Think about how you can scaffold your component parts. We know the image in Figure 15.4 is a ladder. The image is simpler than a scaffold, and ladders are used to climb up scaffolds. So let's use the ladder analogy. Choose three of the rungs on our image of a ladder and write down how you would adjust your activity for each level.

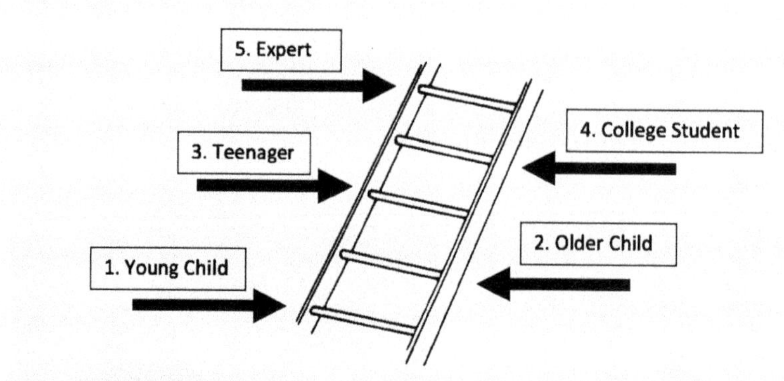

Figure 15.4 Instructions from a manual on ladders: Start at step 1, then go to step 2, then step 3, and so on
Note. Ladder created by Firkin.

Further Reading

1 *You may well be talking to a young child*

The Alan Alda Center for Communicating Science (https://aldacenter.org/) used to run a science communication competition called the Flame Challenge. The competition asked scientists to explain an abstract scientific concept to an eleven-year-old. The fun twist was that the Alda Center actually had classrooms full of eleven-year-olds judging which explanation was the best. (Well, they did have a panel of scientists vet the answers for accuracy before they let the contestants loose on the kids.) The competition is defunct these days, but you can still find many of the winning videos online. As language scientists, our favorite year was 2016, when the target concept was "Sound." Here's a link to the winner for that year: https://vimeo.com/147241241.

2 *What do people think about first when you say "vowel"?*

Here are some things we found when we googled the word *vowel*:

- www.grammar-monster.com/glossary/vowels.htm
- https://teachphonics.blog/2019/10/10/what-are-vowels-and-consonants/
- www.dictionary.com/e/vowels/
- www.youtube.com/watch?v=YU6G6h-wV04

3 *What is a formant?*

Obviously, there's a lot more one could say about vowel formants than what we have in our example! If you want to learn a lot more, we recommend taking a course on phonetics. What we've described in the main text is the "source-filter" model of speech sound production.

If you want to dip your toe a bit further into those waters, here are two websites to try:

- www.voicescienceworks.org/harmonics-vs-formants.html
- www.britannica.com/science/phonetics/Vowel-formants

16 The Three-Legged Stool Approach

OPENING WORKSHEET

At the end of this chapter, we're going to ask you to pull together all the pieces you've been working on for your doable demo and make a set of guidelines to help you (and maybe someone else too) use your activity to engage with the public. To prepare for the worksheet at the end of this chapter, jot down now some responses to the following questions:

- What pieces of your doable demo are in great shape? What are you confident is really good? What are you most proud of?
- What pieces of your demo feel like they still need some work? Are there any pieces you're missing? Is there some part that you're not sure you understand as well as you'd like to?

While you read through this chapter, think about your responses to the questions above. Modify any answers that this reading inspires.

At this point, we've covered all the major things you need in order to effectively engage with the general public: have a conversation, keep it relevant to your audience, balance quality and quantity in your own contributions to that conversation, put given information before new information, and keep your goals in mind but be open to shifting directions. All of these things are important, but it can be hard to focus on all of them at once. And doing your demo with people will be a lot more fun – both for them and for you – if you're not spending your time worrying about how to address each goal. In this chapter, we're going to be doing the integrative level on your scaffold. We're not suggesting you do anything new, but we are going to offer a metaphor to help you connect what you've already learned about how to have successful conversations with people.

Our metaphor is the three-legged stool. Your interactions with others during these special conversations depend on three distinct elements: your materials, your plan, and you. Each of these elements is essential on its own. It's also important that you keep them in balance. If you only depend on one leg of this stool and leave the other two underdeveloped, then your stool will be lopsided and this will affect your interactions.

Leg One: Have Good Materials

The first leg of your stool is the actual stuff that you're going to have with you. If you're working on the IPA, this leg might include blank name tags and a handout for people who'd like to learn more; a clipboard or whiteboard and markers are also helpful. If you're doing a word learning activity, this leg might include laminated pictures of novel objects. If you're doing an activity based on the McGurk effect, this leg might be a video that you show on a laptop with some headphones. Materials like these are what people often remember about activities! You may see your activity as elucidating the IPA, but visitors are likely to remember it as the fun name tag activity. The materials are going to be central to people's experience with you and your activity, so you want to choose them with care.

Make sure that your materials are engaging! In Chapter 6, we talked about sparking interest as a core goal for your activity and using fun materials as a way to generate some excitement (Strand 1). Make your materials stand out. Use big sizing, bold colors, objects that are fun to play with, videos that are lively and maybe even loud! If you want to talk about word learning, don't use tiny black-and-white line drawings of nonsense objects; use large colored pictures of really weird things. If you want to talk about how hair cells are involved in processing sound waves, don't show a picture from a textbook. Instead, consider getting a giant model of the cochlea. If your materials are visually exciting – and visible from a distance – then they will help you attract people. If people hear odd sounds coming from your cart or booth, then they may come over to see what's happening and even start the conversation you want themselves. A crowd often brings more people, and you might end up with lines of people waiting to engage with you and your activity.

Also, don't be afraid to be a bit silly with your materials. Informal learning venues are usually designed to be fun places to go, and you'll fit right in if you're noticeable or even outrageous. Why not wear a T-shirt with your school's name spelled in the IPA? Why not wear a paper model of the brain as a hat? Why not dress up as a banana? And while you're at it, think about ways that your materials can turn into a small token that you give away to people. We've given away temporary tattoos that show off the sound wave for the word *language* spoken in different languages; zipper pulls and colored markers that have the Stroop task printed on the side; headbands with paper brains; and stickers saying everything from "I did language science today" to "Prescriptivism is fun but Descriptivism is funner." We model these materials as well (e.g., having tattoos on our faces) because having fun isn't just for the people you're talking with. Remember that your number one goal is to get people interested and excited. Having fun is a good way to get started.

Try to make your materials show your core points. In Chapter 13, we talked about how videos, pictures, and games can help you demonstrate a phenomenon so that you are well positioned to explain it. So choose materials that do illustrate your topic area. For example, if you want to talk about how we hear different vowel sounds, then a giant model of the ear isn't your best choice. Giant models are great for attracting people, but there's a big gap between an ear and a vowel. A tablet showing off a spectrogram of vowel sounds, on the other hand, is visually interesting and has a direct connection to the acoustics of vowels. Make sure there is a genuine, organic, and clear connection between what your materials show and what you want to talk about.

Be practical with your choice of materials. If your engagement efforts are successful, you will be talking with a lot of people, and that means wear and tear. If you're using pictures, we recommend getting them covered in plastic. If you're using a tablet, buy a shock-resistant case for it with grips on the sides that lets you hold the case while someone else uses the tablet. If you're using headphones, you'll probably want to have dedicated cleaning supplies with you. Backup copies of items can also be especially useful. And stay away from items so small that they could easily get lost (or worse, swallowed by a small child). If your materials involve electronics, you'll also want to pay attention to things like whether your venue includes internet access and electricity (or, just how far away the nearest plug will be). Bring duct tape and spare bags and cords. Bring water and peppermints or lemon drops to soothe throats stressed from a very successful event where you talk with hundreds of people. Label everything. We recommend downloading any videos you want to use and putting them on a looping cycle so you don't have to worry about constantly reloading them.

You'll also want to pay attention to the specifics of your environment. Are you going to be at an outdoor fair? Are you in a tent or out in the wind? What's the weather going to be like? Depending on your setup, you might have a giant table in a quiet room. Or, you might have a sliver of space next to a loud stage. Not all materials will work equally well in all places. It's good to think ahead of time about how the materials will actually be used and to prepare backup plans.

Figure 16.1 iPad in a shock-resistant case
Note. Brutus Buckeye (left) is the mascot for The Ohio State University. He is used to working at sporting events, so it's a good idea to make sure our materials can stand up to some rough-and-tumble interactions.

Leg Two: Have a Plan

In Chapter 4, we talked about the value of clear goals before your start. Related to that, we cannot emphasize this enough: **You need a plan.** Conversations that you have with friends and family in your everyday life don't require much planning, but talking about your science in a free-choice setting is not that kind of conversation. Before you start, you should know what your goals are and how to use your materials; you should have a nice stockpile of juicy questions to ask people and think about questions that people might ask you. Also, have some ideas about where you want to take your conversation. As the American baseball icon Yogi Berra put it, "If you don't know where you're going, you'll end up someplace else."

Of course, just because you have a plan doesn't mean that you can always stick to it. Nevertheless, you still need to have one! As we discussed in Chapter 5, you'll be talking with real people who don't necessarily have the same perspective as you. They will have their own agendas, questions that are off-the-wall to you (but fascinating to them), unanticipated confusions, and various personal concerns. They will have their own funds of knowledge. And, as we mentioned in Chapter 10, it's important that you listen for all of these things and respond to them in a genuine way. You don't want your activity to be a performance where the public's contributions are treated like some random humming that ought to be ignored; these contributions are critical to the conversation too, and you will need to let your conversational partners help steer it. So no matter what your plan was when you started, you will need to be flexible and open to different directions once you're actually interacting with people.

But if you start with a plan, then it will be a lot easier to be flexible! Your goals will always matter, and if you are well practiced with your activities and materials, you will be able to answer a wider variety of questions about them. If you have a planned reserve of key points, exciting examples, and juicy questions to use, then you will have options to draw from no matter what turn the conversation takes. The better you know your plan, the easier it is to steer things in the direction that you want to go; it will also be easier to handle being steered in the direction someone else wants.

For most of our activities, we actually write the plan down as a set of guidelines. These guidelines contain the critical scientific background that someone would need to do the activity (and some suggestions for where to read more on the topic); detailed information about how to use the materials; suggestions for how to engage people with the materials – What are some possible juicy questions? How do you explain how the game works?; and a set of educational messages about the science in the activity and how the science connects to people's everyday lives. You can get a sense of what our guidelines look like in this chapter's Worked Example Box.

We treat our guidelines as a living document. We revise them regularly based on the experiences of the students who use them. There's even a section at the end where we add in the answers to questions that people frequently ask and ways around problems that we sometimes encounter. When our students first do an activity, they tend to stick very closely to the plan laid out in the guidelines: The plan that's there works pretty well for most people. But as they get more comfortable with the activity, our students adapt the plan so that it fits them better, and so that it fits the specific person they are talking with better. Learning the plan will get you off the ground. Mastering the plan allows you to really soar.

Leg Three: You!

You add value to the activity. Without you, it's just a bunch of stuff. If you've got really great materials, your stuff might be reasonably exciting –

interesting objects, a fun game, a super gross video. People might be very happy to interact with your stuff. And if you put an especially informative sign next to your stuff, people might even learn something from it. (Just don't underestimate how hard it is to make such signs!) Museums are typically full of non-staffed displays with signage. And people are capable of learning from these kinds of displays. People are also capable of learning material by reading a textbook. But there's a reason why students attend classes with live teachers in them, and why museums and festivals like to have real people staffing their carts and booths: People matter.

You transform the static materials into a conversation tailored to the person you're talking with. Unlike a sign, you can go in a lot of different directions. Also, you check to make sure people are following the information. You help people engage with the materials so that they experience the relevant phenomena and so they can link its lessons to their own lives. You attend to whether they are enjoying the learning experience. You answer questions. You ask questions! You make the activity fundamentally interactive because people get to interact with you. To put it another way, you can make the activity **fun** in a way that no object or signage can.

You are critical for getting people excited about the topic. As Chapter 2 emphasized, if you are enthusiastic about and interested in your own topic, you will help others feel the same way. People really do feed off your energy: If you are projecting the sense that you think what you're doing is amazing, they will believe you. If you are projecting the sense that what you're doing is boring (or hard, or irrelevant), they will believe that instead. So go ahead and gush about how much you love your science! Your positive energy will carry people along with you, and your enjoyment is likely to be infectious.

You are also critical for helping people learn something about your topic. If you've made great materials, they will help you illustrate information, but people may need guidance to help them think about the illustration in effective ways. In Chapter 10, we discussed how different kinds of questions can help people think constructively about your materials. You are there to ask some juicy questions! You're also there to answer questions that others might ask. You are a critical source of content knowledge. You are also a knowledge monitor – you keep track of whether people are understanding what's going on, and so you are able to guide the conversation to where it will be most helpful.

Finally, you are a representative of your field, and of science more generally. You are putting a human face on what a language scientist – or any kind of scientist – looks like. This role will give you a certain amount of natural authority. You can use that authority to make a positive experience for everyone who you interact with. As we noted in Chapter 8, science has a long history of exclusion. Sadly, this is also true of informal science learning venues. If you don't look like a classic stereotype of a scientist, embrace the fact that just being who you are is helping to make your space more inclusive. And no matter what you look like, remember that "a positive experience" includes welcoming every single person who you meet in your venue to engage in a conversation about your activity.

CRITICAL TAKE-HOME MESSAGE

Your interactions with people depend on three distinct elements: Your Materials, Your Plan, and You. Make sure your materials are engaging, educationally helpful, and practical to use. Make sure your plan is detailed but nimbly supports change if needed. Embrace the fact that you add critical value to the experience through your expertise and your personal style. All three legs of this stool matter.

WORKED EXAMPLE BOX

Our dinosaur communication demo is about communication without language in the animal realm, featuring our favorite animal, dinosaurs. In this box, we provide an excerpt of the guidelines we use for this activity. As you'll see, the guidelines describe the materials you need for the demo (Leg 1), but mostly it constitutes the plan that we want students to use with those materials (Leg 2). And of course, the better you know your plan, the more of your individual you can go into the interaction (Leg 3).

Background readings

General information about how animals communicate:

https://en.wikipedia.org/wiki/Animal_communication

More specific information about Hockett's design features:

https://en.wikipedia.org/wiki/Hockett%27s_design_features

Materials

There are bags of small plastic dinosaurs and laminated cards with the core information summaries and interaction suggestions for each one. Each bag has sets of different dinosaurs and shows off a different type of communicative function. You can do as many (or as few) of the bags as you want,

(cont.)

and you can do them in any order. If you want to give people a choice, you can put out a representative dino toy from each bag (a triceratops, a T. rex, a parasaurolophus, and a stegosaurus) and ask them which one they want to talk about.

Interaction

The laminated cards provide specific information for each communicative function, but the basic interaction components for all of them is the same. Here is the contents of the card for the communicative function of *group identification.*

Dinos to use

Two parasaurolophuses and four (or more) dinos of any other kind.

Figure 16.2 This picture shows what a parasaurolophus looks like
Note. The picture of the parasaurolophus is used under a Creative Commons CC-BY-SA License.

Set up the situation

Give the museum guest one of the parasaurolophus dinos and put all the rest of the dino toys in a loose group. Ask the person: "How can your dinosaur figure out which other dinosaurs are in her group?"

Hints and juicy questions

Suggest that people consider things that the dino might see or do. The parasaurolophus's coloring could be used to identify it as a member of a

(cont.)

particular group; the parasaurolophus might make a distinctive noise. In fact, the crest on its head was part of its nose and the parasaurolophus could breathe through it, and it could make a loud noise like a trumpet. The specific nature of the noise depended on the shape of the crest, which was different for different species.

Suggest that people think about modern animals. The closest living relatives to dinosaurs today are birds. How do birds communicate with other members of their flocks?

Suggest that people think about how humans would solve this task! You can ask people to look around at the people nearby and see if they can spot ways that groups look the same (e.g., matching T-shirts or clothing styles). How do humans communicate with other members of their groups?

Core messages

Critical Take-Home Message: There are lots of ways to communicate information, and animals (probably including dinosaurs!) can signal many different kinds of information to each other.

But wait, there's more: Human language is a special kind of communication. Only humans seem to be able to learn it, and it is capable of communicating some things that animal communicative behaviors cannot (such as abstract meanings like SQUARE, FREEDOM, THINK); it also seems to work differently and relies on symbolic signals, compositional structure, and duality of patterning. Ask them how dinosaurs would communicate more complex ideas such as "See you next week" or "I miss that tree we used to eat from." This is a great way to talk about differences between human language and animal communication, including how the communication abilities of animals are limited.

And one more thing: When scientists make hypotheses about how dinosaurs communicated, they look at the fossil records to figure out what kinds of physical traits and physical abilities these animals probably had. That tells us what kinds of signals they might have been able to make. Scientists also observe how modern animals communicate. Dinosaurs faced similar kinds of situations as today's animals. It is reasonable to think that dinosaurs probably would have arrived at similar kinds of solutions to those communication pressures as modern animals currently do.

Relevance Connection

Many people have pets at home! Ask them to think about the ways their pets communicate – with each other and with their owners. What kinds of

(cont.)

information **can** their pets communicate and what kinds of information can they **not** communicate?

Making a Link

This activity links to core points in the wug test demo. The wug test helps show people how children implicitly know complex rules in their language. That's probably something animals (even dinosaurs) can't do.

This activity links to core points in the dialect demo. Humans also use language to mark their social groups. Dialect differences illustrate that beautifully.

CLOSING WORKSHEET

It's time to make the guidelines for your own doable demo! Your focus here is on making sure you have a strong **plan** for how to use your materials. This worksheet provides a basic template you can use. As you fill in your own details, you may realize that you haven't yet made final decisions about various aspects of your activity. Now is the time to commit! Settle on the specific materials that you want to use and how you think they can best be used. Remember, your guidelines aren't fixed in stone: After you've had a chance to use them with some real people, we recommend that you come back to them and improve them. Every time you engage with other people through your demo, you will learn something new about how to do your activity better – your guidelines are a great place to keep track of what is working. So this is just the start of the living document for your doable demo.

Name of activity

- Background readings:
  Where did you learn about your topic area? It's important that your activity be based in real science, so make sure you can point to one or two sources so you're sure you have the science right!
  [Check out your notes from the worksheets in Chapter 8 and Chapter 12.]
- Materials:
  What are you using to engage people with?
  [Check out your notes from the worksheets in Chapter 6 and Chapter 13.]

- Interaction:
  What are you going to do with your materials?
  What kinds of instructions will you give? What are your juicy questions?
  [Check out your notes from the worksheets in Chapter 3, Chapter 4, Chapter 6, and Chapter 10.]
- Core messages:
  What do you want people to learn?
  How are you adjusting your message depending on who you're talking with?
  [Check out your notes from the worksheets in Chapter 4, Chapter 5, Chapter 9, Chapter 11, and Chapter 15.]
- Relevance:
  How are you planning on connecting with people's everyday lives?
  [Check out your notes from the worksheets in Chapter 5 and Chapter 7.]

Further Reading

1 *Communication without language in the animal realm*

The dinosaur communication demo was created and refined by a former student, Abigail Sarver-Verhey, who has gone on to become a designer of museum exhibits: www.abigailsarververhey.com/. You may remember we mentioned her before with our Mayan glyphs demo. No wonder she went on to work in museums!

2 *Only humans are able to learn human language*

The way we discuss the question of non-human language abilities in our activity is a good example of how being incomplete is not being incorrect. While the generalization that only humans are able to learn human language is broadly true, the picture is more complicated the more you learn about it. There have been attempts to teach animals specific human languages like English or ASL, but those haven't worked out well. On the other hand, many species have abilities that are evolutionarily related to what humans do: There is hierarchical syntax in birdsong; dolphins can use word order to assign thematic roles; the dog Chaser learned labels for hundreds of objects; Alex the parrot could understand some compositional structure, as could Kanzi the chimpanzee. What's more, if one considers animal communication systems on their own terms and not just in comparison to humans' preferred method, they show a range of intriguing properties, such as the specialized alarm calls of vervet monkeys. A good place to get an overview of the breadth of animal communication abilities is Marc Hauser's book *The Evolution of Communication* (Hauser, 1996).

17 Working with a Range of Different Audiences

OPENING WORKSHEET

What kinds of people might respond particularly well to your doable demo? For what kinds of people might your doable demo pose a particular challenge? Think about both your materials and your interactions for these questions.

What kinds of people outside of an informal free-choice learning setting might be interested in the main messages of your doable demo?

Our focus has been on informal learning environments, and the people who you'll interact with in such places vary along just about every dimension. You'll see toddlers and great-grandparents; families with very attentive parents; families where the parents are looking for a place to park their young children while they check their phones; young couples on a date; people who look just like you; people who look very different from you; people who don't speak the language you're most comfortable with; religious school groups; tourists; people who know the region better than you; adults with disabilities; community leaders; retired professionals in your field. Talking with each of these kinds of people is different, and you don't want to have the same conversation with all of them!

You may also want to engage with people outside of informal learning venues as well. And beyond these locations, you might encounter variation of a different sort. You may find yourself wanting to talk about your science with your parents, your neighbors, your boss, potential employers, a local political representative, your child's teachers, or the random person who sits next to you on a bus, train, or airplane. Talking with each of these kinds of people is also different, and you want to vary the conversation with each of these people, too.

In Chapter 15, we emphasized the ways in which you'll modify how scientifically detailed your conversation is depending on who you're talking with. In this chapter, we want to talk more broadly about audience design: How do you change the conversation to make it ideal for different people? We'll discuss how to approach the range of people you'll encounter in informal learning settings, and we'll review how to apply the major lessons of the book to working with different audiences. We'll also discuss how to approach people in the rest of your life who you might want to talk with about language science.

Different Audiences in an Informal Learning Setting

We want to start by saying how you might get an audience in a free-choice learning venue in the first place. As we discussed in Chapter 1, people have choices in these locations, and one of the first things you'll need to do is attract people to your conversation. In Chapters 6 and 13, we talked about some ways to make your activity attractive so that people will approach you, wanting to talk with you. But sometimes, you will have to encourage people to join you.

Making eye contact and smiling are great ways to be welcoming – people generally would rather talk with someone who looks friendly and enthusiastic than with someone who looks bored or uncomfortable. You can also explicitly ask someone to talk with you. In our work, we call this the PITCH (as in, a sales pitch), and it's just a quick comment that serves as an invitation. The pitch can be as simple as "Do you want to see what I've got here?" or it can be something more dramatic, like "Do you want to trick your brain?" or channeling carnival hawkers: "Get your free spectrogram here!" What's important is that you're initiating the interaction and letting other people know that your activity is for them. It will probably seem obvious to you that anybody can come and do your activity, but it might not be so obvious to the people you want to talk with. As the sociologist Emily Dawson has found through her work with visitors in these settings, individuals who come from minority backgrounds or who don't speak the region's dominant language natively may not feel all that comfortable at your venue (Dawson, 2014, 2019). They may worry that your activity requires special skills or involves an uncomfortable social interaction. Your pitch helps make it clear that you want to talk with people, that you're ready to talk with them, and that this person in particular is someone you want to talk with.

Another concern that Emily Dawson noted was financial. Many museums and festivals charge admission fees, so people are primed to worry about cost. On top of that, many special museum events require what's sometimes called an "up charge" and many booths at festivals are selling their wares.

You can see how someone who doesn't have a lot of money to spare might be wary about agreeing to join you in what might end up being a costly situation. You can help alleviate such worry by being very clear that your activity is totally free. Sometimes we actually say that quite directly ("Try this out! It's totally free for everyone!"). Sometimes we tell adults that we're teaching our students how to talk with people and ask if they would be willing to help us out. Sometimes we lead with a giveaway and then move to the demo ("We're giving away some stickers! Here! Do you want to try our game?").

Once you've engaged with a few people, it is usually easier to engage with the next few. Mostly that's just a property of crowd mentality. If people see others having a good time doing something, then they will be interested in checking out what's going on. You don't need to pitch to new people – your satisfied customers are doing the pitching for you! And the more people you talk with, the easier it gets to have these conversations, and the more comfortable you will be approaching more people for the next iteration.

We recommend being conscientious about inclusivity in both your pitches and the conversations that follow. Don't assume that people who look a particular way won't be interested in your activity. Instead, pitch to people who are every gender, every skin color, every age, wearing every kind of religious marker. If someone is at your location, whether that's a festival, a museum, a library, or anywhere else, you should assume that they are open to learning something from you. It is more likely that these people are worried that you don't want to talk to them. So send them all the signals you can that you welcome all kinds of people at your activity. Your goal is to spread your love of language science, and you should want everybody to enjoy it as much as you do.

If you find yourself talking to only one or only a few kinds of people, try giving yourself a pitching rule. Maybe you'll pitch to every person who comes within four feet of you. Maybe you'll pitch to every third person who walks through the entrance. Maybe you'll pitch to everyone you see who is wearing green. So long as your rule will identify people in a reasonably arbitrary way, it will help you approach a real diversity of people and not just those you feel most comfortable with.

Even after you've started your conversation, you should still strive to be inclusive. If you're talking to a group of people, make sure that everyone within the group gets a chance to speak. Direct your juicy questions to different members of the group, and make sure everybody gets some hands-on time with your materials. Don't just talk to the most sophisticated person in the group or entertain the least sophisticated person. Don't just engage with the most dominant or the most enthusiastic person. It's fine to explain your activity multiple times in different ways to the different people in the group. What's most important is that everybody feel like they got to participate.

Some Guiding Principles

Of course, if you are successful at attracting a diverse range of people to your activity, then you have to have some idea about how you're going to have a good conversation with different kinds of people! Exactly how you shift your conversation to match with your audience will depend on what you're talking about, who you're talking with, and who you are. But we can suggest a few principles that will help.

Know Your Goals

In Chapter 4, we talked about the importance of having specific goals. This clarity on your goals will help with audience design a lot. Remember that experts in informal science learning laid out six core goals (or strands). Keeping these goals in mind will help you focus your activity for different people. And just to remind you what those are, we're listing them again!

Strand 1: Generate interest and excitement.
Strand 2: Celebrate scientific knowledge.
Strand 3: Foster observations, explorations, and questions.
Strand 4: Invite people to reflect on science as a process.
Strand 5: Collaborate in using the tools of science.
Strand 6: Encourage people to think of themselves as science learners and as potential scientists.

Not every activity will be equally good at accomplishing all six goals, but you should have a clear idea about how best to use your activity to accomplish as many of these goals as possible. Now combine what you know about how your activity works with what you know about your audience.

If you are talking with a young child, then your main goal might be to generate interest and excitement. If you are talking with an older child, then your goals might include teaching content and fostering observations and questions. If you're working with a group of people of different ages, you might target different parts of your activity to different people in the group. For example, if your activity demonstrates articulatory phonetics, you might encourage the younger children to hold their nose and/or tongue while they say different words (it's fun to do and gets kids excited!). For older children, you can ask the juicy questions that link the fun activity to the content: What kinds of words sound the same/funny when you hold your nose? Can you figure out what those words have in common? A discussion about which words are affected by blocking different articulators leads naturally into explaining how linguists define sounds partly in terms of the place of articulation. And if you have older or more informed people in the group, this point might lead to a discussion of what a phoneme is.

You can think about these strands as creating a kind of scaffold like what we described in Chapter 15. At the foundation of your scaffold is the first strand: Generate excitement. As you move to a more advanced (higher) floor in your scaffold, you can foster observations, explorations, and questions. Introducing content is also something on a mid-level floor of your scaffold. The strands centering on connecting the demo experience to science as a process is on a higher floor yet. Different members of your audience will respond better to different strands. Know your goals and focus on the ones that fit best with the audience you have in that particular conversation.

Think about What's Given and New for Different People

Following the general principles from Chapter 11, you will want to organize your activity so that you're presenting familiar information (given) before you present new information. But also remember that what counts as given and new will be different for different people. Our funds of knowledge differ. So just as you will have different goals in mind for different people, you should also keep in mind that your explanations will need different starting places for different people. Luckily, this principle works well in tandem with the previous one. Just in general, talking about phenomena is a good way to generate excitement **and** it's a good way to establish some common ground that you can build off of. The scaffold that you build to help you move from one goal to the next will also scaffold the information that you want to deliver.

And remember that it's always fine to start at the foundational level. If you're talking with a child, you should assume that no information is given and begin at the very beginning. And for a young child, the lowest foundational rung of the ladder may well be as far as you go. But it is also fine to start at the bottom of the scaffold even if you're talking with someone who needs very little scaffolding. Just be aware that you can move swiftly up the scaffolding if you're talking with someone with more expertise.

Plan Ahead

One element that is embedded into the last two principles is planning! You don't want to figure out how the different pieces of your activity best satisfy the different goals or which information is most familiar while you are having a conversation with people. You'll be more comfortable and they'll be less confused if you figure that out before you start. As Chapter 16 shows, part of creating a good activity is having a plan for how your conversation will go. You should know your goals, know your content, and know different ways to make your activity interesting and connected to the real world. The more you've figured out ahead of time, the more flexible you can be with different people.

If you have a plan, then when you're talking with an individual or a group of people, you can consciously focus on the audience design part of the process. Are you talking with a little boy who is eager to see something shiny? What's in your plan that could get him excited? Are you talking with a grandmother who is curious about why anybody studies this topic? What's in your plan that connects to the real world? Are you talking with a family group with kids of varying ages? How can you order your content so you go from simplest to most complex?

Audience design is never easy, but if you have a good plan in your head – a plan that lets you choose your goals, organize your information, and make connections to the real world – then you can treat the problem like a matching game. Where does this person link to your plan? Of course, you may match someone wrong and focus on the wrong part of your activity. To figure out if you've done that and therefore that you need to focus on a different part of the plan, remember the advice from Chapter 10: Listen to what people say to you. People will give you feedback about what they need. If you have a plan, you will know how to use that feedback!

Some Completely Different Audiences

Throughout this book, we have focused on how to talk with the general public in a free-choice learning environment such as a museum or a festival. In Chapter 1, we explained why we chose this focus. First, these are important locations where a lot of people do a lot of learning. Second, we ourselves have the most experience working with people who visit these locations, and so have the most useful advice to offer for these settings. Third, they are challenging to work in: If you can succeed here, you will have mad skills! And finally, they are places where you'll get lots of opportunities to practice and receive lots of feedback – so you'll have great opportunities to improve.

The lessons from this book apply to other kinds of audiences as well. If you are an effective communicator in the context of a cultural festival, then you already have a lot of the tools that you need to be effective with other kinds of audiences as well. The guiding principles you'll need beyond informal learning venues are actually just the same: Know your goals, Think about what's given and new for your audience, and Have a plan.

Applied Audiences

One kind of audience you might want to talk with are people who actually use knowledge from your science in their work. With language examples, you might want to talk with a teacher about how children learn words. Or you might want to talk with a principal about the value of bilingual education. Or you might want to talk with a lawyer about how dialect influences the believability of a witness. Or you might want to talk with a policy maker about translation practices for new immigrants.

One of the biggest differences between talking with these kinds of audiences and with people in an informal learning venue is that the conversational goals are likely to differ. Often your goal in these contexts will be more about advocacy or activism. You don't just want to get people interested in your topic; you want them to believe something specific about it. To be effective with this kind of audience, you will want to consider very carefully the question of real-world relevance. Why should these people care about your point of view? How does understanding your science better help them? You'll want to be very focused on what your audience cares about so you can make it clear how your knowledge is going to be useful to them.

In Chapter 9, we emphasized the principle that incomplete ≠ incorrect. This matters for these audiences too. If you have something useful to contribute to an applied question, then you will want to state that clearly and straightforwardly. You will almost certainly need to omit a lot of details, a lot of nuance, and a lot of qualifications. You will definitely not be giving people a complete understanding of your topic. But just because you don't talk about everything doesn't mean that what you do say is wrong. You can mention that things get more complicated when you dive into all the details, but what will be persuasive is a clear generalization.

Having a plan is absolutely critical for these other audiences. And in order to be prepared to talk with applied audiences, you need to do your homework. If you're trying to persuade someone, you should know what their current point of view is and why they hold it. What really matters for this audience? It will be imperative that you make your science relevant to their interests, so make sure you know what those are!

Academic Audiences

We often think that academic audiences are composed of people who are a lot like you – they are people who are interested in and knowledgeable about a particular science. And if you go to a language science conference (or an oral defense related to an advanced degree), that may well be true. But there are lots of people in the academy who you may want to talk with who are outside of your immediate field, and talking with them is not that different from talking with the general public. If you are talking with the dean of your college or the president of your university, that person is probably very smart, but odds are that their academic background is different from yours. Even if you're talking with people who you think should have the same background as you – say, you're giving a talk at a seminar or a departmental job talk – it's still the case that many people in your audience will know different things from you. That means that it's up to you to communicate your topic effectively! How can you do that? Use what you know about having a successful conversation with the general public.

Start by knowing your goals. One goal that many people really do have with an academic audience (especially for something like a job talk audience) is to show off how smart they are. Proving you are smart is something you should never have as a goal in an informal learning setting, but establishing your credentials is truly a part of what people expect from a job talk. Still, just being smart isn't going to get you hired. You will do better if you can also show people why your research is exciting and interesting, and you'll do even better if people feel like they can understand what you did and that you are open to discussion. So actually, the goals of informal learning are still pretty useful to keep in mind.

One thing that people often misjudge about talking with academics is what is given and what's new. Far less is given than you may think! Just because academics are experts in one area doesn't mean they are knowledgeable about your topic. In fact, presumably the reason they want to hear from you in the first place is because you know something that they don't! The curse of knowledge that we discussed in Chapter 12 can be especially strong in the academy. If you've just read six journal articles that all use the same technical vocabulary, you may forget that not everybody uses that jargon. Always define your technical terms, and always always always define any abbreviations you use.

Everyone in the academy – students and faculty – has had the experience of listening to an academic presentation and not understanding it. Sometimes the problem is with you as a listener: There are presentations designed solely for high-level experts in a field, and if you aren't one, then you won't get it. It's OK that not every chemist can follow a talk in the music department and vice versa. Academic talks do have relatively narrow target audiences.

But if you are the intended target audience, then you should understand it. If you don't, then the fault isn't with you. Sometimes the fault is with the speaker: The speaker is trying too hard to prove they are smart and not hard enough to be understood. As one of our graduate advisors liked to say: If people don't understand you, that's **your** fault. Being impenetrable isn't a sign of intelligence. It could be a sign of arrogance – maybe the speaker doesn't care if their audience understands them. It could be a sign of duplicity – maybe the speaker has something to hide and is being difficult to understand so you can't tell for sure. Or it could just be a sign of communicative incompetence – maybe the speaker just doesn't know how to explain things clearly.

None of those things are good things to be. The people who are considered **really** smart are almost always good communicators. Even in the academy!

Practice, Practice, Practice

If you're working in an informal learning venue, practice and feedback are built into the process. Each conversation with a new person is pretty short, and you'll have similar conversations over and over (and over) again. By paying attention to how people respond to you, you'll get a lot of feedback about what's working and then you'll get lots more opportunities to practice.

However, if you're talking to an applied audience or an academic audience, your interactions won't be as repetitive. But that doesn't mean you can skip the practicing part. It just means that you'll have to do it ahead of time. You should practice any presentation many times before you actually give it. It doesn't matter how long or short your presentation is. Whether you're practicing the two-minute elevator pitch, the ten-minute advocacy speech, or the forty-five-minute job talk, you should practice over and over (and over) again before you do any presentation for real. Some of your practicing can be done alone in front of a mirror, but ideally some of it should be done in front of a sympathetic audience who can give you feedback. Hard work can make you an effective communicator. Don't skip the work!

CRITICAL TAKE-HOME MESSAGE

Be prepared to talk with a lot of different kinds of people by knowing your goals, thinking about what's given and new for different people, and having a plan.

WORKED EXAMPLE BOX

Our *ghoti* demo is about English spelling. Here's how we might spin it differently for different audiences.

At a museum

First, we spark interest by using an example often (and probably wrongly) attributed to George Bernard Shaw: How would you pronounce the word *ghoti*? Most people say something like "goat-y." We then show them how the letters can be pronounced in different contexts: enough, two women, nation. If those letters were pronounced the same way in *ghoti*, then the pronunciation would be "fish."

For elementary-school children, we make the connection to their real-world experience of spelling tests: This is an extreme example of how English letters don't always link up to sounds. And that is our Critical Take-Home Message: Letters are not sounds.

For older children and adults, we ask them to think about the pros and cons of English spelling. The complicated mapping between letters and sounds is usually brought up as the big con. The pros come out when we bring up something like dialect (Would we really want people in the northern and southern United States to spell the word *pie* differently?). Another pro is the way that spelling can show how some words are clearly related even if you can't hear it in the sounds (*hymn/hymnal; practice/practical; sign/signature*). Those funny spellings help you find other kinds of information.

And for those who are still interested, we might bring up the International Phonetic Alphabet (IPA) and talk about how language scientists need a way to represent sounds for all the world's spoken languages – even ones they don't know. English spelling is doing too many other things for it to be very good at capturing the full range of sounds across languages. Not to mention the fact that some languages have sounds that English doesn't!

For a politician contemplating a spelling reform bill

Reforming English spelling so that each letter represents a single sound is something that periodically captures the public eye. If a politician were considering supporting a bill to change the way we spell words, we might want to use some of the key points from our activity to argue against it.

Something that might matter to a politician would be the regional tensions that might arise. What might happen to national unity if people in different parts of the country not only pronounced words differently

(cont.)

but also spelled them differently (reflecting their pronunciation)? We might even suggest the possibility that if spellings started dividing along regional dialect lines, we might foster a sense of difference between different regions. It could be possible eventually that children wouldn't be able to read the same texts all around the country.

For the principal of a school

Teaching kids how to spell correctly is hard, and thanks to spell-check programs, it can feel like an old-fashioned skill to have. If a principal were looking into how to revise her school's spelling-relevant curriculum, this activity might have some features that could help guide the process.

Some points that might matter for an educator would be the idea that spelling isn't just about arbitrary rules but reflects a fundamental connection between speech sounds and written symbols. Learning that you can represent your speech visually is an important thing in and of itself. Working through the places where letters do and do not match sounds can help children think about how that symbolic connection works. Another point that might matter is the idea that English spelling doesn't just represent sounds, it also represents meaning information that allows children to see connections among words. The connection between *practice* and *practical* is hidden in the sounds, but the spelling helps kids see that those words should have similar meanings.

For the dean when you're applying for a job

Deans usually care about whether your research topic will allow you to get funding and academic publications. If your research is on spelling (or alphabetic systems, or reading more generally), then you might consider using the *ghoti* example as a way to create a striking memory with the dean about your work. *Ghoti* shows us how the history of English is alive and well and living inside of how we currently spell things. It shows us that there is both a bottom-up level to reading (involving letter-to-sound correspondences) and a top-down level (involving meaning-based connections that cut across the lexicon and different dialects). *Ghoti* shows us that there is no way to make a perfect symbolic representation of speech that preserves all of the information that we know about a word – there are always trade-offs between being accurate to the sounds of an individual item and representing an idealized notion of the word across people and situations.

CLOSING WORKSHEET

Reflect on the core lessons of working in a free-choice learning setting: know your goals, consider what's given and what's new for different people, and have a plan. Now, how could you talk about your doable demo topic in a job interview? How could you explain your doable demo topic to your parents or friends?

Further Reading

1 *Applied audiences*

The American Association for the Advancement of Science (AAAS) has compiled a range of articles about different aspects of science advocacy: www.aaas.org/page/center-research. For a more corporate perspective that provides lots of very concrete advice about being persuasive, we recommend *Made to Stick* by the brothers Chip and Dan Heath: https://heathbrothers.com/books/made-to-stick/ (Heath & Heath, 2006). Regardless of whether one is selling good science or the latest widget, it turns out that experts recommend very similar techniques, such as being concrete and using compelling examples, sticking to the point, and not overwhelming people with information. These bits of advice may sound familiar to you if you've been reading this book closely!

2 *Academic audiences*

The Linguistic Society of America runs an annual event called the "Five Minute Linguist" where professional language scientists give brief talks that are supposed to be understandable for everyone in the room. A particularly awesome example of this talk was given in 2019 by linguist Ai Taniguchi (www.utm.utoronto.ca/language-studies/people/ai-taniguchi). You can watch her here: www.youtube.com/watch?v=8Qbqr17L6OY&t=3695s.

3 *An example wrongly attributed to George Bernard Shaw*

The evidence suggests that G. B. Shaw was not the first person to use the *ghoti* example, and in fact, he might never have actually used it at all. You can read about it all here in an article by Ben Zimmer (Zimmer, 2010): www.nytimes.com/2010/06/27/magazine/27FOB-onlanguage-t.html. (Fair warning: The *New York Times* has a paywall and only allows you to read a limited number of articles for free.) We don't necessarily like to maintain the misattribution to Shaw, but since it's a fairly commonly believed myth, it's good to know of it.

4 *Spelling reform*

Probably the most famous attempt to reform English spelling was advanced by Noah Webster (of dictionary fame). Most of his proposed changes were never adopted, but his efforts are one of the reasons for transatlantic differences in spelling words like *color/colour* and *center/centre*.

18 Where Can I Go?

OPENING WORKSHEET

Where can anyone who lives in your community go to learn new things? Try to think broadly – people definitely do learn things in school, but they also learn things in other places! What informal learning settings exist where you live? Jot down a couple of specifics.

Hint: If you don't know where to start, try looking at a tourism website for your local community. Or do a web search on your town's name and words like *museum*, *festival*, and *fun activity*.

If you've been playing along so far, by now you should have put together an activity designed to engage people in a demonstration of your science – perhaps most likely a language science. You've got some materials, some core points, a plan for how to engage with different people that includes questions to ask and to answer, and you've practiced with your friends and family members. You're ready to take this thing live with the general public! So, where can you go to do that? And what do you actually **do** at these venues?

The short answer is that there are lots of opportunities for doing this kind of work if you are open-minded. As for what you do at such venues, that will depend on where you go. As Chapter 19 emphasizes, it's important to be a good partner with the people who organize these opportunities, no matter who they are. In this chapter, we'll talk about some types of places to look for, offer resources for how to find a specific place or event, and address a few practical concerns. We'll also talk about how to modify your activity to make it ideal for different kinds of venues.

We introduced in Chapter 1 the work of science learning experts John Falk and Lynn Dierking. Examining science education over the lifetime, these scholars have found that people from all over the world enjoy a variety of free-choice opportunities to learn about science. Relevant opportunities can be found in libraries, zoos, and aquariums; and a variety of museums, including natural history museums, children's museums, and museums explicitly focused on science or technology. We have also added to these institutions some emphasis on event-based opportunities, including science festivals but also other kinds of festivals. Arts festivals, book festivals, food festivals, children's festivals, and cultural or heritage festivals all have room for public engagement around language (and activities showing off other sciences as well).

Look Close to Home!

Many people reading this book may be affiliated with an educational institution. Although the primary business of schools is formal education, many have a variety of programs that involve informal education for different kinds of people. Such programs may intersect with institutions and events such as those just noted.

One of the populations that colleges and universities care about is their own students. Many schools have cross-campus events that aim to inform their students about different majors or activity groups. Many departments run events aimed at attracting new majors. Dormitories often run programs aimed at expanding the horizons for freshmen. The engagement activity that you put together through this book's worksheets is likely to be a good advertisement for your favorite science-oriented department, and can help you attract new students and/or impress your peer group.

Another population that colleges and universities care about is school-aged children. Many colleges and universities run summer camps for middle schoolers and high schoolers. What's often called a diversity and inclusion office in the United States might run a program to expose youngsters to life in college. There may also be on-site day care centers or after-school programming for children connected with your institution. Ideally, you've made a doable demo that supports good conversations with children of many ages, so any of these kinds of programs could be a good place to engage with people.

On the other end of the spectrum, many colleges and universities also have programming aimed at older adults. These programs may involve talks on campus, social events, or going into nursing homes and community centers. Just as an ideal activity should allow you to talk with children of many ages, so too should it allow you to talk with adults of many ages!

And for some colleges and universities, reaching out to the general public is an important part of their overall mission. This is certainly true if

Figure 18.1 Ohio State University students at Westfest, a university-sponsored science festival

you are at a large university that is part of a national or statewide (in the United States) system. Many of these institutions have an entire office devoted to public outreach and engagement. That kind of an office can help you get connected with all kinds of activities happening on your campus and in your community. If your institution supports this kind of work with small grants, you may find opportunities to get funding for engagement work too!

If you are yourself a member of a college or university community, getting involved with a school-sponsored program is usually pretty easy. We recommend searching through your institution's website. Sometimes it will be easy to find upcoming events whose organizers are looking for people to join them. But sometimes you will instead find programs that have happened in the past. Don't despair if you only find old listings for programs! Check those pages for local contacts and get in touch. Even if someone else is now running that program, you will often be able to find them through the former organizers. Also, it is our experience that while specific programs and events do come and go, the people who work on them often stay the same over time.

RESOURCE LIST: RELEVANT COLLEGE AND UNIVERSITY OFFICES

Every college and university will have a range of offices that aim at connecting with the general public. We have provided a few links to relevant offices at our own home institutions, but every institution works a bit differently. So, these are just examples to help you see the kinds of programs we mentioned in the main text.

- Offices that target student life (incoming students, student activities, dorm life):
  https://housing.osu.edu/get-involved/
  https://orientation.arizona.edu/
- Offices that target lifelong education (for seniors, for community members, for alumni):
  https://asa-tucson.org/lifelong-learning/
  https://olli.arizona.edu/
- Offices that support primary and secondary school programming (after-school programs, summer programs, events to encourage students to come to college, programs for teachers):
  https://science.arizona.edu/community-engagement/k-12-educators
- Offices that promote community engagement or outreach:
  https://engage.osu.edu/
  https://sbs.arizona.edu/community
- Individual departments with engagement efforts (including attracting new majors, or engaging with the general public about their topic area):
  https://u.osu.edu/apop/

Check Out Local Informal Learning Venues in Your Community

Since informal learning is something that happens (by definition!) outside of a formal learning institution, it might also help to think about places in your local community where people go to learn about different things.

If you want to stay close to a school or school-like setting, consider looking into programming run by your local primary and secondary school systems. Many schools run after-school programs and other events where they welcome people who want to add educational value. Other places run after-school programs as well. Consider looking at your local YMCA or YWCA, the Girl Scouts, and local community centers. And don't forget about continuing education! There is also lots of programming out there

Figure 18.2 An Ohio State University student prepared to talk about hearing loss during a Deaf Awareness Day event at the COSI museum

for older adults through community centers, assisted living facilities, and nursing homes.

You can also look for well-established centers of informal learning, such as science museums and children's museums. Many of these kinds of institutions have volunteer programs where people regularly come and do activities with whatever public they target. Some of these places even have special programs aimed at bringing scientists into their space to share their work. However, even if your local museums don't have such programs, you can always approach them to see if they might be interested in starting one. But be aware: Many of these institutions will have their **own** activities for public engagement. Also, their programming is typically handled by museum professionals who are already very savvy about the emphases in this book. If you want to bring your special science activity into their space, you will likely need to work with staff members there well ahead of time to make sure that they are OK with it. We hope you consider such an opportunity a privilege as well because you can learn much of value from these professionals.

Another informal learning institution that is likely in your hometown is the public library. Libraries do far more than lend books – they support a great variety of programming relevant to the community. If you're interested in working with children, try contacting a children's librarian and see if your demo might integrate with the library's story-time sessions. Libraries also support programming for adults – they run book clubs, sponsor lectures, provide skill-building classes. Language science isn't very far away from the core mission of libraries (spreading literacy and the joy of reading), and many language activities will fit right in with this mission.

A relatively recent development on the informal learning scene is the Science Café. Despite the name, these events are often held in bars and pubs. They are fun and intriguing programs for people who just want to learn something about science while enjoying a beer. These people are very much like the Explorers at science museums that we talked about in Chapter 5. Often Science Café events are officially set up as venues where you would give a very interactive talk, but their convivial atmosphere makes them great places to introduce more hands-on activities. Plus, you are allowed to use adult-themed content at these venues, which isn't something you get to do at most informal learning locations!

RESOURCE LIST: TIPS FOR CONTACTING AN ESTABLISHED INSTITUTION

It's easy to identify likely institutions (e.g., schools, museums, libraries), but it can be a little trickier to find the right person at each institution to talk with!

Ideally, you are looking for someone in charge of programming (because you have a program activity to do), events (where your activity might fit in), or volunteers (because that's who you are). Alternatively, many of these venues will have a general contact email for all kinds of open queries. It's fine to start there – it's the place where you can ask who the best person to talk to is.

Science Cafés

You can find established Science Cafés here: www.sciencecafes.org/. The same website has information for organizers and for speakers to help you start something up or to slide into something already set up.

Science-Specific Events

One of the easiest type of venues to get involved with is the science festival. There are lots of these – they are affiliated with schools, communities, national organizations, and more. Many of them have some kind of open call where they invite people to join them and provide programming and presentations. At one of the events that include such calls, you'll typically get assigned a designated space where you get to do your activity. The space is often called a booth, but in reality it might be a table or a tent or maybe even just a taped-off bit of the floor. Whatever it is, it's a space you get to turn into a language science oasis.

One thing to be aware of, though, is that some events will charge a fee for you to get a booth. These events take care of all the logistics – including the advertising needed to bring people to them. And that advertising is worth it! The more prominent science events get terrific attendance. If you are affiliated with a college or university organization, you can often get your home institution to help with the fee if there is one (it's good publicity for them to have you doing science with the public). Alternatively, if you are a student, some events will waive the fee for you.

But the great thing about going to science events is that people come to them to do precisely the kinds of activities and have precisely the kinds of conversations that this book concerns. Truthfully, most people don't expect to see language-oriented content at these locations, but they will be very open to learning about the science of what you do!

Figure 18.3 A scene at a USA Science and Engineering Festival
Note. The University of Arizona's booth at a festival in Washington, DC, that sees many thousands of visitors. Thanks are due to the National Science Foundation for supporting this booth.

RESOURCE LIST: SCIENCE FESTIVALS

There are lots of science festivals out there – far too many to try and list them all! Instead, we've provided links to some sites that provide lists of such events (and descriptions of them) in various parts of the world. You will surely find one near you (or near somewhere you want to travel to).

www.isbglasgow.com/18-biggest-science-fairs-and-festivals-in-the-world/
https://sciencefestivals.org/festivals/
www.astc.org/astc-dimensions/science-festivals-celebrations-of-science-around-the-world/

Non-Science Events

We've emphasized the scientific study of language in this book, but of course, language is a cultural artifact that is critical to our experience of arts and humanities. One big advantage of this multifaceted nature of language is that your engagement activities will fit in well in lots of venues that aren't necessarily oriented to the sciences. You can consider festivals and fairs devoted to specific cultural groups, food, music, community activism, literacy, art, and more. Your local county or state fair is also a great place to consider. And don't be afraid to get creative! You can even find booths devoted to talking about sciences at popular culture venues, renaissance fairs, and *Star Trek* conventions.

Most of these events encourage booths devoted to education and entertainment, and they likely have some kind of online application for prospective programming. It's generally good to check out their websites several months ahead of time so you can register properly and find out more about the schedule and other requirements for the event.

One thing to keep in mind about these kinds of events is that they will have some stated focus, and it's unlikely to be science. To help you keep your activity relevant to the interests of the people at the event, you may need to tweak it some. Often you don't have to change very much, but these changes will make a big difference. One thing that is easy to change is the example items you use. If you're going to an agricultural fair, consider using words and sentences related to farm animals. For example, if your doable demo is on regular rules in morphology, then you can illustrate regular plurals with cows and ducks and irregular ones with oxen and geese! If you're going to a Greek festival, consider incorporating some specific Greek language facts into your activity. For example, if your doable demo uses the International

Figure 18.4 Teaching Navajo demo at the Tucson Festival of Books
Note. This University of Arizona student made traditional Navajo bread dough while teaching festival-goers some words in Navajo.

Phonetic Alphabet (IPA), you could start by contrasting the English and Greek alphabets.

We also recommend finding an educational point that is especially relevant for the venue you are in. If you're at a festival devoted to books, think about what your activity has to say about literacy. If you're at a music festival, think about what your activity has to say about the relationship between language and music. In the Worked Example Box, you'll see a few ideas about how to shift your activity to connect it to different venues.

RESOURCE LIST: CULTURAL FESTIVALS OF ALL SORTS

There are even more non-science festivals and similar events out there than science ones! We recommend that you start with your local tourism board to check out the ones that are in your hometown. And here are a few lists of festivals out there in case you need some ideas.

https://en.wikipedia.org/wiki/List_of_festivals_in_the_United_States
www.travelawaits.com/category/3093/activities-and-interests-festivals-and-special-events/
https://en.wikipedia.org/wiki/List_of_festivals_in_Europe
https://allexciting.com/culture-art-festivals-europe/
https://en.wikipedia.org/wiki/List_of_festivals_in_Asia

Practical Concerns

As you can see, there are lots of different kinds of places where you can do your activity. How do you choose? Here we offer some practical things to keep in mind when you're weighing your choices. Which ones matter most to you will depend on who you are and what kinds of resources you have access to. But it's useful to think about the full range of issues so you're making an informed choice.

One-Time Event vs Recurring Events vs Established Venues

How often do you want to do this kind of work? If you're just dipping a toe into the water, you might want to start with a single visit at an annual fair or festival that has well-established protocols for new applicants. Such an event will likely take up one whole day (or maybe just an afternoon) of your life, and then you can decide later if you want to do it again. But if you are trying to develop a regular presence in some community, then you might want to look for events that recur more often – like a weekly after-school program or story time at the library. Working more regularly will give you more practice (or will give your students more practice), but it means you have to put in a larger time commitment overall.

Established venues like science museums or children's museums often have one-time events (like an "ask a scientist" event) where you can try things out. But these institutions are often also open to the possibility of creating a regular gig where you can come and do your activity on a recurring basis. Most museums don't have dedicated programs to help you with that, so if you want an ongoing presence at one of their events, you will have to do a bit of work to build a relationship with the museum staff. In Chapter 19, we'll talk about how to be a good partner with such venues and the people who you collaborate with in order to participate in their programming. Building a long-term connection requires you to do all the things a good partner does, but in a somewhat more intensive manner. You should expect that it will take a substantial time commitment.

Registration, Rules, and Fees

As we noted, going to a one-time event requires a fairly low time commitment. However, you do need to make sure that you come prepared! Annual events often require you to register months in advance, and you might even have to submit a description of what you are planning on doing or a blurb to be used for advertising your booth. You can't just walk into one of these events on the day they happen and expect to be allowed to offer your activity. Some events, especially large national ones, are competitive – more people want to offer programs than they have space for. Many smaller events are happy to have lots of activities, but they still will want to know ahead of time who will be coming.

Also be aware that all of these places will have rules of one sort or another. They may have a general dress code or require that you wear one of their T-shirts. They may require that your booth be staffed whenever the event is going on. They may only allow you in for certain hours to get set up. They may charge you for "extras" (and those extras could be as simple as electricity or access to your assigned space ahead of time). They may expect you to give away small prizes with your activity, or they may prohibit you from giving away small prizes.

Even if you're looking at a program in a local institution such as your own school or a library nearby, you should expect that there will be some rules to follow. We'll talk a bit more in Chapter 19 about why this is so. But if you are interested in being able to return to a venue for another event, it is critical that you follow their rules.

In addition, many venues, especially fairs and festivals, charge fees in order for you to work there. Fee structures vary dramatically depending on a range of factors: How big is the event? Do they charge their audience to attend? What kind of space are they in? What resources will they be giving you? We have worked at events that have no fees at all as well as events that cost us a thousand dollars to have a booth. These places aren't shy about what the rules and the fees are – most of it will be found on their websites or told to you explicitly.

But don't despair if there is a fee involved! If the fee is large, then most likely the venue is better suited for a whole team (probably sponsored by a faculty member or department). In that case, you may qualify for an educational discount or be able to get your home institution to pay for you to be there. Public outreach is a desirable activity for the academy, and you might be doing them a favor that they are willing to pay for.

Space and Other Resources

The venues we have mentioned vary dramatically in terms of the space and other resources you will have access to. A typical sized space at a festival is about six feet square, and you might be expected to stay inside your zone. You're likely to get a folding table and a few chairs to work with, but often there won't be a designated place for you to safely store equipment and so on. A big tablecloth makes that space under the table useful in this regard. If the event is indoors, you might have access to electricity, but if it is outdoors, you might not. Usually, if you're outdoors, you'll have some kind of overhead protection to help with the sun or rain. Internet access is also something that varies a lot by location. You should always feel free to ask the organizers what the situation is so you don't have any unfortunate surprises when you get there.

If you're working in a venue that is not specifically dedicated to doing these kinds of activities, like a school or library or dormitory common room or bar, then you will have access to whatever is typically in those spaces. Electricity is likely to be there and so is the internet. But you might need to get creative about your physical arrangement – you could be working on the floor or on a comfy couch surrounded by people. If your activity does have critical physical constraints (e.g., you need a table to lay out some cards, or electricity, or space to set up a map or a poster), then make sure you discuss that with the venue ahead of time.

Audience

A big difference across these venues is the nature of the audience. As we noted in earlier chapters and as the Worked Example Box shows, some of these venues have a topical focus and you can expect that your audience is there because they have some interest in that specific topic. These people are very much like the Hobbyists that we talked about in Chapter 5. Different venues also attract different audiences, so if there is some group you especially do (or do not) want to interact with, choose your location wisely.

Some audience differences will be pretty obvious – you'll find kids at after-school programs and library story times; you'll find college students at university functions; you'll find older adults at nursing homes. And different kinds of cultural events often attract very diverse audiences: A Juneteenth celebration is likely to have a lot of African American attendees, while a Cinco de Mayo festival is likely to have a lot of Mexican American attendees.

But sometimes there are other, less obvious factors that might matter to you. Some venues attract primarily high-income attendees while others bring in a more economically diverse crowd. For example, many museums have high admission fees that restrict who can attend them. But many of these same museums also run free events or have days with discounted admission fees.

It is perfectly OK to ask the people in charge of your target venue what kind of people you can expect to encounter. They will know if their programming attracts low- or high-income families, monolingual or multilingual individuals, old people or young people, locals or tourists. As we discussed in Chapter 7, a great way to make your activity relevant is to connect it to people's regular lives. But in order to do that effectively, it does help to know a little bit about what those lives might look like.

Your Logistics

A final set of things to think about is what makes sense **for you**. You'll want to think about what's involved with doing your activity and what kind of resources you have to make this happen.

Some people have activities that are quite extensive and require special equipment. We've done an activity where we record people saying their names, make a spectrogram of the recording, and then print the image out for them. Doing this activity requires a computer with easy-to-use speech analysis software such as Praat, some connecting cables, a printer and paper, extra ink, electricity, and a table to put everything on. We also find it's useful to have some markers around so that we (or the guest) can write extra things on the printout (such as the person's name in the IPA or in a traditional spelling). And sometimes we bring along IPA charts so we can talk a bit more about how linguists think about speech sounds with people who are interested.

That's a lot of stuff to bring to a venue! When we bring that spectrogram activity to an event, we think a lot about how we're going to transport our materials, who's going to carry what, and what the venue will supply (electricity is an absolute must for this one!). We also think about how far we might have to carry heavy things, how we're going to protect our materials when we take a lunch break, and how we're going to control our materials so little children don't accidentally break anything.

Our answers end up largely being common sense (we like plastic bins with labels on them, we try to find out layouts of event spaces ahead of time, and we make sure everyone on our team knows what they are responsible for). But having a plan for how to work the details will make everything go more smoothly.

RESOURCE LIST: A CHECKLIST OF USEFUL THINGS

- Stay organized!
  - Bring a list of materials that you need to do each demo – you don't want to leave anything behind!
  - Label your pieces, including cords, boxes, folders, and miscellaneous electronics.

- Scheduling your people:
  Stagger people's shifts so you don't leave gaps and so there are no abrupt turnovers.
  Have someone in each shift who knows where all the supplies are and how everything works.
  Consider who's comfortable with what languages.
  Build in breaks so individuals can get meals and explore the venue.
- Stuff that's always useful:
  Tape – duct tape, masking tape, Scotch tape.
  Power cords and/or chargers for everything you're using. Also consider an extension cord and power strip.
  Pens, markers, clipboards, binder clips, small boxes to organize items.
  Peppermints or lemon drops – and encourage people to bring water bottles!
  A large tablecloth (it makes the space look better and will help hide your stuff).
- Promotional items:
  Consider bringing T-shirts, signs, or banners that advertise your school (or any other sponsor you might have).
  Small items related to your demo that you can give away.

You might discover that you can't make a reasonable plan for all kinds of venues. If you have a lot of equipment, then you might want to restrict yourself to venues that you can drive a car to (as opposed to going by plane or train). If your team is very small (maybe you're a team of one!), then maybe you want to design an activity that involves fewer items or involves very lightweight materials. If you are terrified of working with children, maybe you want to stay away from venues where they are the primary audience. There is no one right answer for what makes a particular venue a good one for you to work at. It always depends on what makes sense for you and your team.

CRITICAL TAKE-HOME MESSAGE

When you're looking for places to reach the general public, there are many options. Do your homework to find out the rules, and be flexible about the range of places you might work.

WORKED EXAMPLE BOX

How can you take an activity and modify it so that it feels more relevant for different venues?

The McGurk effect

In Chapter 14, we laid out how to do this activity. To remind you, the Critical Take-Home Message for this demo is that our perception of speech sounds is not just an auditory act done by the ears; it is done by the brain, which is integrating information across multiple domains. Here we show how you might do the same activity in very different kinds of spaces!

1 College dorm event

Do you want to trick your brain? Can you think of any other places where you're matching auditory and visual speech signals? What about dubbed movies? What about other kinds of visual information, like what a person looks like?

2 A book festival

What can this tell us about the difference between reading a physical book and listening to an audiobook? How does your experience of a book change depending on how you get the words?

3 A Science Café

Ever tried to talk to your friends in a noisy bar? What do you do to help you hear better? What kinds of things do you mishear in a noisy place?

CLOSING WORKSHEET

Find three locations or events where you might be able to do your demo! It's fine if you find some that involve traveling, but make sure at least one of them is close to where you are now.

Write down what you found. Include dates (for events) and information about who to contact for more details, as well as any requirements that you discovered for getting into the location or event. Sketch some logistical details related to your doable demo. For example, do you need to inquire about electricity? Can you bring everything you need for the demo into the venue on your own?

Further Reading

1 *Popular culture venues*

In fact, engaging with people outside of a traditional science venue can be a good way to expand people's minds about science and language. Vaughn James reports interviewing people at different sci-fi fan conventions (like Dragon Con and Awesome Con) where science communicators had set up booths (James, 2020). Many of the fans reported that they found it "eye-opening" to see scientists in this context and the experience made them more interested in trying out more science content.

2 *Having a plan will make things go more smoothly*

Of course, no matter how much you plan, things can still go wrong! While preparing for the Tucson Festival of Books one year, CM's team made a huge board for the syntactic ambiguity demo. We got permission to set it up on the grass several feet out from our tables under a tent that we shared with about a dozen other exhibitors. We practiced for weeks to make sure everyone knew how to use the new and improved board. The first day of the festival was extremely windy, and the festival organizers brought sandbags around for everyone who had this kind of material. But it wasn't enough! The wind picked up our board and blew it onto one of our team. Although we were incredibly glad the board hadn't hit a member of the visiting public, we were seriously concerned for the University of Arizona student (he was fine).

Another year at the same festival, we hauled a huge monitor to our area so we could use materials like the video of the beatboxer and the opera singer more effectively. We hadn't tested this setup outdoors. And, even though we were shaded by a huge tent, the light was so bright that people who could hear these amazing sounds coming out of the speakers couldn't see the associated video on the monitor.

19 Being a Good Partner

OPENING WORKSHEET

Think about some experiences where you have worked with other people – paid or volunteer jobs, group projects in school, sports teams, and so on.

Who do you like to work with? Why?

Write down three things that people do that make them fun or easy to work with.

Who do you **not** like to work with? Why?

Write down three things that people do that make them unpleasant or hard to work with.

This chapter is about how you can be a good partner with the venues you're going to be working at, whether it's a science festival, an art museum, or a university library.

Choose Your Team Wisely

Before you start thinking about how you work with others, it's worth reflecting on who exactly **you** are. While it is possible to do public engagement as a solo act, it generally works better as a team sport. Working with a group of people has a lot of advantages. You get to pool your ideas and give each other feedback on the activities you are developing. Also, watching someone else do 'your' activity can teach you ways to improve it when you do it yourself next. Plus, the best way to develop your conversation skills is to have someone to talk with. Moreover, going into a free-choice learning environment is probably not something you're used to doing and going with a group of people will give you mutual support. A group will also make your presence more visible and more exciting: One person doing an activity is nice; three people doing activities is an event!

And it doesn't hurt that having more people will allow you to maintain a presence even over lunch time and bathroom breaks.

But like any group activity, it will be more fun and more successful if everyone in the group is a team player. In this case, that's going to mean not only that everyone comes when they say they will and prepares their activity ahead of time; it also means that all of you are committed to providing a good public engagement experience. You should all be striving for activities that are interesting and informative; you should all have plans for how you're going to make your topic relevant and have a stockpile of juicy questions to get people talking; you should all be enthusiastic about having real conversations with people. You should also all strive to be supportive of each other.

Having anyone on your team who isn't really trying to have good conversations with people, or who doesn't really care whether people understand what they are saying, or who is listless and bored, is no good. It's not good for team morale, and it will drag down your own sense of fun. It is also not good for building a solid partnership with the venue that you're in. Informal learning venues want you to add value for the people who go there, and if they don't think you're even trying, they won't be enthusiastic about having you back.

Trust Your Partner

When you're working in an informal learning venue, remember that you're on someone else's home turf. Even if you're doing a program at your own university, you're still likely to be working in a part of the school that isn't about the formal classroom. The people who run these informal learning spaces care about them and probably have strong ideas about how they are supposed to work. And if that informal venue is any good, those ideas are probably excellent.

That last bit bears repeating: Ideas about public engagement that we learn from the people who run the very places and events we're trying to join are probably very good ideas! Scientists coming from an academic or industry background have a reputation for parachuting into an informal learning situation and assuming that they know better than do the people who spend their lives educating the general public. Nobody questions whether these scientists know more about their own science than the educators at these venues. But it is critical to realize that scientists are **not** experts in accessible communication. The people who run informal learning institutions are.

What does that mean? It means you should listen to them. In the next section, we'll tell you that you should follow all the practical rules they lay down for you. But it is also important that you listen to them when they offer general advice or feedback about your demo and your interactions with people. If they think you are using words that their target audience might not know, or materials that aren't appropriate for that audience, or that your activity takes too long, or that your materials are a choking hazard – pay attention! They have a lot more experience than you do at working with people who come to these places for fun and learning, and you should trust their judgment about how your activity will go over with the audience that they know well.

It can also help to realize that there are complicated power dynamics between you and the staff at informal learning venues. You might feel that you are contributing a lot: You made an awesome demo, you bring knowledge about your science, and most likely, you are volunteering your time. With that in mind, you might feel like you are owed some kind of special treatment as recognition for what you are doing.

But it's important to think about the situation from the point of view of your partners. They do work hard all the time to minimize risks in their interactions with the public and to make their venue a success. If you're working at a one-time event like a festival, someone had to arrange the physical space and all the booths, organize general staff for the event, address potential safety concerns, advertise the event, coordinate with local officials for scheduling and permits and who knows what else, fundraise to get things going, and much more. If you're working at an established institution like a museum, someone had to make and maintain the ongoing functioning of the venue, train the staff, advertise for visitors, coordinate all the different internal programming, and fundraise.

When you come into these spaces, you are adding value to their mission. But you are just one piece in a very big puzzle. For some of these places, they don't actually need you in particular – they may have lots of options for ways to bring scientific content into their space. In fact, they may see themselves as doing a favor for **you**. Their job is promoting accessible communication with the public, and they are allowing you access to their resources so that you can promote your favorite message.

The staff at these venues won't expect any kind of special treatment from you, but they do deserve your respect and your appreciation. They are not your employees who have created an entire festival just so you can do your demo. They are your partners. Respect their expertise and their opinions about communicating with the public. And treat them like the professionals that they are.

Be a Good Citizen

Nobody likes a party guest who breaks the furniture and won't follow the house rules. Consider yourself a guest at these venues and play nice. It also doesn't hurt to say things like "Please" and "Thank you" to the people who help you out.

You should also trust the staff at these venues about how the logistics work. If they ask for a risk assessment, then address that. If they want you to show up at a certain time, then be there at that time. If they recommend that you stay within your booth's designated area, then stay there. If they don't want you to eat while you're doing your activity, then take your snack and meal breaks somewhere else. Some of their requests and rules may seem arbitrary to you, but have some faith that they reflect lessons the venue has learned from past experience.

Another part of being a good citizen is being positive and enthusiastic about the nature of the place you are in. You are unlikely to be doing language science outreach in a venue that is specifically devoted to language. So learn to make the most of being in an environment that's **not** explicitly about language. We both do a lot of our activities at venues that are geared toward traditional physical sciences such as biology, physics, and chemistry. We've done our activities next to people demonstrating bomb-sniffing mice and people talking about the space shuttle and people controlling what look like the world's funnest explosions. If you are at a cultural festival, you might be surrounded by sculptors, beer makers, booksellers, or klezmer and mariachi bands.

You want to be part of the positive vibe of your venue, so be supportive of the people around you. If you are enthusiastic about your activity, people will come and talk with you and learn from you, no matter who else is around you. But it will undercut your number one goal (to generate interest and excitement) if you are dismissive (or worse, denigrating) of the other attractions around you in the venue. At festivals, we like to check out what is happening at other booths or tables so that we can suggest other fun activities for people to do once they finish with us and so that we can help them find connections to other sciences. We often get ideas for our own work from experiencing how other scientists are sharing other domains. In short, promoting an overall positive community helps everybody there.

And being a good citizen can be a self-interested act. If you want to be invited back (or allowed back) to the venue, it helps if people there remember you well.

It's a Different Conversation: But It's Still a Conversation

The key to being a good partner is, in the end, the same key to successful communication with the public: Have a conversation. The goal of your conversation with a museum professional or festival organizer will be a bit different from what we've been discussing so far. With these conversational partners, your goal is to make sure that each of you understands what the other is contributing and what is expected of you. But the core principles for having a good conversation that we laid out in Chapter 3 still apply!

The first maxim for cooperative conversation is Quality: Tell the truth. In this context, you should be honest about both your own level of experience and the nature of your demo. If you're doing your demo for the very first time, go ahead and tell your partner that! It will help them adjust the amount of information and feedback that they give you. Also be honest about your demo. Be clear about the things you absolutely need to make it work (a table? internet access?) and the things that are genuinely optional (does it have to be a big screen TV, or can you show those movies on an iPad?). Your partner may have to do extra work to get what you ask for, so be respectful of their contribution by only asking for the things your activity truly requires.

The second maxim is Quantity: Say as much as you need to and not more. In this context, that means answering all the questions put to you in a thoughtful manner – whether those questions are on an application form or being asked in person. Don't cut corners and assume that they don't really need all the information that they are requesting. Make sure that you're telling the venue everything they want to know.

The third maxim is Relevance: Stick to the point! For this one, it helps to think about the venue from your partner's perspective. Most likely, they don't need to know the details of the science behind your demo. But they very likely will want to know how many people you're going to have in their space and when those people can be there. Try to think about what is relevant for them, not just for you!

The last maxim is Manner: Be clear. In this context, it is very important to remember that you are coming from a very different background from your partner. That means that what is given and new will be very different for each of you. For example, you may think that it is obvious (a given) what your role is on your team, but that may be news to your partner. For example, at a university, it's pretty common for a faculty member to be in charge of financing engagement activities but for a student to be the person who is doing the organizational work. Your partner may not be clear on who has decision-making powers and who they should be talking to about different issues. On the other side, it may be obvious (a given) to your partner that you will bring small tokens to give away to everyone who you interact with (a sticker, a pen, a small toy), but you might not have expected that at all. In fact, we have found that different venues have very different rules about the use of giveaways. Some forbid it entirely, while others consider it virtually mandatory. Your partner may not realize that you haven't thought about the question one way or another.

The best way to have a smooth partnership is not to have just a single conversation, but instead to have many good conversations with your partner. The more you talk with them, the better you will understand their perspective, and that will make it easier for you to be a good citizen. The reverse is just as true. The more you talk with them, the better they will understand your perspective, and that will make it easier for them to provide good support for your activity. What's most important is that you realize that you are partners – you're in this together and you should be working together to create the best experience for the public.

A Partnership Case Study

In Chapter 1, we mentioned CM's work with Children's Museum Tucson on a demo about vowels and mouth shapes. The way this demo and the related research were developed illustrates our core lessons about trusting your partner as you build such collaborations. This museum was interested in relating play-based engagement to science practices in two- to five-year-olds. The university group had expertise in research and in young children's language development. So far, so good! But the museum's mission and daily operations differed in important ways from what the university-based team was accustomed to.

First, the museum's primary audience was young children **and** their families. So the demo needed to be a game that even toddlers could do and that caretakers could appreciate as well. Also, places like museums do keep an eye on their bottom line, so how fun it was mattered for both the children and the adults who accompanied them. Both partners also wanted the demo to support research on children's science practices and on parents' views of such activities. Although CM's own research focuses on syntax, she and her colleagues decided that an activity based on mouth shapes and speech sounds would address the museum's interests best and that the research would be feasible through a course giving research-focused community experience to university students.

Next, the museum wanted the university-museum co-sponsorship to be clearly identified. Museum staff also wanted to integrate the demo and associated research into the rest of the museum's operations. It wasn't going to be a permanent exhibit, so everything associated with the demo had to fit onto one of the museum's science carts. To make that happen, the university-based team followed the museum's protocols for its own staff who work on roving exhibits (e.g., attire, name tags, signing in and signing out, cart cleaning) and instantiated the museum's core values, such as learning through play and helping families. For example, the university students learned the museum's physical layout so they could direct visitors to bathrooms and water fountains and so on. From the perspective of the museum visitors, the university researchers were the same as museum floor staff, and they behaved accordingly.

Third, the museum wanted the research to maintain their standards for a high-quality visitor experience. For example, this museum uses giveaways to help parents take play-based learning home, so the university team developed a miniature version of the mouth shape game that parents could use later to guide the activities themselves off-site. The museum wanted anyone to be able to engage with the demo when the cart was on the floor, even if they didn't want to participate in the research. The university team therefore had to be able to guide the game as either a conventional science cart activity or as a research study. That the demo needed to be an option for all visitors also required some modifications to the research protocol. For example, some of the museum's visitors did not read or speak English, and modifying the protocol to accommodate these visitors required the university team to do extra work with their ethics review board.

Figuring out the details so they would meet the research standards of the university team and the requirements of the museum took time. The university and museum teams met weekly for several months, alternating locations to learn about each other's spaces and to gain clarity on each other's missions.

The end result was an engaging demo about vowel sounds. A child doing this demo chooses a face on a metal game board. After 'discovering' that the face lacks a mouth, the child and the researcher then 'read' three mouth-shaped magnets, being very silly while exaggerating [i], [u], and [ɔ]. Next, the child finds the mouth shape magnets needed to say the words *see*, *sue*, and *saw* and chooses one. Together, she and the researcher find more words using the vowel represented with that mouth shape. With the [u] mouth for example, three-year-old Spanish-English bilinguals offer words like *blue*, *moo*, *tu*, and *su*. The research component asked parents to observe their children moving their mouths and saying new words to go with different vowels. Parents answered survey questions about their children while observing the demo. The giveaways emphasized that children's moving their mouths and hearing what changes are examples of exploration and observation, science practices that very young children can do and that parents can easily spot and encourage. If parents wanted further discussion, that conversation could also link various ways of playing with various science practices.

Figure 19.1 Vowel mouth shapes demo at Children's Museum Tucson
Note. A child has just put the [ɔ] mouth shape magnet on a face (for the vowel in the word *saw*). The child's mother (with green-cased survey iPad) is leaning over to see her face as a University of Arizona student points to the [ɔ] mouth shape because the survey asked parents to code their children's participation in science practices.

CRITICAL TAKE-HOME MESSAGE

Be a good citizen at the informal learning venues you work at! Bring a good team, play by the rules, and show respect.

WORKED EXAMPLE BOX

In Chapter 18, we covered a few ways that you could tailor your activity to fit with the focus of a particular venue. If you can do that, you are ahead of the game at integrating yourself into your community.

But sometimes, you may want to go even further and choose a topic just so that it will fit into the venue you're working in. Here are some ways that we've developed new content expressly to emphasize a connection with where we were.

(cont.)

- One of us (LW) works regularly in the same venue – the Center of Science and Industry (COSI). Within the museum, there are a variety of permanent exhibits, including one that is devoted to dinosaurs and another one that is devoted to space travel. Neither one of these domains is obviously about language, but interesting links can be found! For example, you may have noticed that we have highlighted a few activities that featured dinosaurs: In Chapter 5 we discussed how to use dinosaur names to do a morphological analysis activity, and in Chapter 16 we discussed an activity about nonlinguistic communication also using dinosaurs. Both of these activities were designed so that we could build off of a popular experience in the museum. In both cases, museum visitors (especially children) are drawn to the activity because they are already thinking about dinosaurs. And they don't seem to mind learning a little bit about language along the way.

  The space travel exhibit in the museum might also seem like a stretch for a language-related point, but some students figured out the angle: astronaut hand signals. It turns out astronauts use a system of hand gestures to communicate information for when they are floating around in space or walking around on the moon. These signals are fun to teach and can lead to interesting discussions about why astronauts need special modes of communication (hint: sound waves need air to travel through!). You can read a bit more about them here: https://mdrs141.weebly.com/blog/eva-hand-signals.
- One of us (CM) volunteers at an agricultural heritage museum called Mission Garden, which features edible plants of the Sonoran Desert in Arizona, California, and Mexico. Mission Garden hosts a variety of demonstrations, including ones about unusual domestic arts. Even in a demonstration of how to make your own liqueur, it is possible to add some language science fun. For example, an easy-to-make liqueur is the Italian favorite, *limoncello*. In Italy, it's obvious what fruit is at the heart of this liqueur because *limone* means lemon in Italian. Interestingly, many Americans call this drink "lemoncello," which suggests that people like such names to be meaningful and also that they have done some morphological analysis of the word! After trying a few other liqueurs made from other fruits growing in this garden, people doing this activity spontaneously name them with terms like "Mexican sweet

(cont.)

lime-cello" and "Seville orange-cello" and "pomegranate-cello." Without flashing a technical term, it's easy for anyone in this conversation to find other examples of the morphological process of back-formation (e.g., *alcoholic, chocoholic, workaholic*; *Watergate, Volgagate, wine-gate*).

CLOSING WORKSHEET

Choose one of the locations or events that you identified in Chapter 18. Think about how you would get involved with that venue so that you could do your doable demo. Consider the following questions:

- What are their rules for getting involved? (If you don't know, see if you can find out!)
- What are their goals? Do they have a mission statement or a description of their aims that you can read?
- Who is their core audience? Who else is likely to be at this venue?
- What will they expect from you? What will they want you to do for them?
- What will they want to know about you? What will they want to know about your activity?
- What can you do for them? How does your activity address their goals?

This will be hard, but we're nearing the end and you've thought about your demo a lot by now. What permutation on your demo might make it fit your target venue especially well?

Further Reading

1 *Treat them like the professionals they are*

Readers wanting to partner with museums will appreciate Alpert (2013). This example-packed guide for starting and stewarding university-museum partnerships also includes lessons that are useful for all partners that differ in core mission, financial model, internal organization, daily operations, and more. One of our favorite examples from this booklet shows how **not** to start (Alpert, 2013, p. 2):

> Hello. My name is Professor __. I'm calling from the __ department at __ University. I was just hoping to get in touch with you today regarding this very large grant proposal that we're putting together and actually submitting by the

> end of the day ... and one thing that was suggested and that would be great would be if we could establish some links with the Museum. If you can give me a call back ...

As Alpert gently notes, this approach launches without a plan or a budget. It assumes that the university-based researcher's schedule and goal are paramount. Just as this book has emphasized learning and respecting your conversational partner's perspective, Alpert's guide suggests something similar for institutional partners. Conversations about each other's perspectives can function as feasibility tests and also strengthen a budding partnership. Even if you're not ready for the parts of this guide concerning research and education grants, this section may help you think about issues such as hidden labor (e.g., training university students on museum protocols) and the value of time management and regular communication.

Another useful resource related to such partnerships is Moore (2021). Leslie Moore is a university researcher who successfully created a partnership with a science museum for a project looking at dual language learners in museum and educational contexts. In this chapter, she describes how she built and maintained the relationship over time. She presents a clear-eyed perspective on both the advantages and the difficulties of these sorts of partnerships.

2 *Venues specifically devoted to language*

While venues devoted to language aren't nearly as common as broader science centers, children's museums, or cultural festivals, a wide range of language-focused venues do in fact exist around the world. In the United States, we have been excited about Planet Word (https://planetwordmuseum.org/). And this collection from the Centre of Norwegian Language and Literature has many other suggestions for museums around the world that feature language (Grepstad, 2018): www.nynorsk.no/wp-content/uploads/2020/02/814-20180314-Language-museums-OG.pdf

3 *Connections to other sciences*

Here's an example of the serendipitous connections we often find in our booth or table assignments. The University of Arizona team once participated in a Summer Science Saturday emphasizing planetary sciences. We were in the Earth-Is-Special room, which featured insects and people. Our team showed that "people are special" because we talk, and one of our activities started with spectrograms. It being largely an astronomy event, we emphasized how spectrograms could represent frequencies in several types of signals and sent visitors to booths where they could see light spectrograms. When we invited visitors to link spectrograms to their interests, some children asked to compare the noises of the neighboring Madagascar hissing cockroaches to human speech sounds. The entomologists did not want to subject their bugs to that indignity, so we did the hissing ourselves.

20 Finale

OPENING WORKSHEET

Now that you've just about finished this book, write down the most useful thing that you learned and the thing that surprised you the most.

Our goals with this book were to inspire you to want to talk more with the public, and to give you some tools that would help you do that in a successful way. If you've been using the book systematically – and doing the worksheets in each chapter – you should by now have in your possession one fully realized language science activity that you could use at an informal learning event. We hope that you do!

Our Critical Take-Home Messages

As you probably noticed, we like distilling things down to their essence. So here's what we see as five Critical Take-Home Messages for this book.

1 Have a Cooperative Conversation

Formal classrooms are often about one-way communication from a teacher to a student, but informal learning works much better when the communication is done in the form of a conversation. Great conversations are ones where you're truthful, relevant, and clear. They allow everybody to participate and work together to understand each other. Have **that** kind of conversation!

2 Value the People You Are Talking With

The people you're having that conversation with are worth your time. They have important funds of knowledge, and they are worth listening to. They will learn more from you if you pay attention to them and respect what they say to you. Plus, you just might learn something from them if you do those things.

3 Organize Your Information for Your Audience

Apply what language scientists have figured out about how people process information, and organize what you say in ways that make it easy for people to track. Find good ways to establish common ground, and provide given information before new information.

4 Incomplete ≠Incorrect

Don't worry about explaining everything about your topic area to anyone! You're not cheating people by just giving them part of the story. It's most important to get them excited about your science, even if it means you're just sharing a basic piece of it. That excitement will provide a foundation from which they can learn more. If your activity has motivated them to learn more, they'll keep going.

5 Have Fun

Seriously. We mean it. We didn't include a whole chapter about having fun, but we hope that you've figured out by now that you will be a more effective communicator if you're enjoying the conversations in your public engagement. But more than that, you're more likely to actually do it if you have a good time. While we know that there's no way to guarantee that you'll enjoy yourself, we do think it helps if you are expecting to have fun.

It's Not Rocket Science! (It's So Much Harder Than That)

We don't want to highlight stereotypes about physics vs language science vs science communication. But we do know that rocket science is often thought of as being extremely challenging and the kind of thing that only really really smart people can do. And we know that people are less likely to think you need to be a genius to study language than physics, let alone to engage in science communication. But if you think about it, just the opposite is true.

Rocket science is relatively well understood – we actually know how to make rockets that can launch people into space and bring them back home again. By contrast, there is an immense amount about human language that is still not well understood. For example, language scientists still don't know how children learn language, or why chimpanzees don't, or whether the iconic status of some signs helps signers of ASL process language more efficiently. The intricacies of the human mind and how it creates and uses language are at least as hard as rocket science.

As for science communication, it just might be harder still! We are currently living through a period when trust in science is not high, and science misinformation proliferates across every type of media. Organizations like the American Association for the Advancement of Sciences (AAAS) have been arguing for decades that we need experts who are better skilled at communicating with the public in an accessible way to foster trust and understanding. Despite the fact that many people have long recognized science communication as a critical area in need of skilled users, it is still the case that most experts, including most language scientists, do not receive the training they need to do it well. Talking with the public about scientific concepts is very, very hard to do well.

This book has described how to do effective science communication, but just reading this book will not make you good at it. Communicating with the public is a skill that requires practice. You have to do it over and over again to become adept at it. It's less like rocket science and more like riding a bicycle. Or playing a musical instrument. Or becoming an athlete. You have to actually practice science communication in order to do it well.

LAST THOUGHTS

We hope you take the lessons of this book to heart, and go out and practice using your doable demo with people in an informal learning location near you!

WORKED EXAMPLE BOX

Share your work!

We think that engaging with the public is something our entire community should be doing. We know about some people who are already doing it, but we always like to hear about more people doing it.

So please tell us – and everyone else – about your efforts! Please consider making a record of your activities: Take pictures, make a video, keep a blog, write an essay. And please consider making those records public, whether that means posting them to a website, or putting them up on social media, or publishing them in a journal.

Or, if you're too shy to go public, consider just emailing us and letting us know!

CLOSING WORKSHEET

Practice is a great thing, but practice with structured and constructive feedback is even better! Here is a set of questions that you can give to a practice audience to find out how well you're doing. Remember that audience design is **your** responsibility! If people can't give you good answers to these questions, then you need to think about how to change your activity so that your conversational partners are having the experience that you want them to have. Do your demo with a practice audience and then ask these questions:

(1) What do you think you were supposed to learn from this activity?
(2) Identify at least one point where my demo was interactive. That is, when did you get to participate?
(3) What questions did I ask you? What questions did you ask me?
(4) Were any technical words used in this activity? Please list as many as you can remember. From your list, circle the **one** technical word that you think was absolutely indispensable for this activity.
(5) When were technical terms first introduced? Were they presented before or after you understood the concept that each described?
(6) What was the most enjoyable thing about this activity?
(7) Was there anything about the topic of this activity that connected to your everyday life? What was it?
(8) What was one thing that you found confusing in this activity?
(9) What is one thing that you would definitely change in this activity?
(10) What is one thing that you thought was done exactly right in this activity?

Further Reading

1 *One-way communication from a teacher to a student*

King (1993) referred to this approach as the "sage on the stage" and contrasted it with an approach using a "guide on the side" analogy. In the conversations that we encourage here, you will be that guide on the side.

2 *People are less likely to think you need to be a genius to study language*

The psychologists Andrei Cimpian and Sarah Jane Leslie have investigated which fields people perceive as requiring natural brilliance or innate genius in order to succeed, and the implications of those perceptions on who goes into those fields. In one study they investigated people's belief that you need "field-specific abilities" in order to succeed, and correlated that with how many women get PhDs in the field. The graph in Figure 20.1 is from Meyer et al. (2015); it shows that people believe strongly that physics is a field where you need natural talent to succeed while education is a field where you can succeed just by working hard (linguistics rates between those two). You'll also notice that there are a lot more women getting PhDs in education than physics, which is one of the main points of this line of research. Just in general, these researchers found that the more a field is associated with needing a particular kind of genius or brilliance for success, the less likely women and African Americans are to be members of that field (Cimpian & Leslie, 2017).

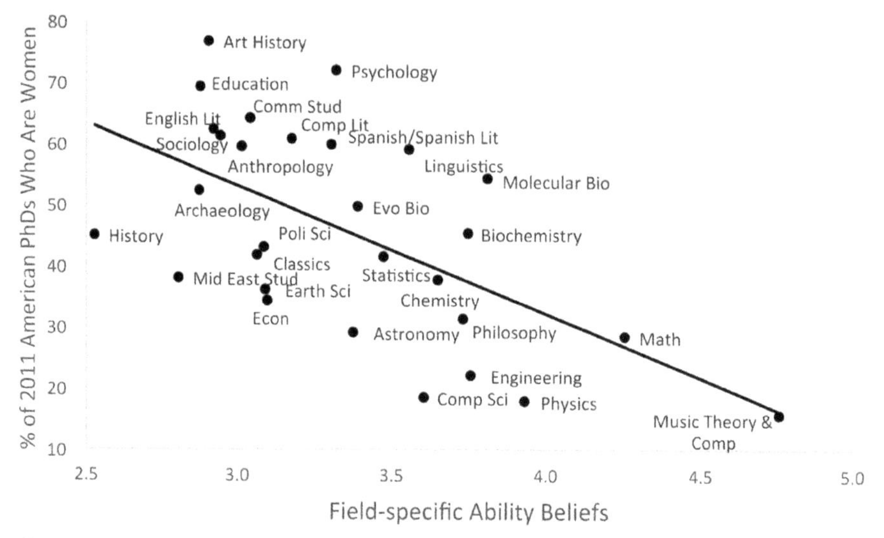

Figure 20.1 Relationship between perceived brilliance and women's participation in academic fields
Note. This graph from Meyer et al. (2015) shows that the more people believe you need special abilities to succeed in a field, the fewer women there are who get PhDs in that field. Reprinted with permission.

3 *Rocket science is relatively well understood*

To be impressed with what rocket scientists can do, see this video from NASA showing how it collected a sample from the asteroid Bennu: www.youtube.com/watch?v=RkJo6BXfbmA.

4 *Science misinformation proliferates across every type of media*

If you want to know more about what the general public does and does not believe, one source to keep an eye on is the Pew Research Center. This organization regularly surveys large groups of people around the world about different topics, including trust in science. In a 2020 report (www.pewresearch.org/science/2020/09/29/science-and-scientists-held-in-high-esteem-across-global-publics/), Pew found that only 38 percent of Americans trusted scientists "a lot" to do what is right, and 36 percent of Brazilians trusted scientists "not too much/not at all" to do what is right. The picture is worse when you look at the issue of misinformation, as Pew did in a related report: www.journalism.org/2018/06/18/distinguishing-between-factual-and-opinion-statements-in-the-news/. Around a quarter of Americans were almost totally unable to distinguish between a "fact" (something where objective evidence determines if something is true) and an "opinion."

APPENDIX
Teaching with This Book

One of our goals for this book is as a text for a university course running a whole quarter or semester, ideally ending with an event where students do demos that they have developed through the course. As noted in Chapter 1, reading the book straight through presents the full story. Moreover, the book incorporates various elements that could be used to generate homework assignments and in-class discussions, including guiding students in helping to improve each other's demos. We realize that teachers have their own styles and favorite strategies, but we wanted to lay out our ideas for how different components of this book might be used in a course. In case you'd like to apply some of Chapter 15's ideas to your own course, Vanderbilt University's IRIS Center has excellent resources on instructional scaffolding: https://iris.peabody.vanderbilt.edu/module/sca/cresource/q1/p01/.

Suggestions for Non–Language Scientists Using This Book

The title of this book includes the word *language*, and we emphasize examples from the language sciences because we ourselves are linguists. But the core lessons in this book apply to any science communication, perhaps even to any discourse between experts in some area and people who lack that particular expertise (but surely have some other expertise). That is, all such communication benefits from cooperative conversations where we are truthful, relevant, and clear. All such communication benefits from adjustments to how people process information where we establish common ground, provide given information before new information, and recognize that incomplete ≠ incorrect. Valuing whoever we engage with and having fun while doing this work are also critical for any such communication.

Short chapters articulate these core lessons, which should make it easy for a teacher to choose reading assignments. Elements of the book that are focused on making new demos, such as the Opening and Closing Worksheets, have little explicit reference to the language sciences and so should be relatively easy for anyone to use. For example, these worksheets ask readers to reflect on stereotypes (e.g., of experts and audiences), credibility, and misunderstandings; or they ask readers to develop concrete materials, to organize information, and to write guidelines for their own demos. The Worked Example Boxes that supplement each chapter's main text can be modified to resonate better with experts on topics other than language. As this might be challenging for teachers who are themselves just starting this kind of work, examples from other sciences can be found on websites and in publications referring to the "strands of science learning."

Opening Worksheets

The worksheets that start each chapter are designed to inspire readers to consider their own motivations and experiences. We've provided a list at the end of this section that summarizes all of these worksheets in one place. Some of them ask people to think about things that they might find personal – their strengths and weaknesses, their experience with arguments, their views of different kinds of people, times they have faced difficulties. We do believe that asking students to actually write down their answers to the prompts in the Opening Worksheets is an important way to get them to engage thoughtfully with the questions. However, we don't recommend asking students to turn in anything written for the Opening Worksheets. In fact, letting students know that you won't collect their responses might encourage more honest reflections. Instead, we see these worksheets as suggesting seeds or icebreakers for class discussions. You might ask students to volunteer answers, or offer experiences of your own to start the ball rolling. But more important than specific answers that students put down is getting them to think about why they (and others) gave the kinds of answers that they did, and how their reflections connect to the text.

Main Text

We've written the main text in a style that we hope is "breezy" and therefore fairly readable. We avoided on purpose sprinkling the main text with academic citations of the scholarship behind our points. Our intention, even in the chapters discussing theoretical and empirical work related to linguistics, is to keep the barrier to entry quite low. We want all kinds of readers to understand our main points!

If you stick to the main text, you will get the full story. An important part of that story is that the language sciences make critical contributions that are relevant for public engagement. In particular, the central themes of this book are (1) the principles behind successful conversations (i.e., the Gricean Maxims), and (2) the information structure underlying ideal communication (i.e., Given before New). We return to these themes frequently, and we repeat explicit references to our discussion of them across chapters to emphasize how these themes underlie many different features that we discuss. But to provide pedagogical flexibility, we wrote each chapter to stand on its own without wobbling too much. The consistency of the themes allows the chapters to be assigned in different orders and facilitates the use of this book for shorter programming, such as a single module in a semester-long course on professionalism, or in a two-week workshop on science communication, or as a source for icebreakers during orientation to any language science event.

Worked Example Boxes

These boxes highlight examples that unpack practical details of the lessons in the main text. In many cases, the examples will be mentioned briefly in the main text, and then we use the boxes to provide more relevant detail. In other cases, we use these boxes to augment the main text. They may be thematically linked to what was discussed in the chapter, but some won't necessarily be discussed as such. These boxes are one of the easiest places to swap in new material if you are so inclined. We chose examples that reflect who we are – our own experiences, our favorite demos, our interests in language. But if your students are more likely to resonate to different examples, by all means use your own worked examples!

Closing Worksheets

The worksheets that end each chapter work as a coherent set and build systematically toward the reader's creation of a doable demo. We've provided a list at the end of this section that summarizes all of these worksheets in one place. If you do want your students to make a demo as a result of your course (and we really hope you do!), then we strongly recommend that you assign these worksheets and ask students to turn in the products. When we introduce these worksheets in Chapter 1, we suggest that the reader keep a written record of their responses. Having something written down that can be referred to for later worksheets will help with developing the activities we have in mind. Obviously, there are many ways to implement these assignments, and the best way will depend on your specific situation. We've designed these worksheets as if each student is doing their own demo, but the worksheets also work well if you are having students work in groups. As noted in Chapter 19, public engagement activities often succeed as a team sport. They also work well as in-class small group activities if you are "flipping" your class and want to use class time for hands-on work.

About the Further Reading Sections

You may notice that there is a separate section at the end of each chapter that provides notes on additional things to read. These come in various flavors. Some provide more information on the literature that we are breezing through in the main text. If you're looking for background about that literature, more specific sources, or justifications for some of our terminology, you'll find some of that in the further reading notes. Other notes provide more examples. We tried to minimize URLs in the main text, so some of them went into the Resource Lists within the main text and the rest ended up in the Further Reading sections. Finally, some of the notes are a bit more conversational in nature. We had a good time writing this book, and you'll get some hints about our personal senses of humor through a few of these notes as well.

The Doable Demos

We use the doable demo as an organizing idea throughout this book. We ourselves have already established venues where students can develop and use demos like this, but we appreciate that not everyone has a science museum on call or ongoing relationships with local festivals. The later chapters in this book (Chapters 18 and 19, especially) are designed to help someone get, and nurture, access to a free-choice learning environment for themselves. In our experience, creating and building such relationships is probably best done by a faculty or staff member – someone who has institutional stability, which most students do not have. And we strongly encourage you to seek out places or events where you can use these demos, not only for the good of your students, but also for yourself! It really is fun to teach students within these environments.

However, even if you don't have established access to such venues for your students, there are many options you can use to help your students practice their demos. You'll notice that many of the venues we mention in Chapter 18 are relatively easy to connect with, particularly those that are already associated with your institution. If even these seem too difficult, we recommend requiring students to practice with their peers and family members, or with any group that they individually have access to (children they babysit, a scout troop they supervise, members of their religious congregation). The lessons of this book are best solidified by practice, so any opportunity your students can get is worthwhile.

Learning Outcomes

What is reasonable to expect from a student who has gone through this book? Obviously, if you're using the worksheets closing each chapter as we suggest, it is reasonable to expect that your students will make a doable demo, including some kind of written guidelines that support its use. Moreover, we hope that your students also gain greater appreciation for the importance of public engagement and end up with some strategies for doing such engagement effectively. If you can provide an opportunity for students to practice their demos (or demos that you've made for them) with actual members of the general public, you can expect more substantial learning outcomes. When one of us (LW) teaches this course, she provides students with regular access to practice over the semester and when she assessed the course outcomes, the number one outcome was improved confidence in public speaking. She was also able to document high levels of proficiency in communicating with the public and some mild improvements in dispelling common language myths (you can read the details in Wagner et al., 2021).

Quick Guide to Opening Worksheets

Chapter	
1	What does public engagement mean to you? Why are you reading this book?
2	What does an expert look like? What are some strengths and weaknesses of your favorite experts, and of yourself?
3	Think about a misunderstanding you've had and the factors that contributed to it.
4	Compare classroom and free-choice learning environments.
5	Think about the kinds of people you might interact with and what they would get out of your demo topic area.
6	What got you interested in your chosen language topic?
7	How might language matter (be relevant) for different kinds of people?
8	Think about a person you find credible and what makes them credible.
9	Think about what steps are really needed to explain something – specifically, how to make lentil soup!
10	Think of questions on your topic that different audiences might have about it.
11	Think about what information is common ground for your demo – for people who are similar and dissimilar to you.
12	Learn about something unfamiliar. See how your knowledge changes.
13	Explain a complex diagram and think about what kinds of information images are good (and not so good) at conveying.
14	Practice coming up with alternative words for things, including the content of your demo.
15	Practice breaking down a topic with a Lalana Chinantec morphology problem.
16	Evaluate the readiness of your demo's various components.
17	Think about how your demo will work with different audiences. Consider what audiences outside of a free-choice learning setting might be interested.
18	Where do people in your community go to learn new things?
19	Think about people you do, and don't, like to work with. What makes someone a good partner?
20	What have you learned from this book? What seems most useful and what's been most surprising?

Quick Guide to Closing Worksheets

Chapter	
1	How to use the worksheets to make a doable demo. Brainstorm topic ideas.
2	Choose your topic!
3	Connect the Gricean Maxims of Quality, Quantity, Relevance, and Manner to your chosen topic.
4	What funds of knowledge do others bring to your topic? Connect your topic to at least two strands of science learning.
5	How can you make your demo interactive and fun? Link your topic to someone who is an Explorer, a Hobbyist, and an Experience Seeker.
6	Revise your ideas about how to make your demo interactive and fun.
7	Connect your topic to features of people's everyday lives.
8	Identify three things that you do know about your topic area and three things that you do not know about it.
9	Pare down the explanation of your topic. Identify the Critical Take-Home Message of your demo.
10	Write juicy questions for your demo.
11	Write down the steps in an ideal interaction for your demo. See what happens when you rearrange the order of these steps.
12	Find out whether key concepts in your demo are likely to be familiar to other people.
13	Identify the materials that you will need to make your demo work.
14	Use an online jargon filter on your demo explanations.
15	Rework your demo interaction for different rungs on a ladder.
16	Create written guidelines for your demo.
17	Pitch your topic area to different audiences, such as a job interview or your parents.
18	Identify three locations where you could take your demo.
19	What would make you be a good partner in the location you identified in the previous closing worksheet?
20	Practice your demo with others! This worksheet has a set of structured questions that will help you get good feedback.

References

Allen, S., & Gutwill, J. (2009). Creating a program to deepen family inquiry at interactive science exhibits. *Curator: The Museum Journal, 52* (3), 289–306.

Allopenna, P. D., Magnuson, J. S., & Tanenhaus, M. K. (1998). Tracking the time course of spoken word recognition using eye movements: Evidence for continuous mapping models. *Journal of Memory and Language, 38*(4), 419–439.

Allum, N., Sturgis, P., Tabourazi, D., & Brunton-Smith, I. (2008). Science knowledge and attitudes across cultures: A meta-analysis. *Public Understanding of Science, 17,* 35–54.

Alpert, C. L. (2013). *A guide to building partnerships between science museums and university-based research centers.* Nanoscale Informal Science Education Network. www.nisenet.org/partner_guide

Babineau, M., de Carvalho, A., Trueswell, J., & Christophe, A. (2021). Familiar words can serve as a semantic seed for syntactic bootstrapping. *Developmental Science, 24*(1), e13010. https://doi.org/10.1111/desc.13010

Baez, B., & Boyles, D. (2009). *The politics of inquiry: Education research and the "culture of science."* SUNY Press.

Bauer, L., & Trudgill, P. (Eds.). (1998). *Language myths.* Penguin UK.

Bell, A. (1984). Language style as audience design. *Language in Society, 13*(2), 145–204.

Berko, J. (1958). The child's learning of English morphology. *Word,* 14 (2–3), 150–177. https://doi.org/10.1080/00437956.1958.11659661

Besley, J., Dudo, A., & Shupei, Y. (2018). Scientists' views about communication objectives. *Public Understanding of Science, 27*(6), 708–730.

Birch, S. A., & Bloom, P. (2007). The curse of knowledge in reasoning about false beliefs. *Psychological Science, 18*(5), 382–386.

Brown, B. A., & Ryoo, K. (2008). Teaching science as a language: A "content-first" approach to science teaching. *Journal of Research in Science Teaching, 45*(5), 529–553.

Bush, V. (1945). *Science: The endless frontier.* National Science Foundation.

Byun, T. M., Hitchcock, E. R., & Swartz, M. T. (2014). Retroflex versus bunched in treatment for rhotic misarticulation: Evidence from ultrasound biofeedback intervention. *Journal of Speech, Language, and Hearing Research, 57*(6), 2116–2130. https://doi.org/10.1044/2014_JSLHR-S-14-0034

Callanan, M., Cervantes, C., & Loomis, M. (2011). Informal learning. *Wiley Interdisciplinary Reviews: Cognitive Science, 2*(6), 646–655.

Carey, S. (2009). *The origin of concepts.* Oxford University Press.

Carr, J. R. C. (2019). *Linguistic landscapes.* Oxford University Press.

Carroll, L. (2010). *Through the looking glass and what Alice found there.* Penguin UK. (Original work published 1871.)

Caselli, N. K., & Pyers, J. E. (2020). Degree and not type of iconicity affects sign language vocabulary acquisition. *Journal of Experimental Psychology: Learning, Memory, and Cognition, 46*(1), 127–139.

Caswell, E. (2016, May 19). *Rapping, deconstructed: The best rappers of all time.* Vox. www.vox.com/2016/5/19/11701976/rapping-deconstructed-best-rhymers-of-all-time

Cépeda, P., Kotek, H., Pabst, K., & Syrett, K. (2021). Gender bias in linguistics textbooks: Has anything changed since Macaulay & Brice (1997)? *Language, 97*(4), 678–702.

Chomsky, N. (1957). *Syntactic structures* Mouton de Gruyter.

Chomsky, N. (1965). *Aspects of the theory of syntax.* MIT Press.

Chomsky, N. (1993). *Lectures on government and binding: The Pisa lectures.* Mouton de Gruyter. (Original work published 1981.)

Chute, E. (2009, February 9). STEM education is branching out. *Pittsburgh Post-Gazette.* www.post-gazette.com/news/education/2009/02/10/STEM-education-is-branching-out/stories/200902100165

Cimpian, A., & Leslie, S. J. (2017). The brilliance trap: How a misplaced emphasis on genius subtly discourages women and African-Americans from certain academic fields. *Scientific American, 317,* 60–65.

Clark, H. H. (1992). *Arenas of language use.* University of Chicago Press.

Clark, H. H. (1996). *Using language.* Cambridge University Press.

Clark, H. H., & Wilkes-Gibbs, D. (1986). Referring as a collaborative process. *Cognition, 22,* 1–39.

Clawson, J. G. (2008). *Managing discussions* (Darden Case No. UVA-PHA-0049). https://ssrn.com/abstract=1283345

Clemens, L., & Coon, J. (2018). Deriving verb-initial word order in Mayan. *Language, 94*(2), 237–280.

Condit-Schultze, N., & Huron, D. (2017). Word intelligibility in multi-voice singing: The influence of chorus size. *Journal of Voice, 31*(1), 121.e1–121.e8. https://doi.org/10.1016/j.jvoice.2016.02.011

Cowie, B., Jones, A., & Otrel-Cass, K. (2011). Re-engaging students in science: Issues of assessment, funds of knowledge, and sites for learning. *International Journal of Science and Mathematics Education, 9*, 347–366.

Crystal, D. (2007). *How language works: How babies babble, words change meaning, and languages live or die.* Penguin.

Curzan, A. (2014). *Fixing English: Prescriptivism and language history.* Cambridge University Press.

Dalchand, N. (2021, February 25). How I transformed myself into a confident presenter – thanks to Lady Gaga. *Science.* https://doi.org/10.1126/science.caredit.abh2491

Dawson, E. (2014). "Not designed for us": How science museums and science centers socially exclude low-income, minority ethnic groups. *Science Education, 98*(6), 981–1008.

Dawson, E. (2019). *Equity, exclusion and everyday science learning: The experiences of minoritized groups.* Routledge.

Dawson, H., & Phelan, M. (2016). *Language files: Materials for an introduction to language and linguistics* (12th ed.). The Ohio State University Press.

Degen, J., & Tanenhaus, M. K. (2019). Constraint-based pragmatic processing. In C. Cummins & N. Katsos (Eds.), *The Oxford handbook of experimental semantics and pragmatics* (pp. 21–38). Oxford University Press.

Denham, K., & Lobeck, A. (2010). *Linguistics at school: Language awareness in primary and secondary education.* Cambridge University Press.

Dorfner, T., Förtsch, C., & Neuhaus, B. J. (2020). Use of technical terms in German biology lessons and its effects on students' conceptual learning. *Research in Science & Technological Education, 38*(2), 227–251.

Duncan, S., Manners, P., & Miller, K. (2017). *Reviewing public engagement in REF 2014: Reflections for shaping the second REF.* University of Bristol/National Co-ordinating Centre for Public Engagement. www.publicengagement.ac.uk/sites/default/files/publication/reviewing_pe_in_ref_2014_final.pdf

Dweck, C. S. (2008). *Mindset: The new psychology of success.* Random House Digital.

Falk, J. H., & Dierking, L. D. (2010). The 95 percent solution. *American Scientist, 98*(6), 486–493.

Falk, J. H., & Storksdieck, M. (2010). Science learning in a leisure setting. *Journal of Research in Science Teaching: The Official Journal of the National Association for Research in Science Teaching, 47*(2), 194–212.

Fenichel, M., & Schweingruber, H. A. (2010). *Surrounded by science: Learning science in informal environments.* The National Academies Press.

Ferreira, V. S. (2019). A mechanistic framework for explaining audience design in language production. *Annual Review of Psychology, 70*, 29–51.

Fox, M. (2013, April 2). John J. Gumperz, linguist of cultural interchange, dies at 91. *New York Times*. www.nytimes.com/2013/04/03/education/john-j-gumperz-linguist-of-cultural-interchange-dies-at-91.html

Fredrickson, B. L., & Branigan, C. (2005). Positive emotions broaden the scope of attention and thought-action repertoires. *Cognition & Emotion, 19*(3), 313–332.

Fromkin, V., Rodman, R., & Hyams, N. (2018). *An introduction to language*. Cengage Learning.

Fuls, A. (2019). *Deciphering the Phaistos Disk and other Cretan hieroglyphic inscriptions: Epigraphic and linguistic analysis of a Minoan enigma*. Tredition.

Gann, T. M., & Barr, D. J. (2014). Speaking from experience: Audience design as expert performance. *Language, Cognition and Neuroscience, 29*(6), 744–760.

Gernsbacher, M. A. (1990). *Language comprehension as structure building*. LEA Press.

González, N., Amanti, C., & Moll, L. (Eds.). (2005). *Funds of knowledge: Theorizing practices in households, communities, and classrooms*. Erlbaum.

Greenberg, J. B. (1989, April). *Funds of knowledge: Historical constitution, social distribution, and transmission* [Paper presentation]. Meeting of the Society for Applied Anthropology, Santa Fe, NM.

Grepstad, O. (Ed.). (2018). *Language museums of the world*. Centre for Norwegian Language and Literature. www.nynorsk.no/wp-content/uploads/2020/02/814-20180314-Language-museums-OG.pdf

Grice, H. P. (1975). Logic and conversation. In R. Cole & J. Morgan (Eds.), *Syntax and semantics: Speech acts*. Academic Press.

Gutwill, J., & Allen, S. (2012). Deepening students' scientific inquiry skills during a science museum field trip. *Journal of the Learning Sciences, 21*(1), 130–181.

Hauser, M. D. (1996). *The evolution of communication*. MIT Press.

Heath, C., & Heath, D. (2007). *Made to stick: Why some ideas survive and others die*. Random House.

Heerman, V. (Director). (1930). *Animal crackers* [Film]. Paramount Pictures.

Hendriks, F., Kienhues, D., & Bromme, R. (2015). Measuring laypeople's trust in experts in a digital age: The Muenster Epistemic Trustworthiness Inventory (METI). PloS ONE, *10*(10), e0139309. https://doi.org/10.1371/journal.pone.0139309

Houston, S. D. (1988). The phonetic decipherment of Mayan glyphs. *Antiquity, 62*(234), 126–135.

James, V. (2020). Science communication efforts and identity at popular culture conventions.

Science Communication, 42(3), 395–418.

Jensen, E., & Buckley, N. (2014). Why people attend science festivals: Interests, motivations and self-reported benefits of public engagement with research. *Public Understanding of Science, 23*(5), 557–573.

Jurafsky, D. (2014). *The language of food: A linguist reads the menu.* W. W. Norton & Company.

Kaminsky, M. (2008). *The secret history of Star Wars.* Legacy Books Press.

Kaplan, A. (2016). *Women talk more than men.* Cambridge University Press.

Kensinger, E. A. (2009). Remembering the details: Effects of emotion. *Emotion Review, 1*(2), 99–113.

Keysar, B., Lin, S., & Barr, D. J. (2003). Limits on theory of mind use in adults. *Cognition, 89*(1), 25–41.

King, A. (1993). From sage on the stage to guide on the side. *College Teaching, 41*, 30–35.

Koenecke, A., Nam, A., Lake, E., Nudell, J., Quartey, M., Mengesha, Z., Troups, C., Rickford, J. R., Jurafsky, D., & Goel, S. (2020). Racial disparities in automated speech recognition. *Proceedings of the National Academy of Sciences, 117*(14), 7684–7689.

Kuhn, T. S. (1962). *The structure of scientific revolutions.* Chicago University Press.

Landau, B., & Gleitman, L. R. (1985). *Language and experience: Evidence from the blind child.* Harvard University Press.

Lane, H. (1989). *When the mind hears.* Knopf Doubleday.

Martínez, A., & Mammola, S. (2021). Specialized terminology reduces the number of citations of scientific papers. *Proceedings of the Royal Society B, 288*(1948), 20202581. https://doi.org/10.1098/rspb.2020.2581

McCulloch, G. (2020). *Because internet: Understanding the new rules of language.* Riverhead Books.

McGurk, H., & MacDonald, J. (1976). Hearing lips and seeing voices. *Nature, 264*, 746–748. https://doi.org/10.1038/264746a0

McKee, C., Zimmer, E., Fountain, A., Huang, H. Y., & Vento, M. (2015). Public outreach in linguistics: Engaging broader audiences. *Language and Linguistics Compass, 9*(9), 349–357.

Metz, C. (2020, March 23). There is a racial divide in speech recognition systems, researchers say. *New York Times.* www.nytimes.com/2020/03/23/technology/speech-recognition-bias-apple-amazon-google.html

Meyer, M., Cimpian, A., & Leslie, S. J. (2015). Women are underrepresented in fields where success is believed to require brilliance. *Frontiers in Psychology*, 6, 235. https://doi.org/10.3389/fpsyg.2015.00235

Michel, J.-B., Kui Shen, Y., Aiden, A. P., Veres, A., Gray, M. K., Brockman, W., The Google Books Team, Pickett, J. P., Hoiberg, D., Clancy, D., Norvig, P., Orwant, J., Pinker, S., Nowak, M. A., & Aiden, E. L. (2010). *Quantitative*

Analysis of Culture Using Millions of Digitized Books. Science (Published online ahead of print: 12/16/2010).

Mielke, J., Baker, A., & Archangeli, D. (2010). Variability and homogeneity in American English /r/ allophony and /s/ retraction. *Laboratory Phonology, 10*, 699–730.

Moll, L. C., & Greenberg, J. (1990). Creating zones of possibilities: Combining social contexts for instruction. In L. C. Moll (Ed.), *Vygotsky and education* (pp. 319–348). Cambridge University Press.

Moore, L. C. (2021). Building partnerships and expanding repertoires of practice: Working with and in museums to improve informal science education for linguistically diverse young children. *Extending Applied Linguistics for Social Impact: Cross-Disciplinary Collaborations in Diverse Spaces of Public Inquiry*, 35.

Moore, L. C., Seilstad, B., Ridley, J., & Kim, S. (2019). Engaged second language research: Studying stakeholders' perspectives on preschool DLLs' science and language learning. In *2017 Second Language Research Forum* (pp. 127–143). Cascadilla Proceedings Project.

Munroe, R. (2015). *Thing explainer: Complicated stuff in simple words*. Hachette UK.

National Research Council. (2009). *Learning science in informal environments: People, places, and pursuits*. The National Academies Press. https://doi.org/10.17226/12190

Nordquist, R. (2020, August 26). *Definition and examples of mondegreens*. ThoughtCo. www.thoughtco.com/what-is-a-mondegreen-1691401

Okrent, A. (2009). *In the land of invented languages: Esperanto rock stars, Klingon poets, Loglan lovers, and the mad dreamers who tried to build a perfect language*. Random House.

Oxford University Press. (2013). Audience. In *Oxford English Dictionary* (3rd ed.). Retrieved April 1, 2020, from https://www.oed.com/

Oxford University Press. (2013). Mondegreen. In *Oxford English Dictionary* (3rd ed.). Retrieved April 1, 2020, from https://www.oed.com/

Pullum, G. (2014). Fear and loathing of the English passive. *Language & Communication, 37*, 60–74.

Quine, W. V. O. (1960). *Word and object*. MIT Press.

Rakedzon, T., Segev, E., Chapnik, N., Yosef, R., & Baram-Tsabari, A. (2017). Automatic jargon identifier for scientists engaging with the public and science communication educators. *PloS One, 12*(8), e0181742. https://doi.org/10.1371/journal.pone.0181742

Rapp, C. (2010). Aristotle's rhetoric. In E. N. Zalta (Ed.), *The Stanford encyclopedia of philosophy* (Spring ed.). https://plato.stanford.edu/archives/spr2010/entries/aristotle-rhetoric/

Raupp, A. B. (2020, June 19). *Defining moment: The STEM and EdTech convergence that will change everything*. Forbes. www.forbes.com/sites/forbestechcouncil/2020/06/19/defining-moment-the-stem-and-edtech-convergence-that-will-change-everything/?sh=4e4d24d764f6

Reiss, J., & Sprenger, J. (2020). Scientific objectivity. In E. N. Zalta (Ed.), *The Stanford encyclopedia of philosophy* (Winter ed.). https://plato.stanford.edu/archives/win2020/entries/scientific-objectivity

Rendell, P. G., Phillips, L. H., Henry, J. D., Brumby-Rendell, T., de la Piedad Garcia, X., Altgassen, M., & Kliegel, M. (2011). Prospective memory, emotional valence and ageing. *Cognition & Emotion, 25*(5), 916–925.

Roberts, C. (2012). Information structure: Towards an integrated formal theory of pragmatics. *Semantics and Pragmatics, 5*, article 6. https://doi.org/10.3765/sp.5.6

Rogoff, B., Callanan, M., Gutierrez, K. D., & Erickson, F. (2016). The organization of informal learning. *Review of Research in Education, 40*(1), 356–401.

Schaefer, A., & Philippot, P. (2005). Selective effects of emotion on the phenomenal characteristics of autobiographical memories. *Memory, 13*(2), 148–160.

Schatz, P. (2011). Finger tapping test. In J. S. Kreutzer, J. DeLuca, & B. Caplan (Eds.), *Encyclopedia of clinical neuropsychology*. Springer. https://doi.org/10.1007/978-0-387-79948-3_178

Sedivy, J., & Carlson, G. (2011). *Sold on language: How advertisers talk to you and what this says about you.* John Wiley & Sons.

Seymour, P. H. K., Aro, M., & Erskine, J. M. (2003). Foundation literacy acquisition in European orthographies. *British Journal of Psychology, 94*, 143–174.

Shohamy, E., & Gorter, D. (Eds.). (2009). *Linguistic landscapes: Expanding the scenery*. Taylor & Francis.

Singham, M. (2020, September 7). The idea that a scientific theory can be falsified is a myth. *Scientific American*. www.scientificamerican.com/article/the-idea-that-a-scientific-theory-can-be-falsified-is-a-myth/

Sobel, D. M., & Jipson, J. L. (eds.). (2015). *Cognitive development in museum settings: Relating research and practice*. Routledge.

Sperber, D., & Wilson, D. (1986). *Relevance: Communication and cognition* (vol. 142). Harvard University Press.

Stevens, S., Andrade, R., & Page, M. (2016). Motivating young Native American students to pursue STEM learning through a culturally relevant science program. *Journal of Science Education and Technology, 25*, 947–960.

Stroop, J. R. (1935). Studies of interference in serial verbal reactions. *Journal of Experimental Psychology, 18*(6), 643–662.

Tan, S.- L. (2015, October 7). *Six reasons pop singers pronounce some lyrics in odd ways*. Psychology Today. www.psychologytoday.com/us/blog/what-shapes-film/201510/six-

reasons-pop-singers-pronounce-some-lyrics-in-odd-ways
Tannen, D. (1984). The pragmatics of cross-cultural communication. *Applied Linguistics*, *5*(3), 189–195.
Tannen, D. (1986). *That's not what I meant! How conversational style makes or breaks your relations with others*. Morrow.
Tatman, R. (2017). Gender and dialect bias in YouTube's automatic captions. In *Proceedings of the First ACL Workshop on Ethics in Natural Language Processing*. Association for Computational Linguistics. https://github.com/rctatman/personal-website/blob/master/files/Tatman_2017_GenderAndDialectBias.pdf
Tiippana, K. (2014). What is the McGurk effect? *Frontiers in Psychology*, *5*, 725. https://doi.org/10.3389/fpsyg.2014.00725
Ugwu, R. (2015, October 6). *Selena Gomez's "Good for You" and the rise of "Indie pop voice."* BuzzFeed. www.buzzfeednews.com/article/reggieugwu/what-is-indie-pop-voice#.biXnELLoX
Vélez-Ibáñez, C. G., & Greenberg, J. B. (1992). Formation and transformation of funds of knowledge among U.S. Mexican households. *Anthropology and Education Quarterly*, *23*(4), 313–335.
Wagner, L., Moore, L. C., & Campbell-Kibler, K. (2021). Training students to conduct outreach in an informal science learning environment. In D. Farland-Smith (Ed.), *Enhancing learning opportunities through student, scientist, and teacher partnerships*. IGI Global.
Wagner, L., Speer, S. R., Moore, L. C., McCullough, E. A., Ito, K., Clopper, C. G., & Campbell-Kibler, K. (2015). Linguistics in a science museum: Integrating research, teaching, and outreach in a language sciences research lab. *Language and Linguistics Compass*, *9*, 420–431.
Walkden, G. (2012, November 8). *English VP fronting and the syntax of Yoda* [LinguistMix presentation]. University of Manchester. http://46.32.240.35/walkden.space/Walkden_2012_Yoda.pdf
Warneken, F., & Tomasello, M. (2006). Altruistic helping in human infants and young chimpanzees. *Science*, *311*(5765), 1301–1303.
Wright, S. (1954, November). The death of Lady Mondegreen. *Harper's Magazine*, *209*, 48–51.
Yegiyan, N. S., & Yonelinas, A. P. (2011). Encoding details: Positive emotion leads to memory broadening. *Cognition & Emotion*, *25*(7), 1255–1262.
Zimmer, B. (2010, June 25). On language: Ghoti. *New York Times*. www.nytimes.com/2010/06/27/magazine/27FOB-onlanguage-t.html
Zimmer, E. (2016). *Children's awareness of syntactic ambiguity* [Unpublished doctoral dissertation]. University of Arizona.
Zwaan, R. A. (2008). Time in language, situation models, and mental simulations. *Language Learning*, *58*, 13–26.

Index

For EU product safety concerns, contact us at Calle de José Abascal, 56–1°,
28003 Madrid, Spain or eugpsr@cambridge.org.

www.ingramcontent.com/pod-product-compliance
Ingram Content Group UK Ltd.
Pitfield, Milton Keynes, MK11 3LW, UK
UKHW030904150625
459647UK00022B/2823